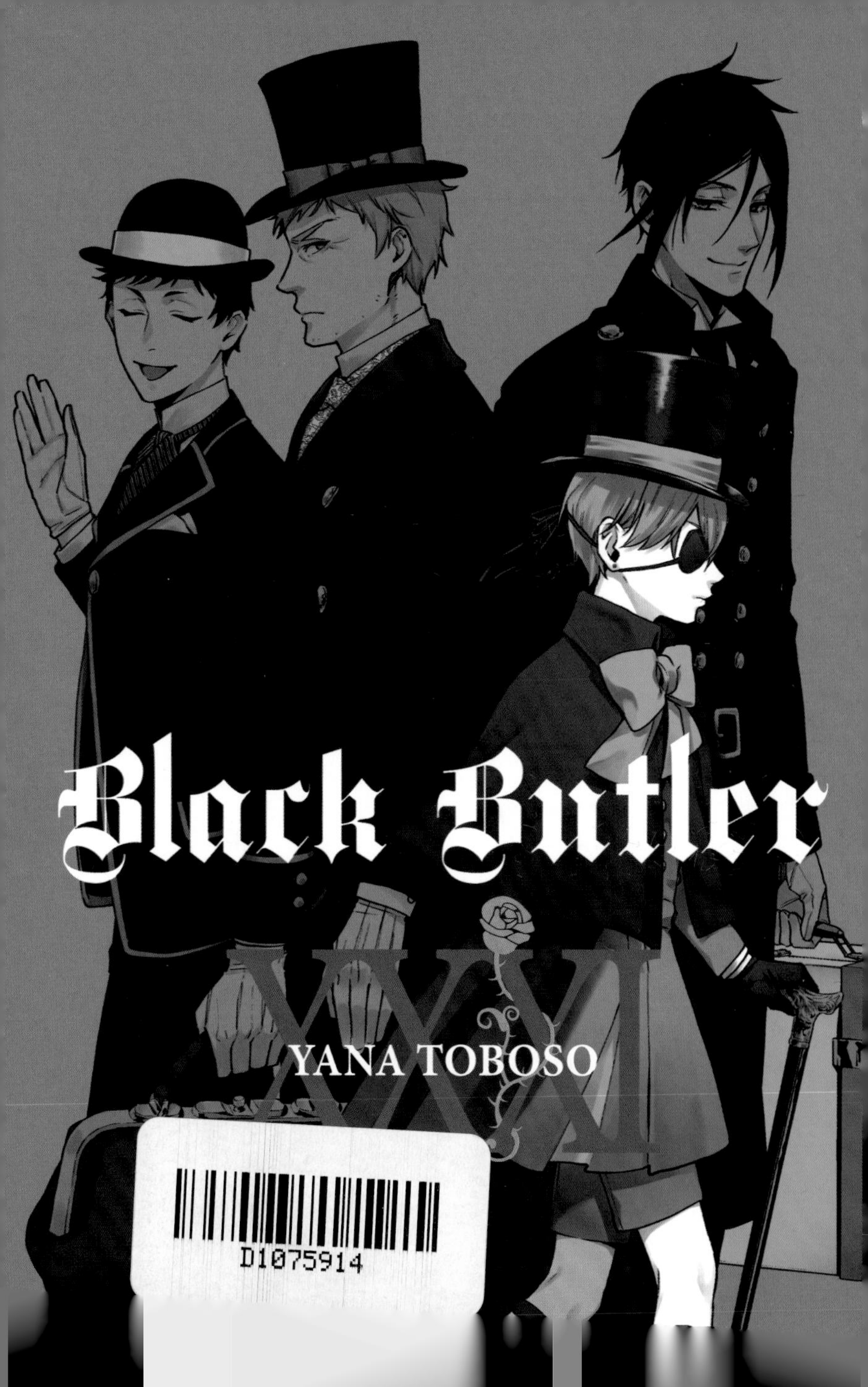
Black Butler
XXI
YANA TOBOSO

Contents

Chapter 166
At dawn: The Butler, Unidentified

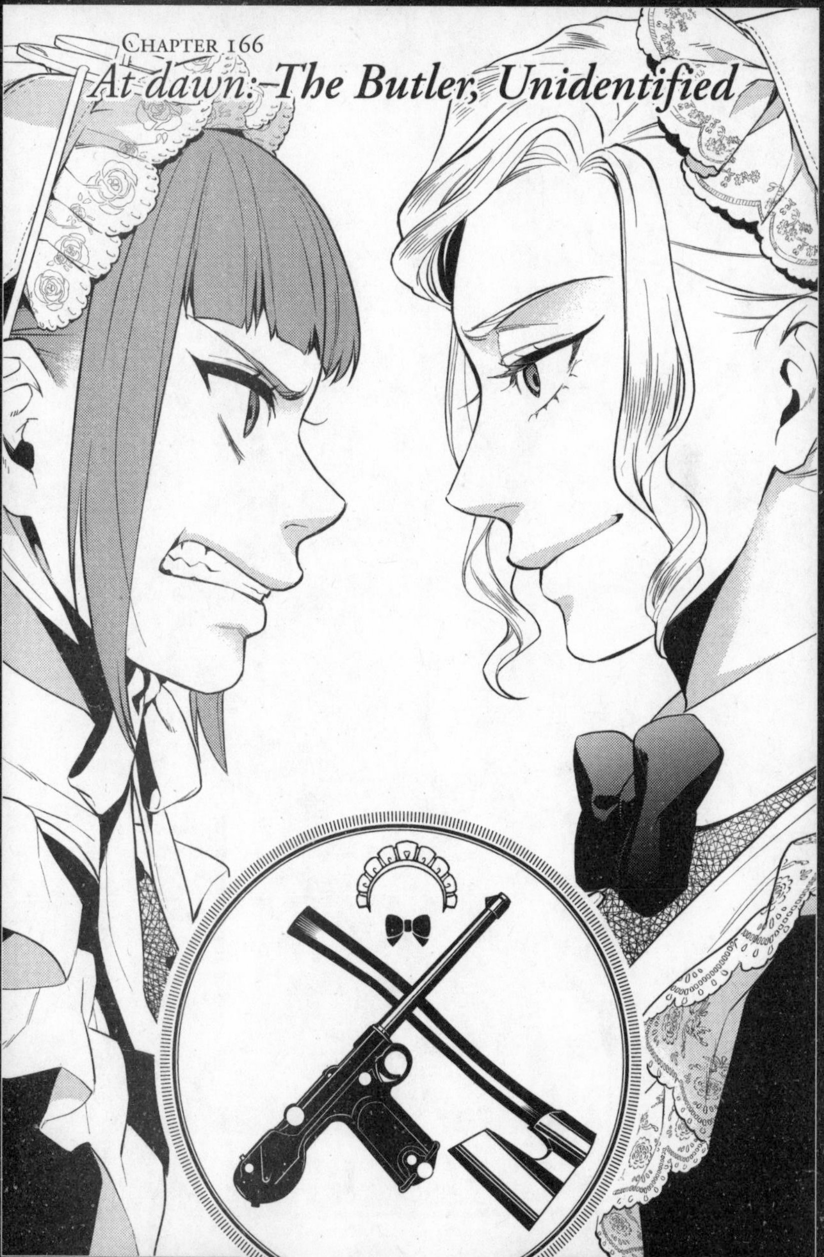

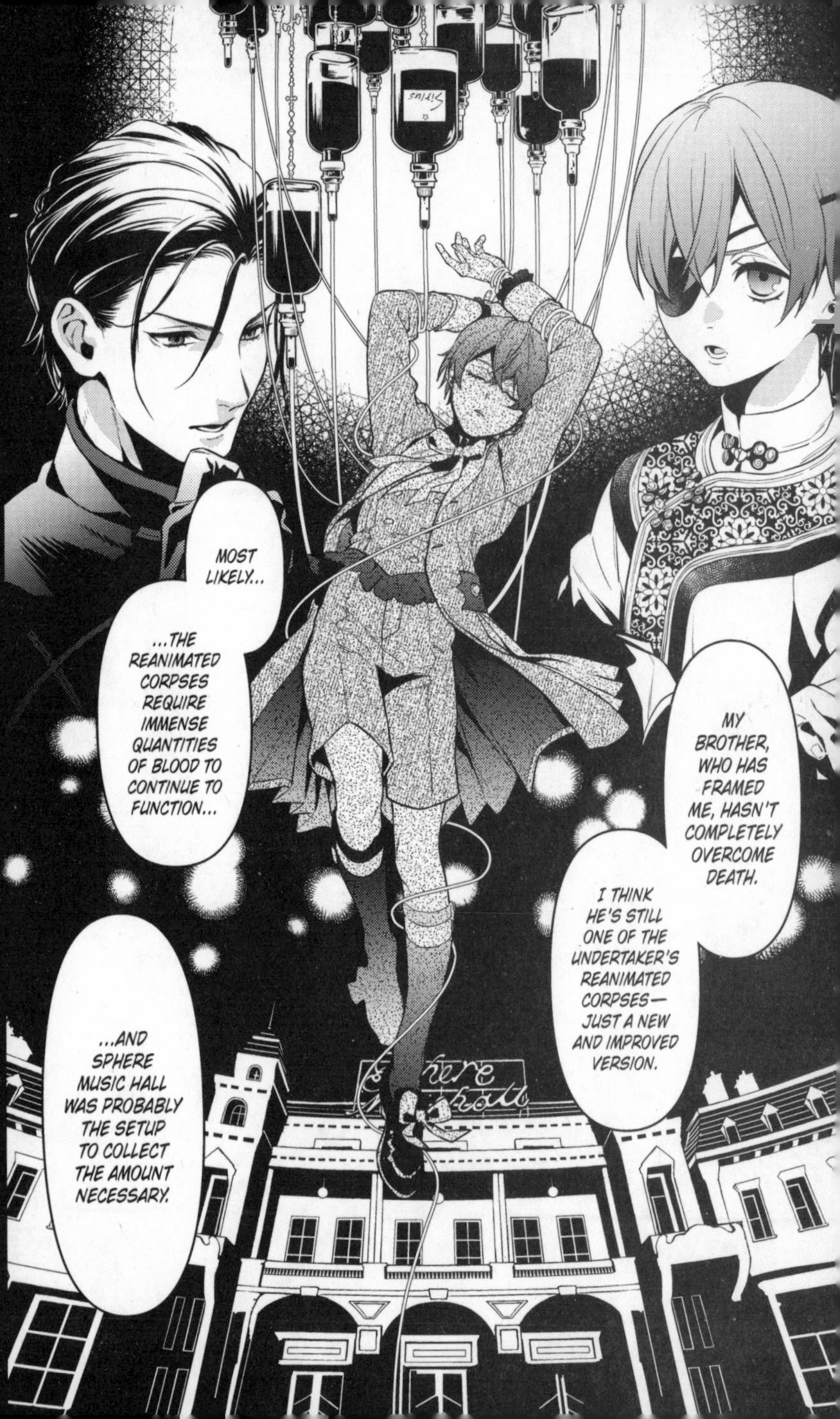
MY BROTHER, WHO HAS FRAMED ME, HASN'T COMPLETELY OVERCOME DEATH.
I THINK HE'S STILL ONE OF THE UNDERTAKER'S REANIMATED CORPSES—JUST A NEW AND IMPROVED VERSION.
MOST LIKELY...
...THE REANIMATED CORPSES REQUIRE IMMENSE QUANTITIES OF BLOOD TO CONTINUE TO FUNCTION...
...AND SPHERE MUSIC HALL WAS PROBABLY THE SETUP TO COLLECT THE AMOUNT NECESSARY.

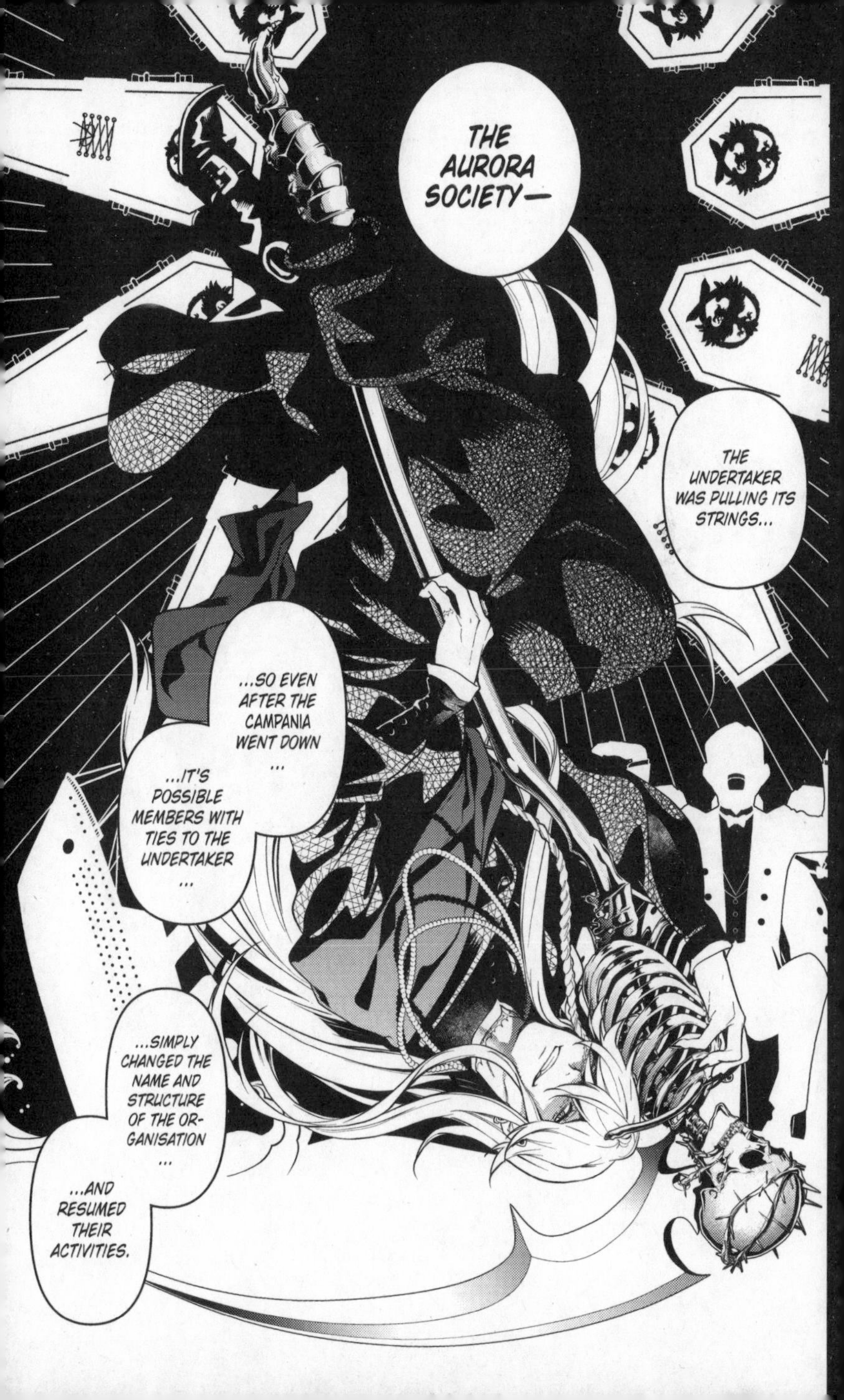
THE AURORA SOCIETY—
THE UNDERTAKER WAS PULLING ITS STRINGS...
...SO EVEN AFTER THE CAMPANIA WENT DOWN ...
...IT'S POSSIBLE MEMBERS WITH TIES TO THE UNDERTAKER ...
...SIMPLY CHANGED THE NAME AND STRUCTURE OF THE OR-GANISATION ...
...AND RESUMED THEIR ACTIVITIES.

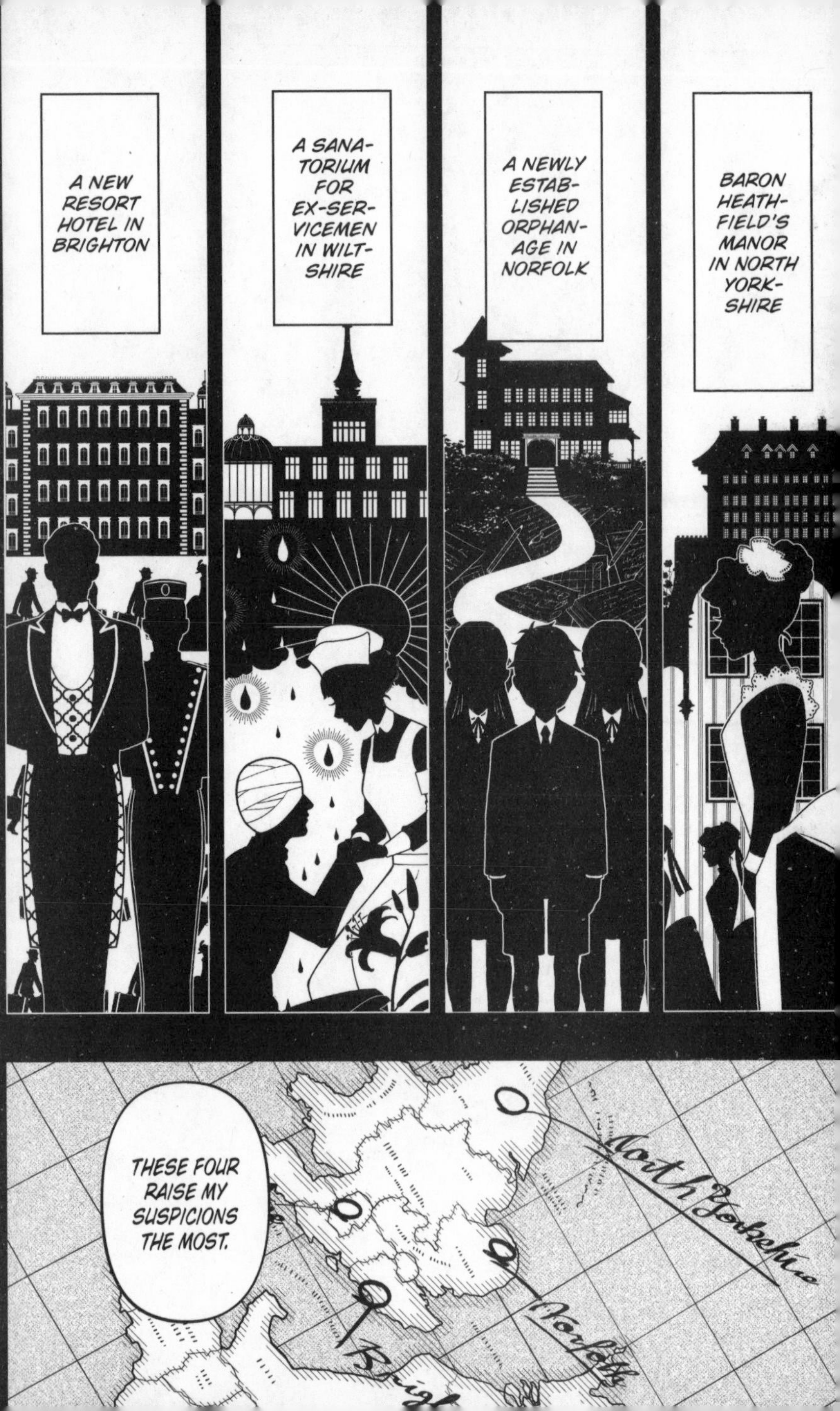
BARON HEATH-FIELD'S MANOR IN NORTH YORK-SHIRE
A NEWLY ESTAB-LISHED ORPHAN-AGE IN NORFOLK
A SANA-TORIUM FOR EX-SER-VICEMEN IN WILT-SHIRE
A NEW RESORT HOTEL IN BRIGHTON
THESE FOUR RAISE MY SUSPICIONS THE MOST.
North Yorkshire
Norfolk

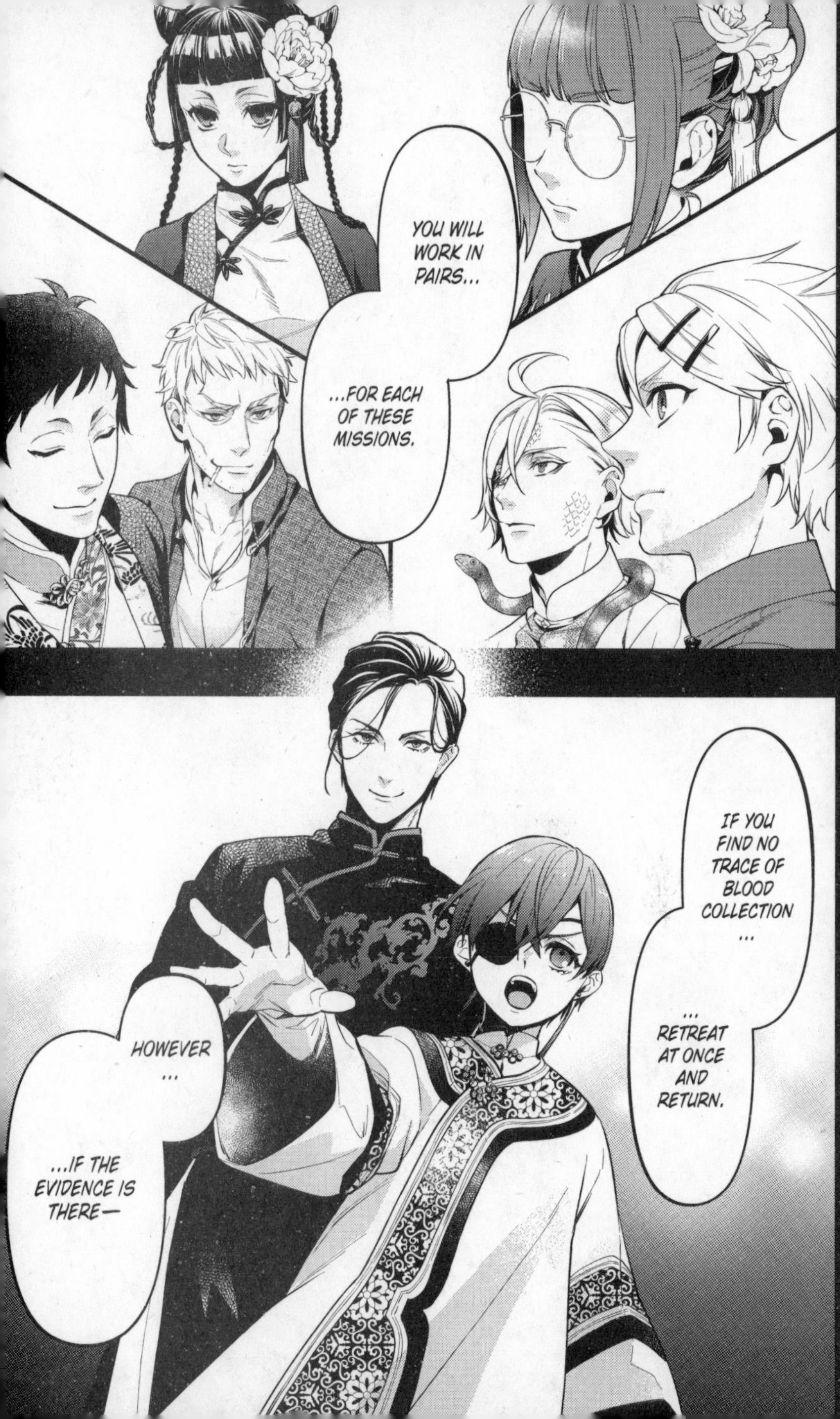
YOU WILL WORK IN PAIRS...
...FOR EACH OF THESE MISSIONS.
IF YOU FIND NO TRACE OF BLOOD COLLECTION ...
... RETREAT AT ONCE AND RETURN.
HOWEVER ...
...IF THE EVIDENCE IS THERE—

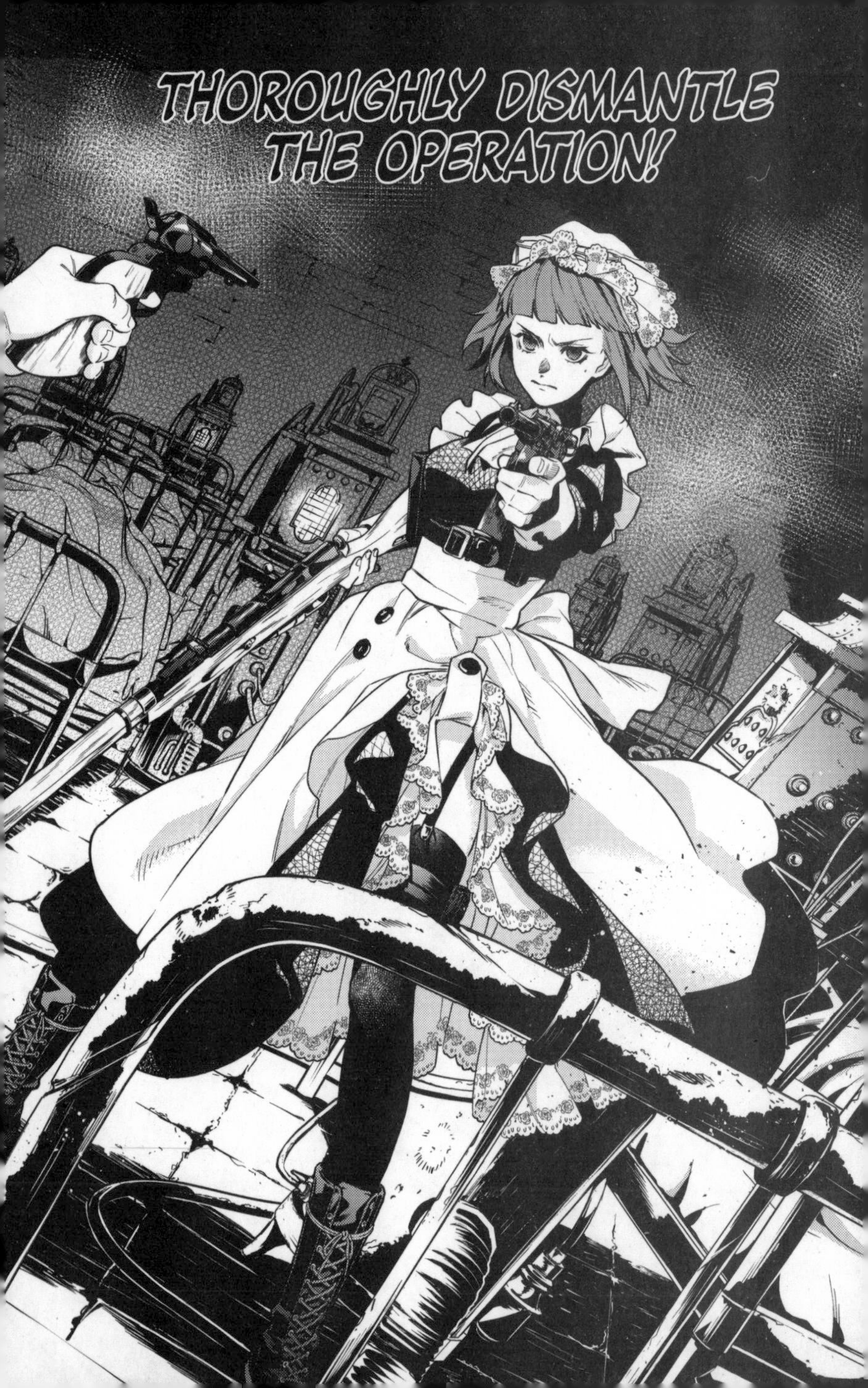
THOROUGHLY DISMANTLE THE OPERATION!

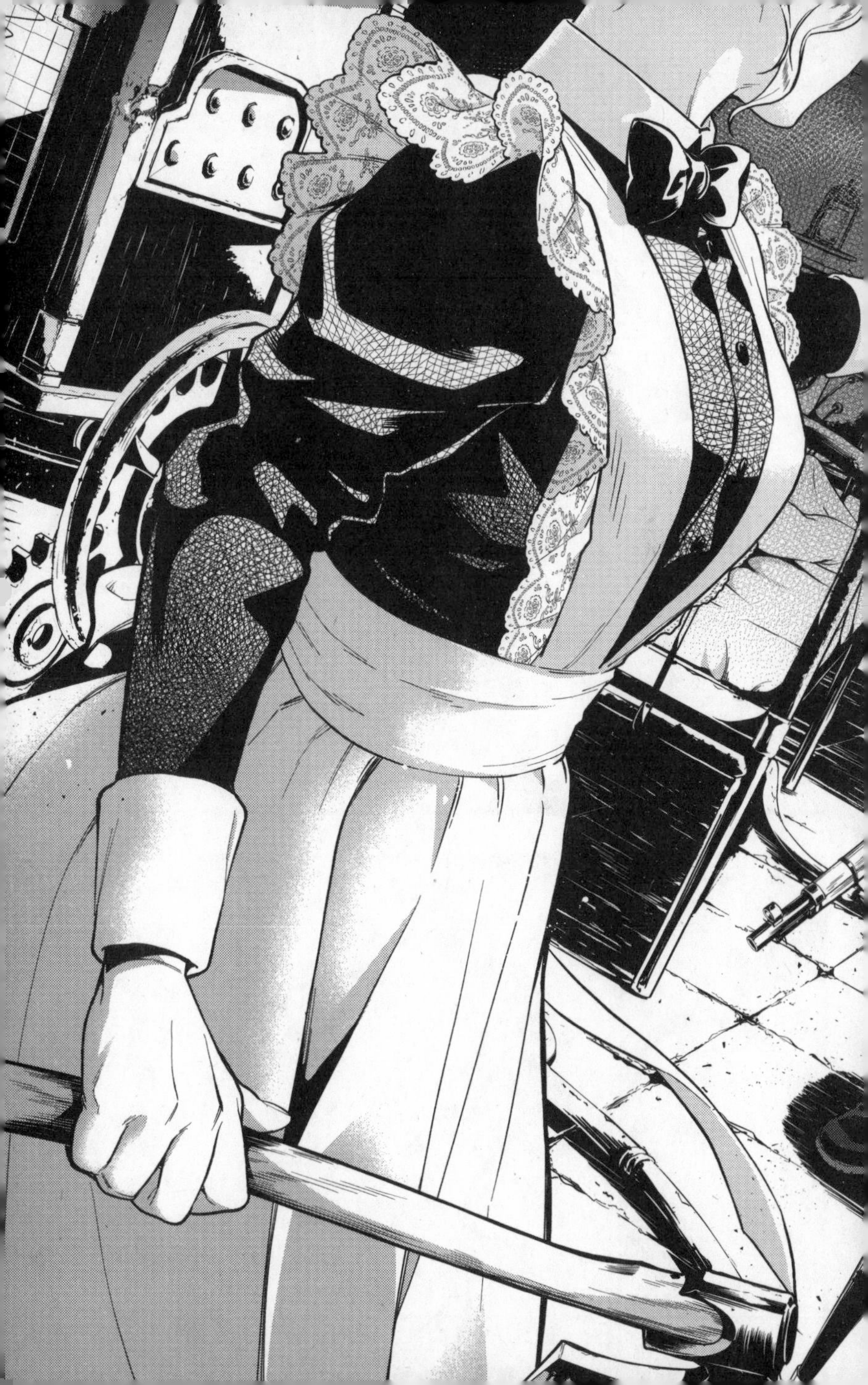

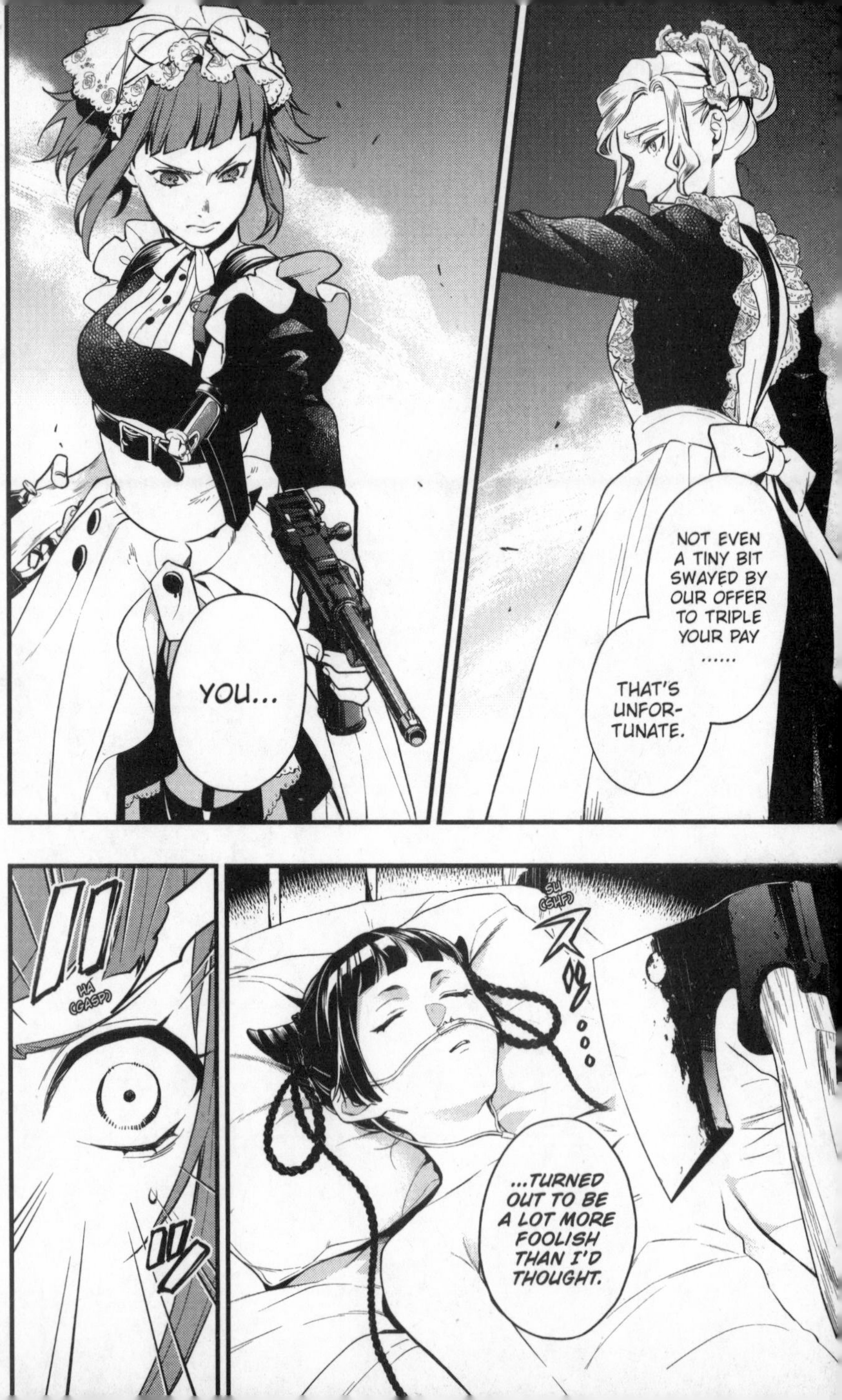
NOT EVEN A TINY BIT SWAYED BY OUR OFFER TO TRIPLE YOUR PAY ......
THAT'S UNFORTUNATE.
YOU...
SU (SHP)
...TURNED OUT TO BE A LOT MORE FOOLISH THAN I'D THOUGHT.
HA (GASP)

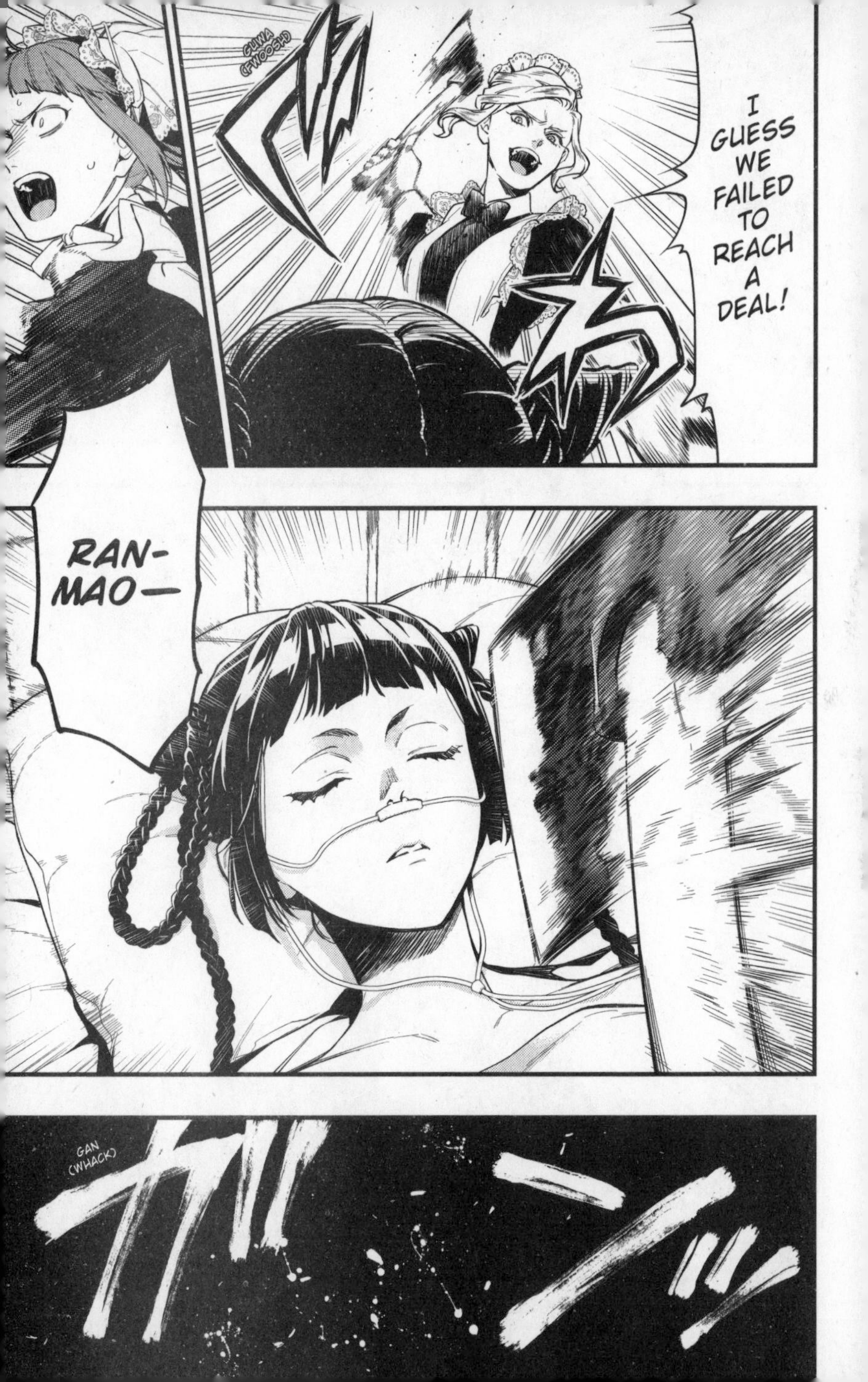
I GUESS WE FAILED TO REACH A DEAL!
GUWA (FWOOSH)
RAN-MAO—
GAN (WHACK)

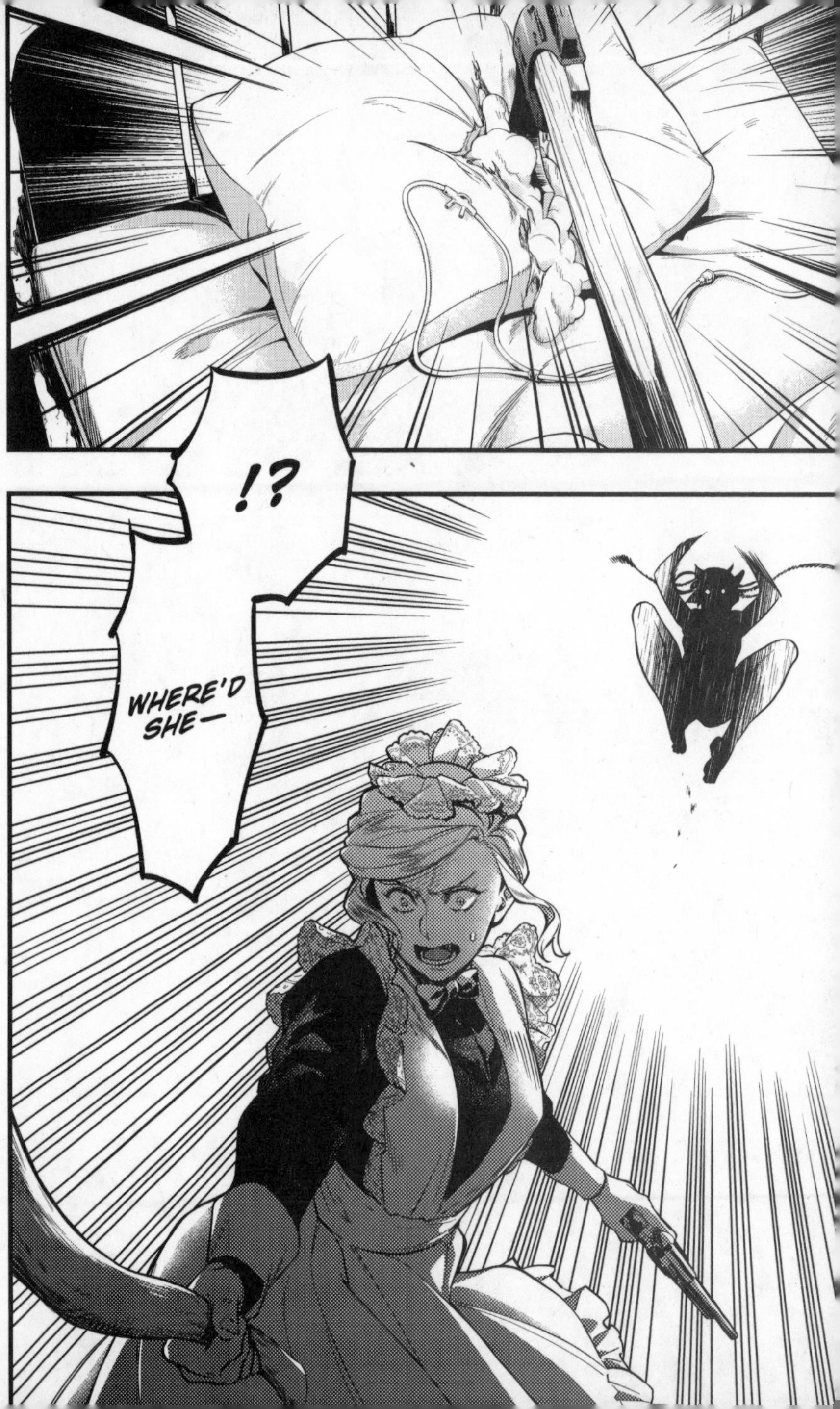
!?
WHERE'D SHE—

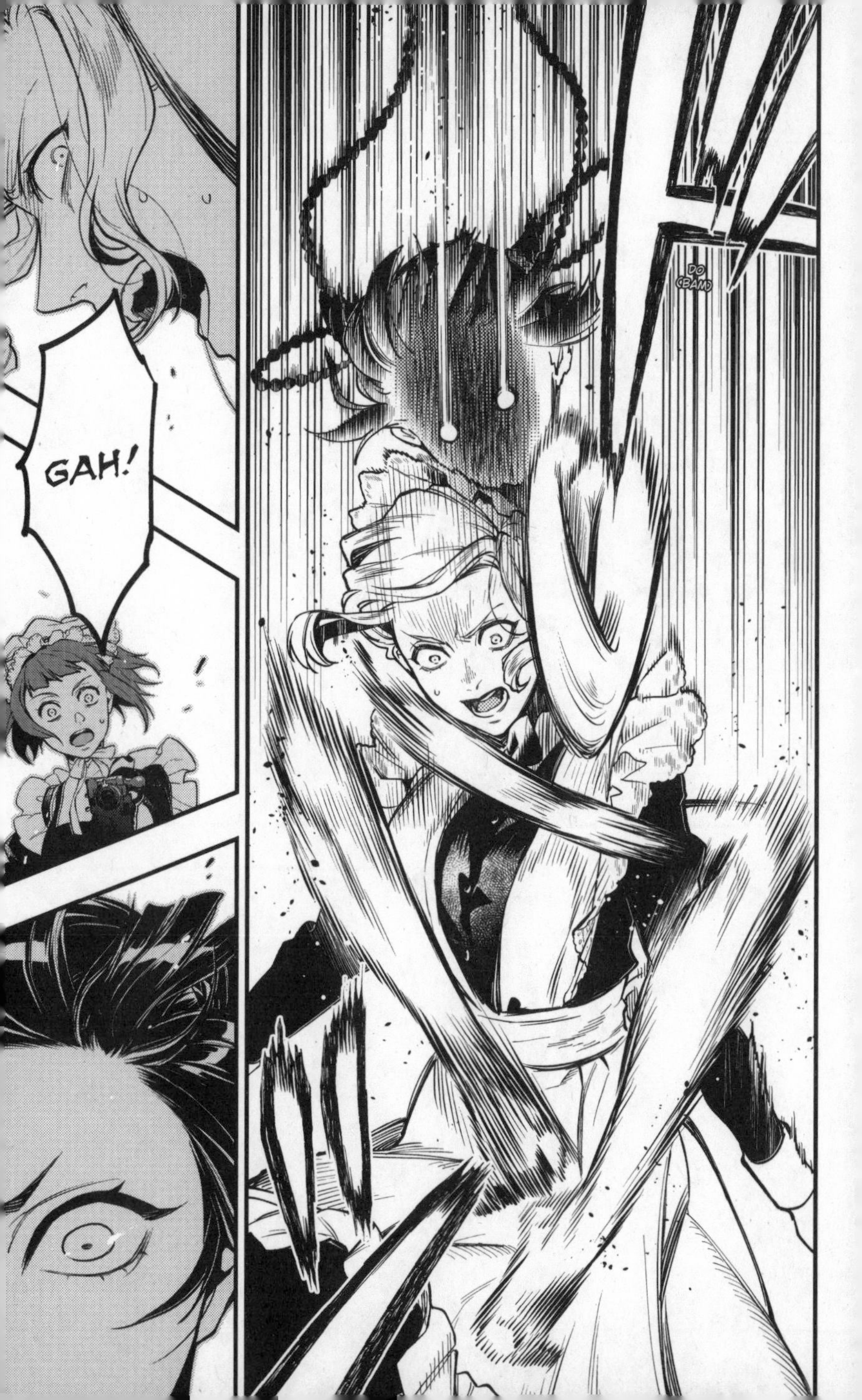
DO (BAM)
GAH!

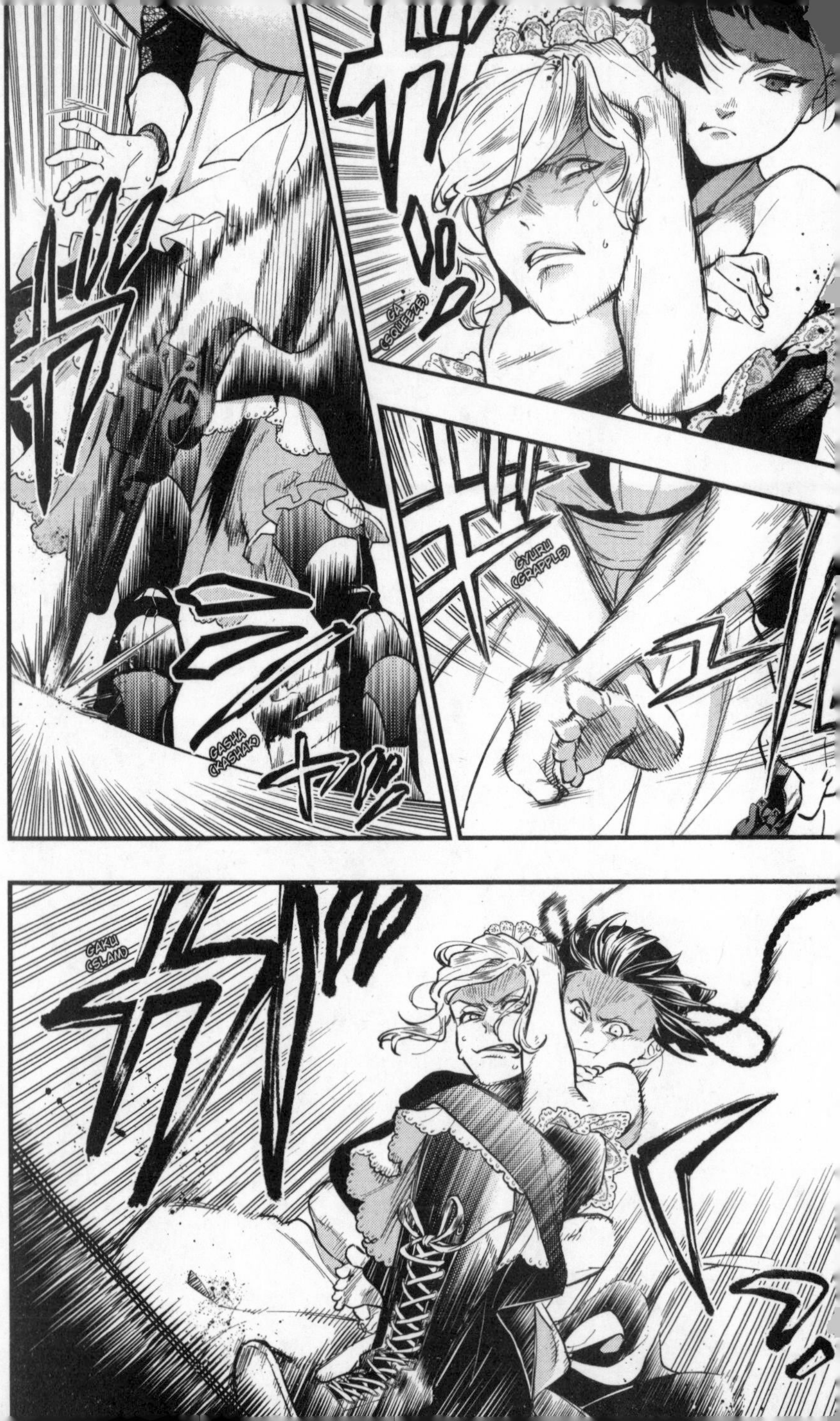
GA (SQUEEZE)
GYURU (GRAPPLE)
GASHA (KASHAK)
GAKU (SLAM)

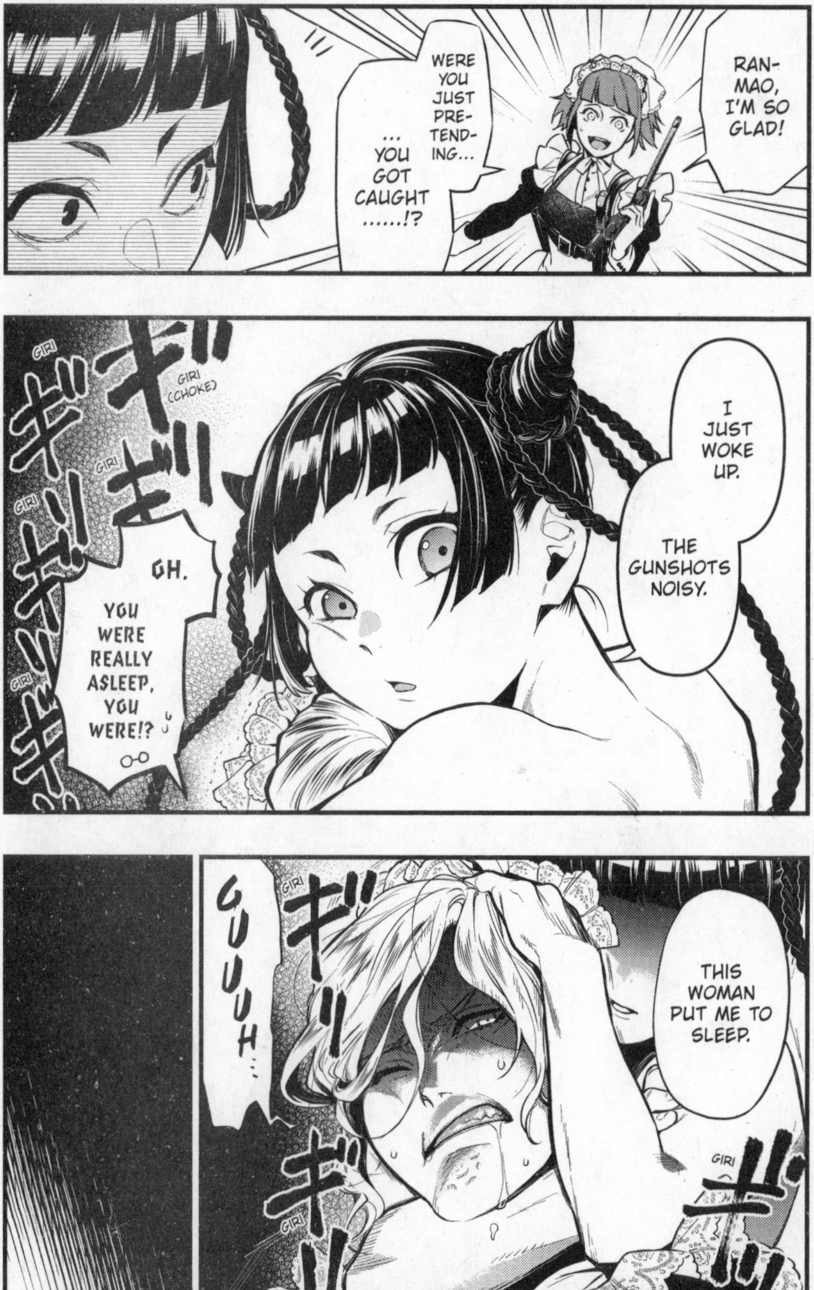
RAN-MAO, I'M SO GLAD!
WERE YOU JUST PRE-TEND-ING...
...YOU GOT CAUGHT ......!?
I JUST WOKE UP.
THE GUNSHOTS NOISY.
GIRI GIRI (CHOKE) GIRI GIRI GIRI
GH.
YOU WERE REALLY ASLEEP, YOU WERE!?
THIS WOMAN PUT ME TO SLEEP.
GIRI
GIRI GIRI
GUUUUH...

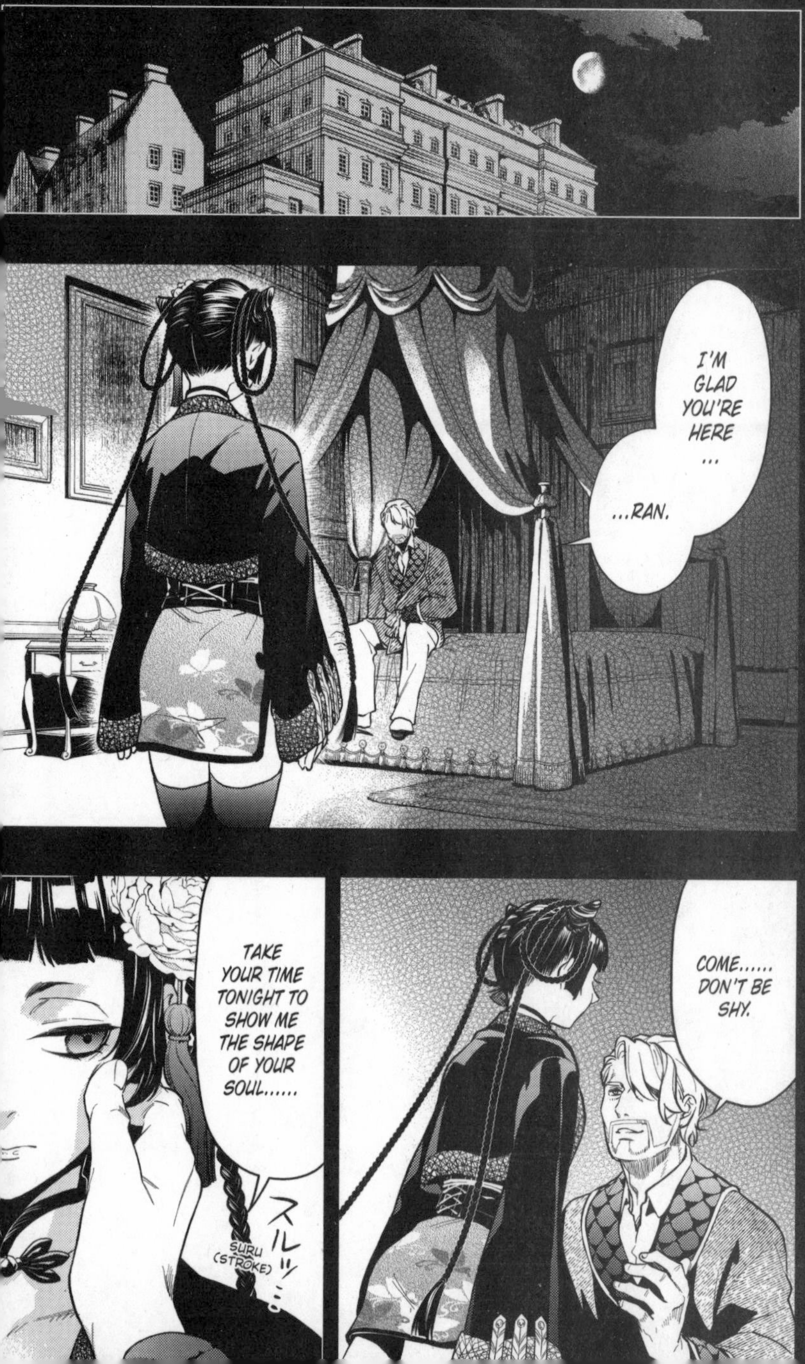
I'M GLAD YOU'RE HERE ...
...RAN.
COME...... DON'T BE SHY.
TAKE YOUR TIME TONIGHT TO SHOW ME THE SHAPE OF YOUR SOUL......
スルッ
SURU (STROKE)

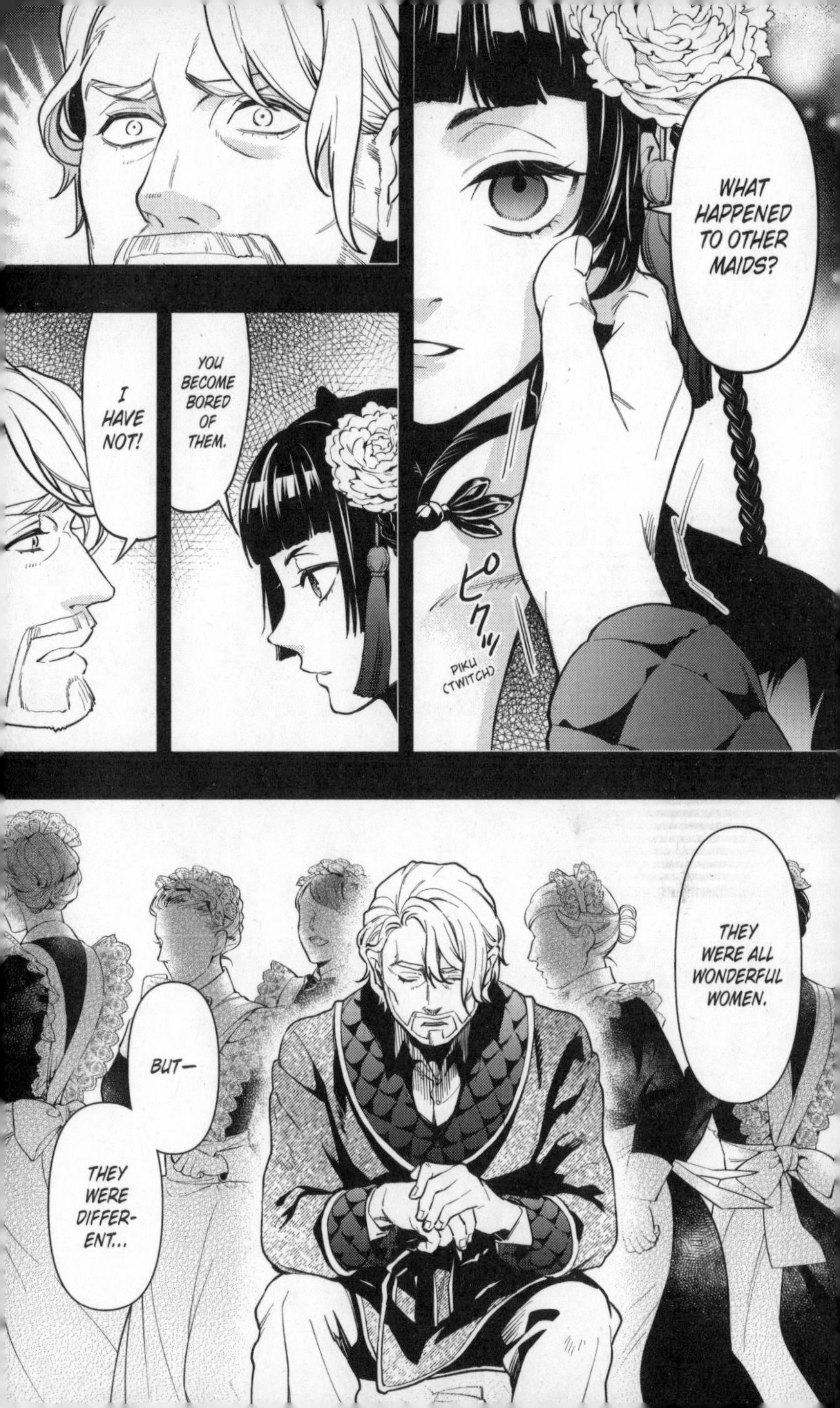
WHAT HAPPENED TO OTHER MAIDS?
ピクッ
PIKU (TWITCH)
YOU BECOME BORED OF THEM.
I HAVE NOT!
THEY WERE ALL WONDERFUL WOMEN.
BUT—
THEY WERE DIFFERENT...

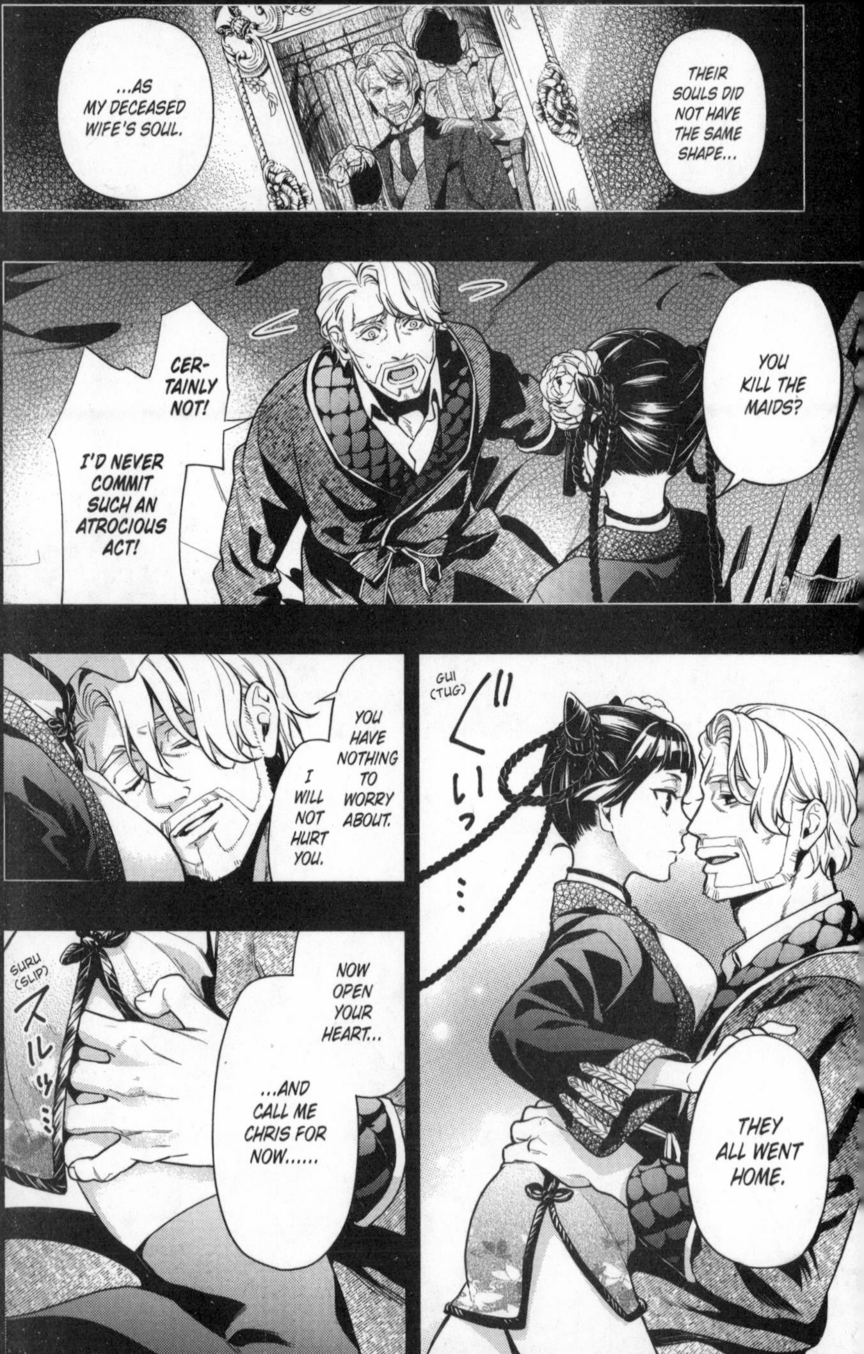
THEIR SOULS DID NOT HAVE THE SAME SHAPE...
...AS MY DECEASED WIFE'S SOUL.
YOU KILL THE MAIDS?
CER-TAINLY NOT!
I'D NEVER COMMIT SUCH AN ATROCIOUS ACT!
GUI (TUG)
THEY ALL WENT HOME.
YOU HAVE NOTHING TO WORRY ABOUT.
I WILL NOT HURT YOU.
SURU (SLIP)
NOW OPEN YOUR HEART...
...AND CALL ME CHRIS FOR NOW......

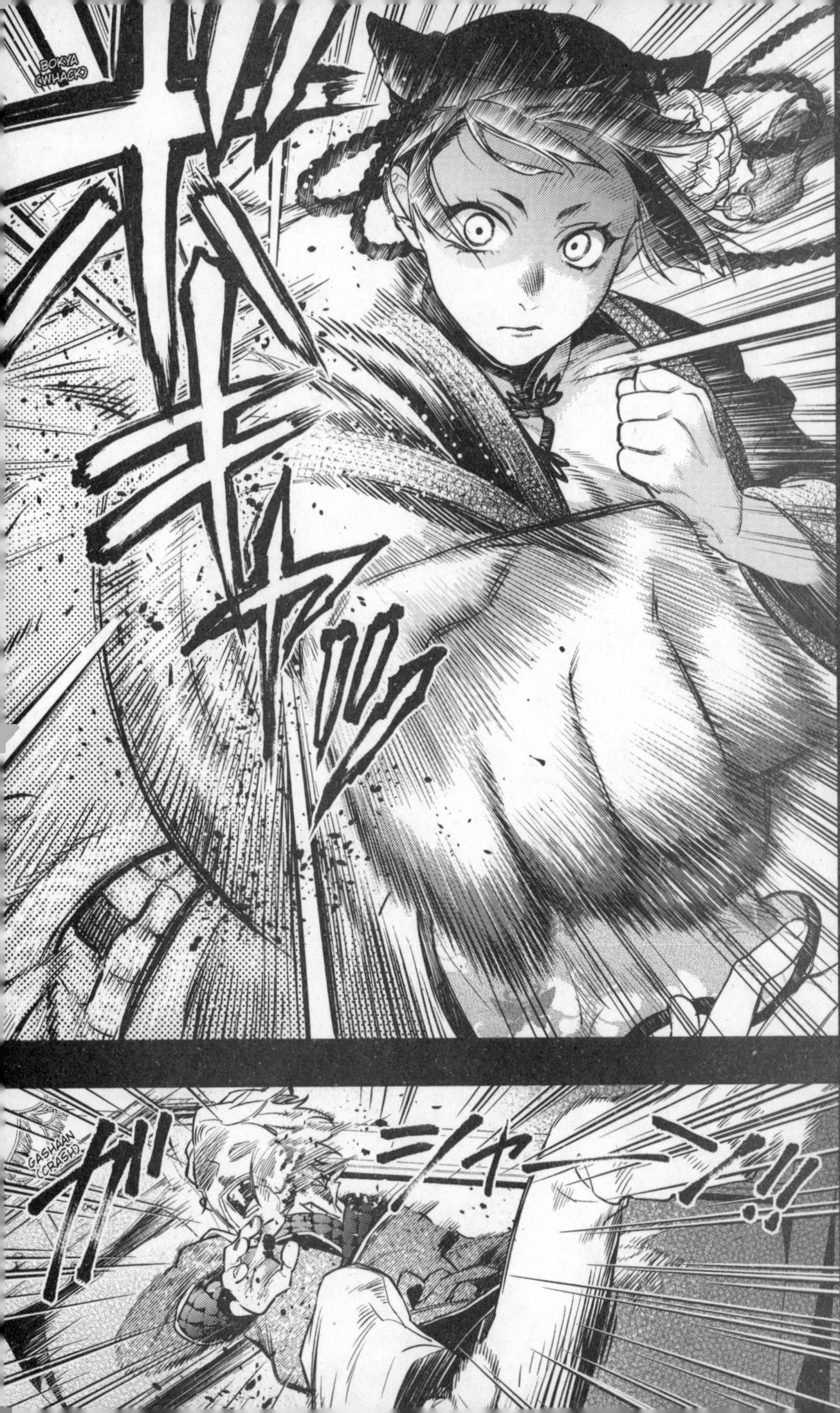
BOKYA (WHACK)
GASHAAN (CRASH)

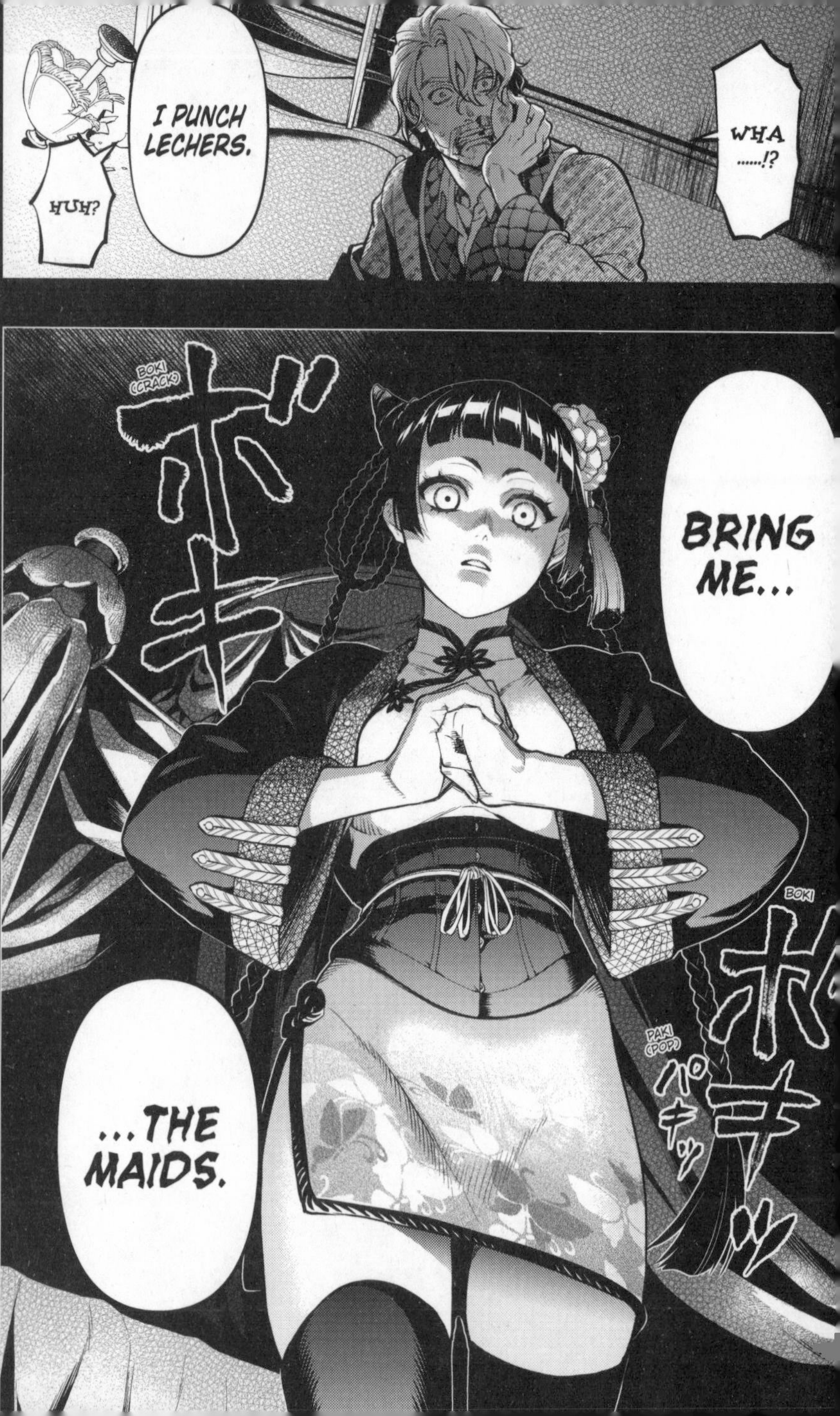
WHA ......!?
I PUNCH LECHERS.
HUH?
BRING ME...
BOKI (CRACK)
ボキ
BOKI
ボキ
PAKI (POP)
パキッ
...THE MAIDS.

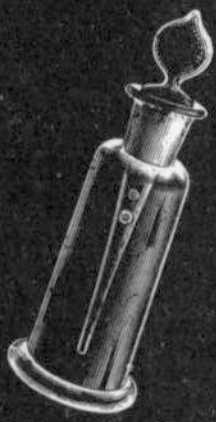

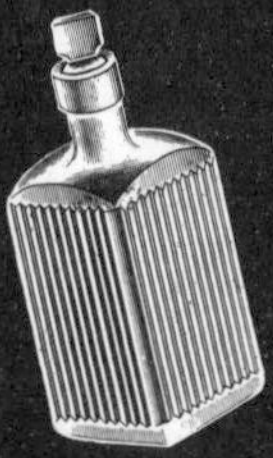

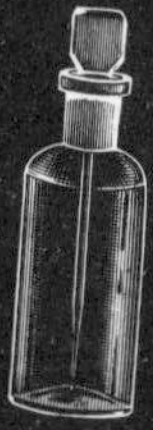

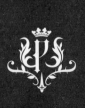

Black Butler

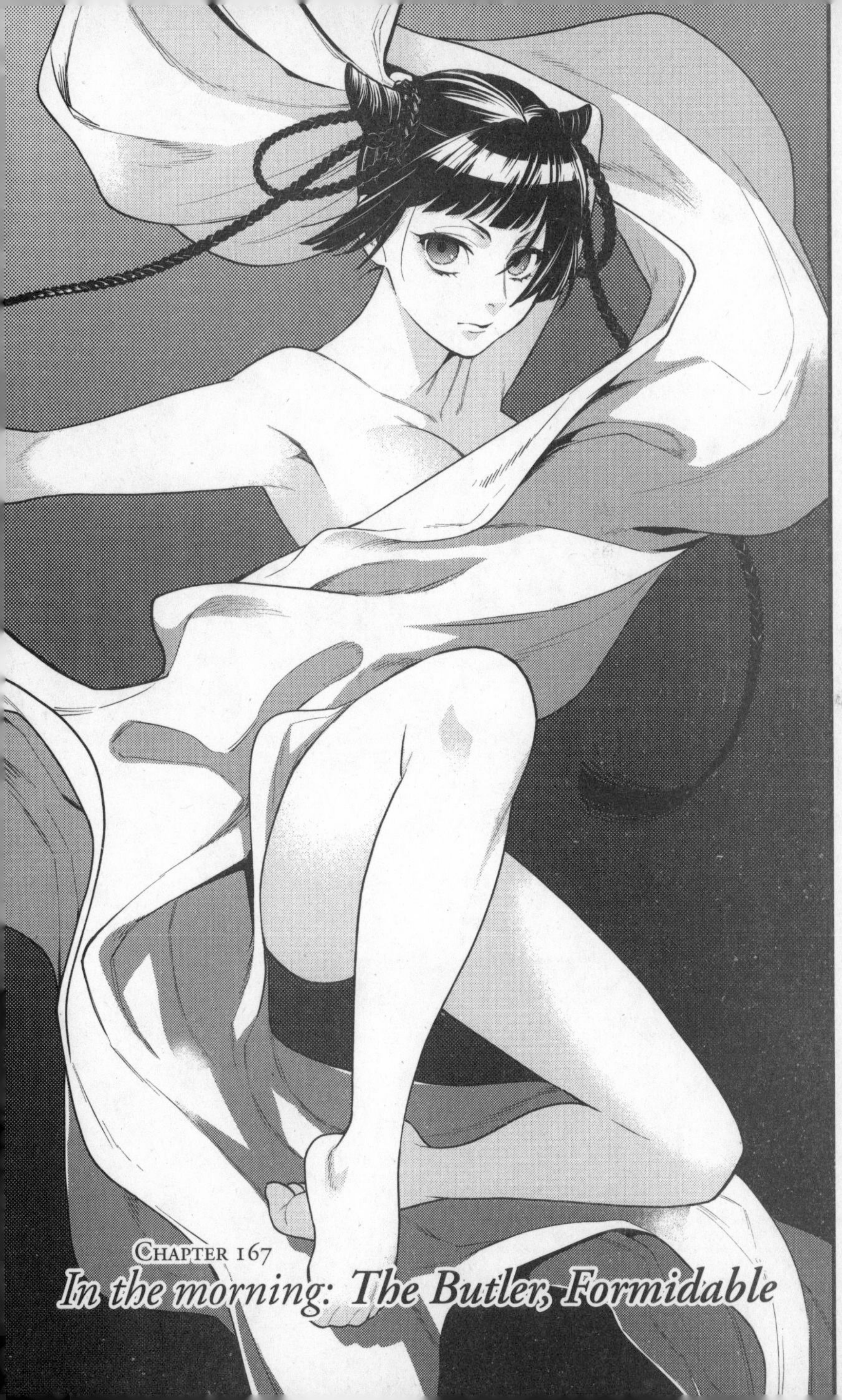

Chapter 167

In the morning: The Butler, Formidable

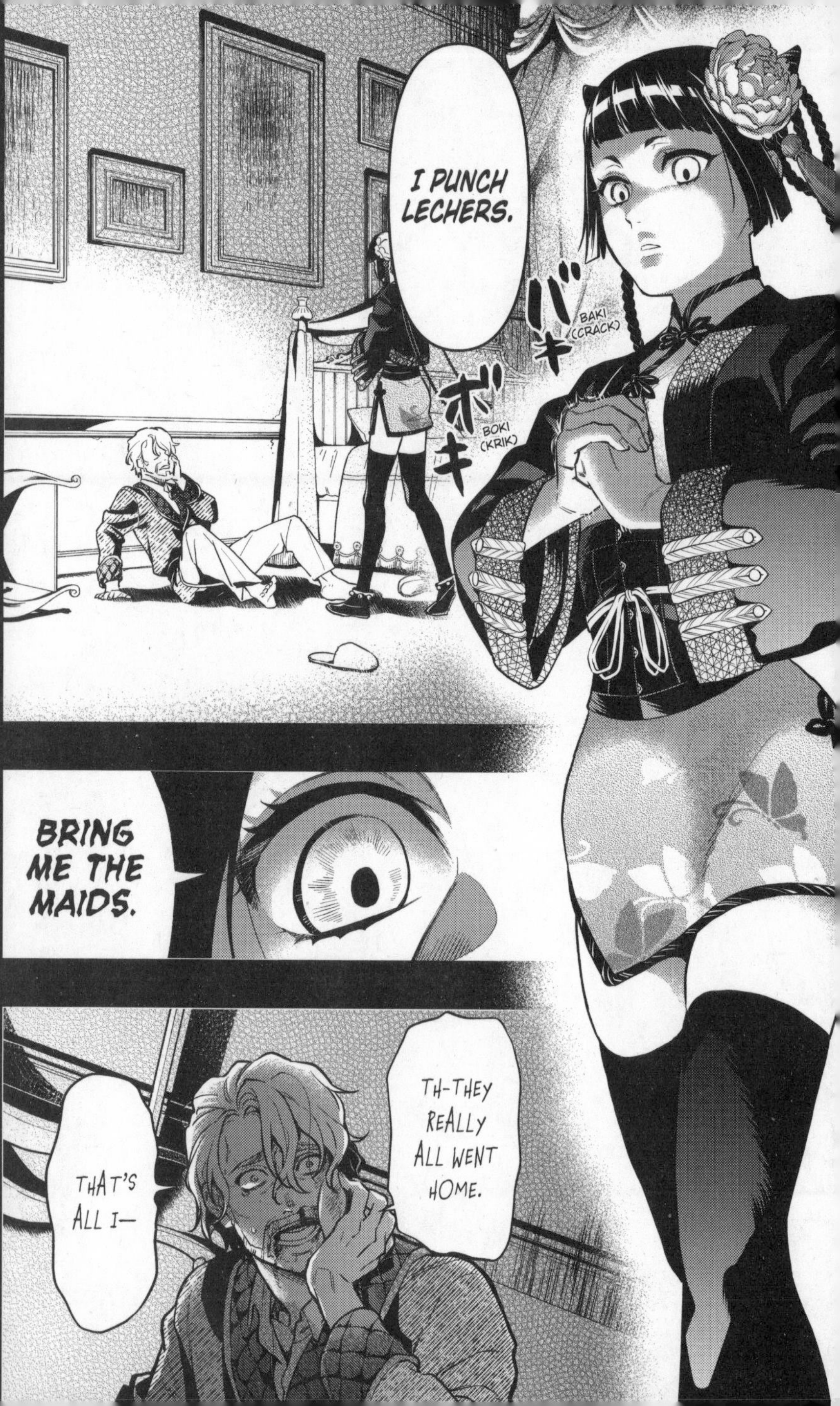
I PUNCH LECHERS.
バキ
BAKI (CRACK)
ボキ
BOKI (KRIK)
BRING ME THE MAIDS.
TH-THEY REALLY ALL WENT HOME.
THAT'S ALL I—

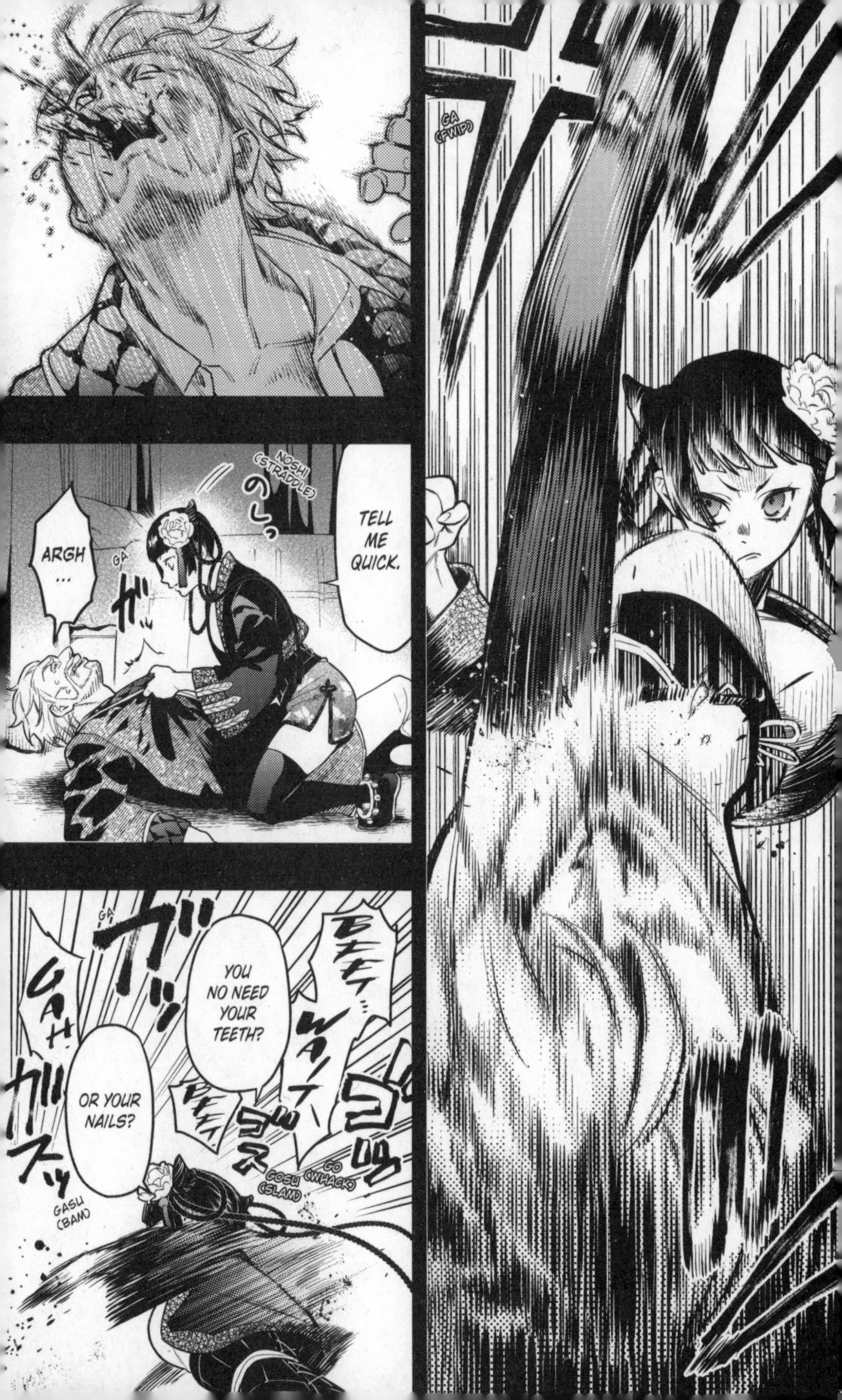
GA (FWIP)
TELL ME QUICK.
NOSHI (STRADDLE)
GA
ARGH ...
WAIT
YOU NO NEED YOUR TEETH?
GO (WHACK)
GOSU (SLAM)
OR YOUR NAILS?
GA
UAH!
GASU (BAM)

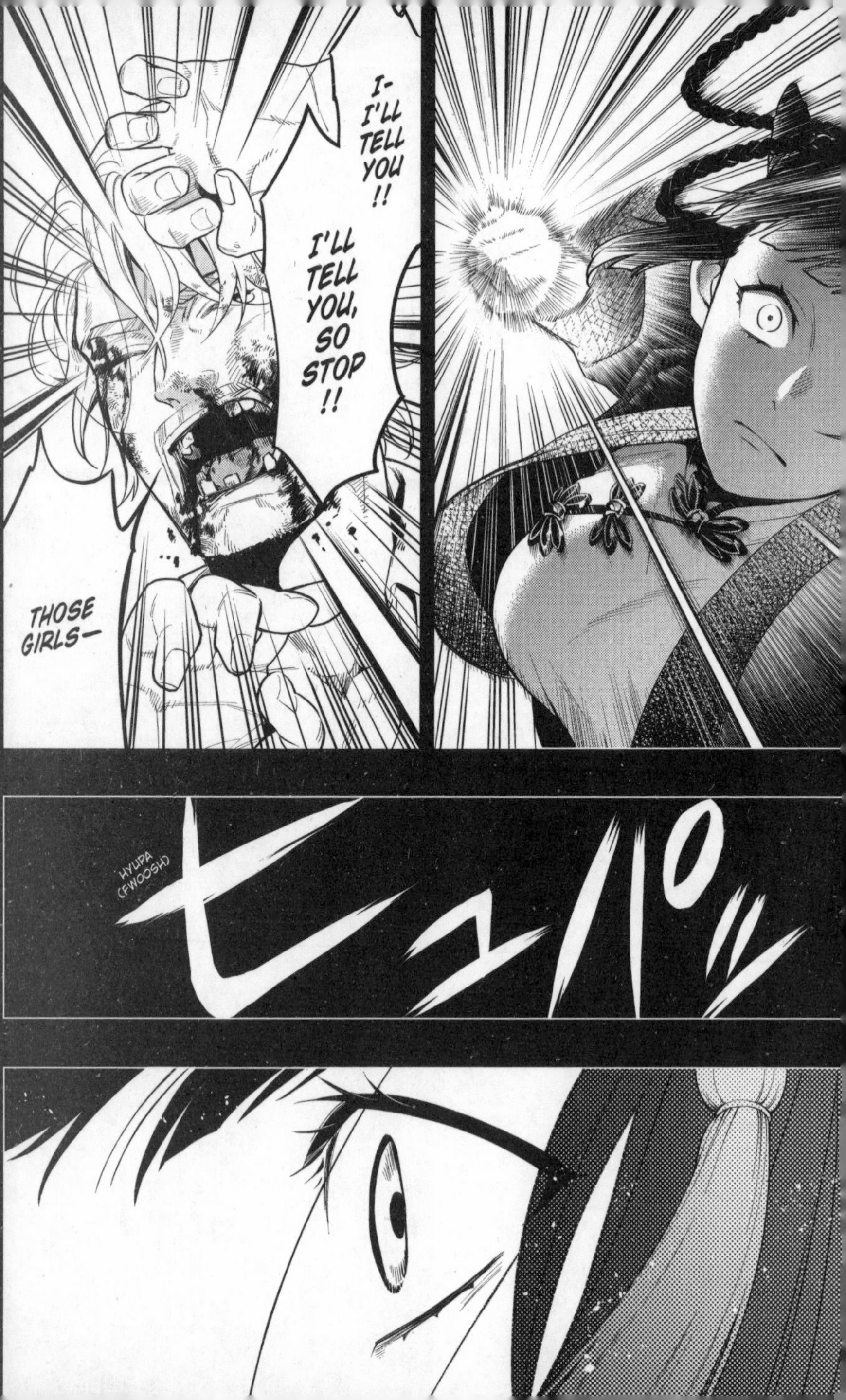
I- I'LL TELL YOU !!
I'LL TELL YOU, SO STOP !!
THOSE GIRLS—
ヒュパッ
HYUPA (FWOOSH)

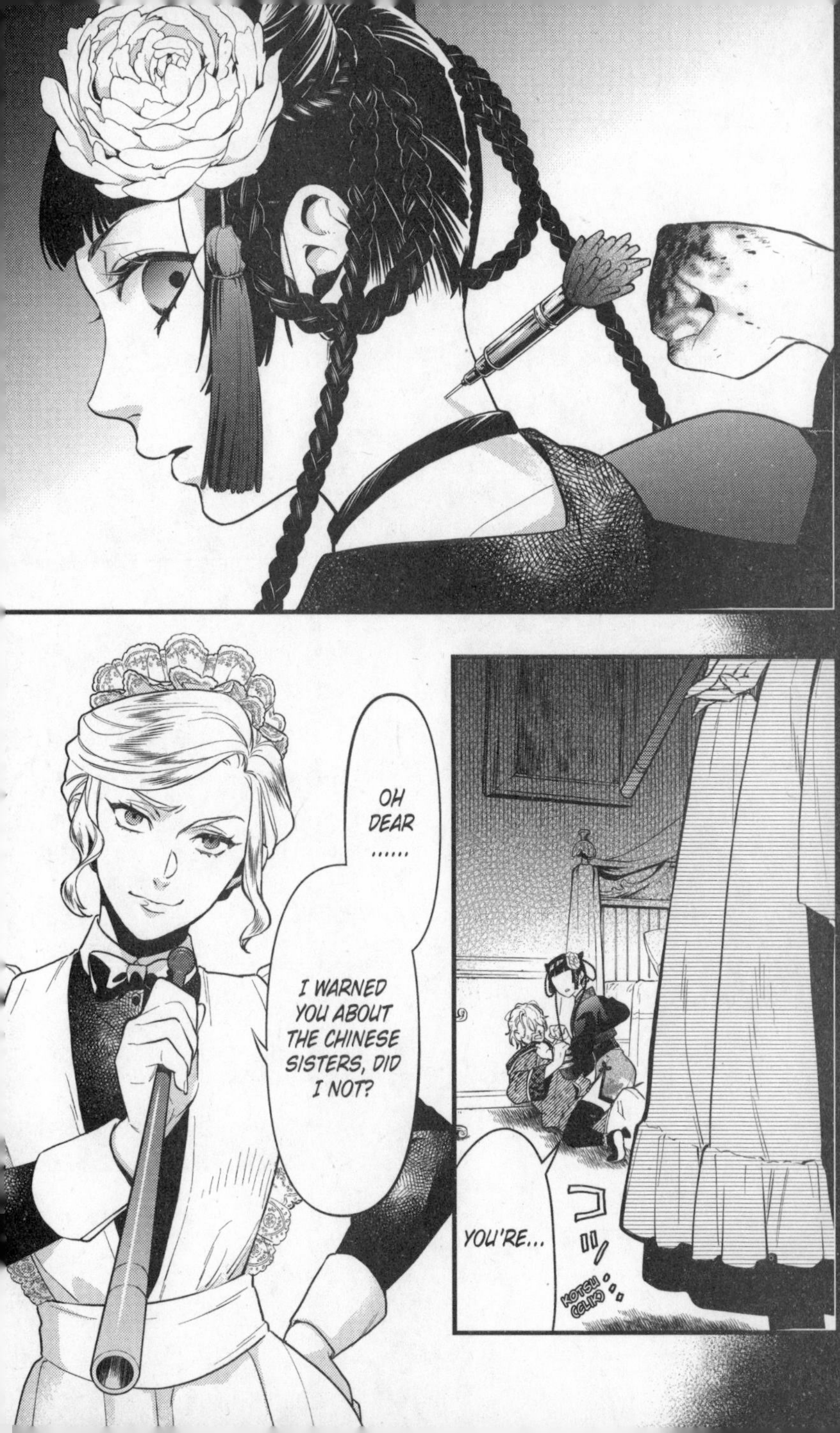
コツ
KOTSU (CLIK)
YOU'RE...
OH DEAR ......
I WARNED YOU ABOUT THE CHINESE SISTERS, DID I NOT?

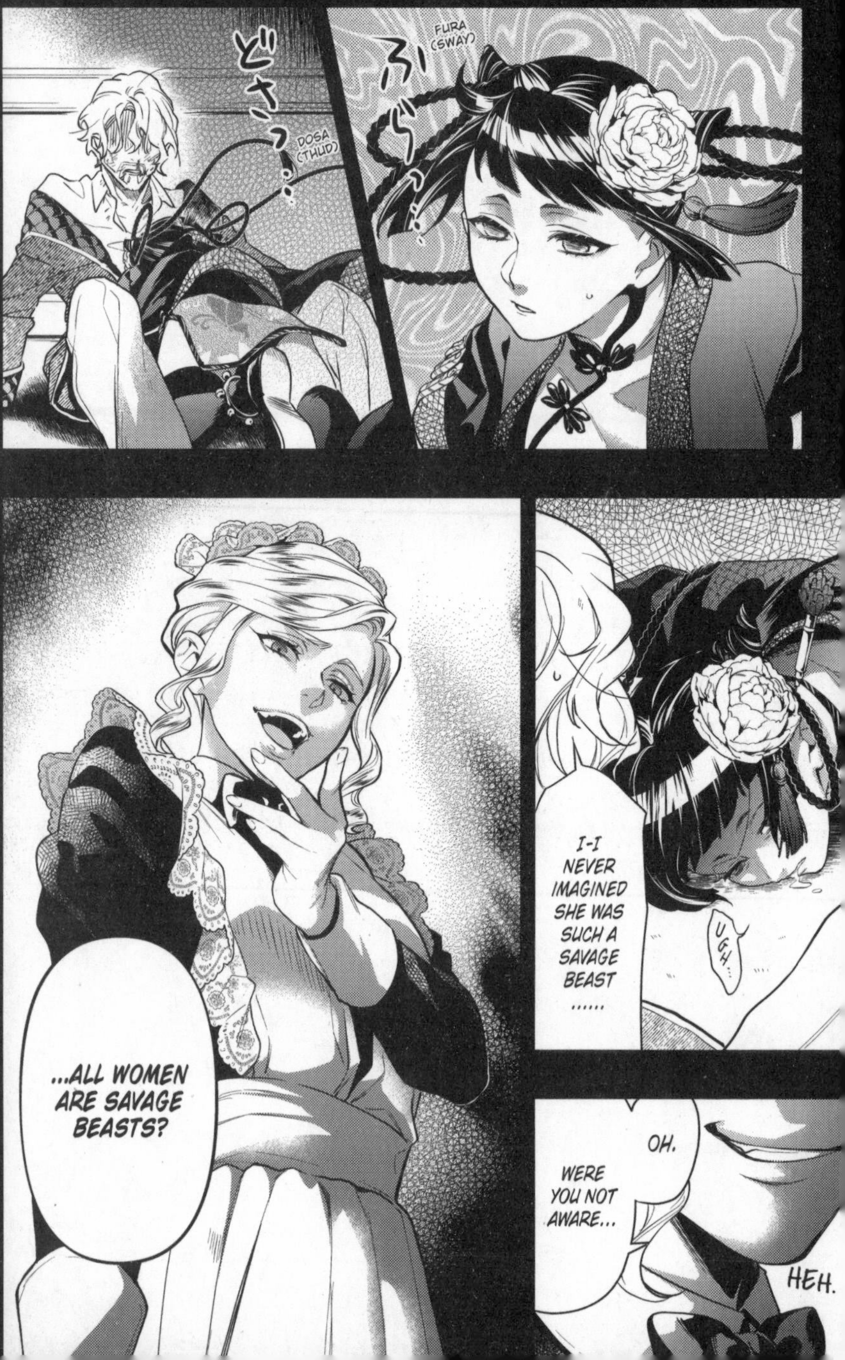

FURA (SWAY)
DOSA (THUD)
I-I NEVER IMAGINED SHE WAS SUCH A SAVAGE BEAST ......
UGH...
OH.
WERE YOU NOT AWARE...
HEH.
...ALL WOMEN ARE SAVAGE BEASTS?

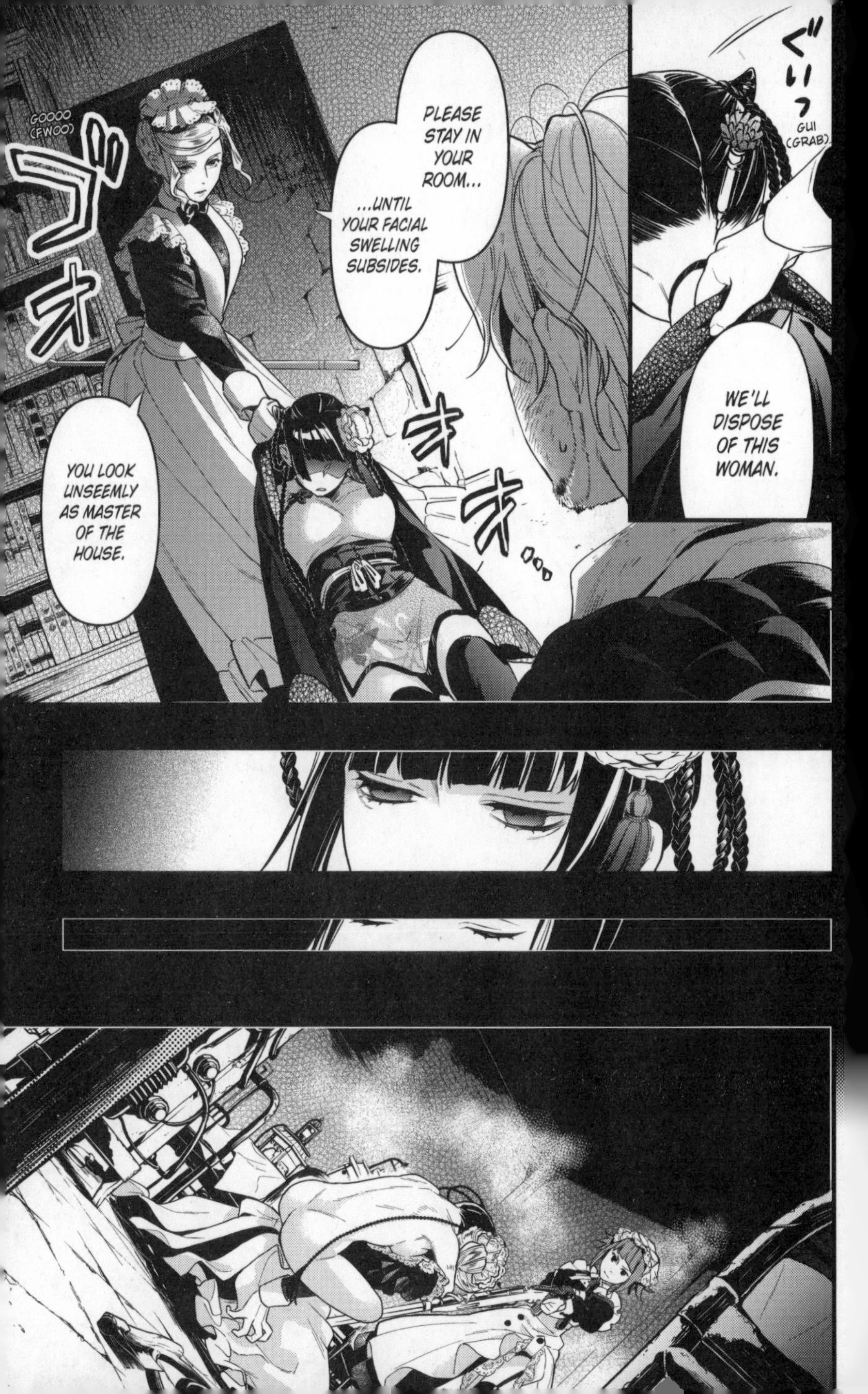
ぐいっ
GUI (GRAB)
WE'LL DISPOSE OF THIS WOMAN.
PLEASE STAY IN YOUR ROOM...
...UNTIL YOUR FACIAL SWELLING SUBSIDES.
GOOOO (FWOO)
YOU LOOK UNSEEMLY AS MASTER OF THE HOUSE.

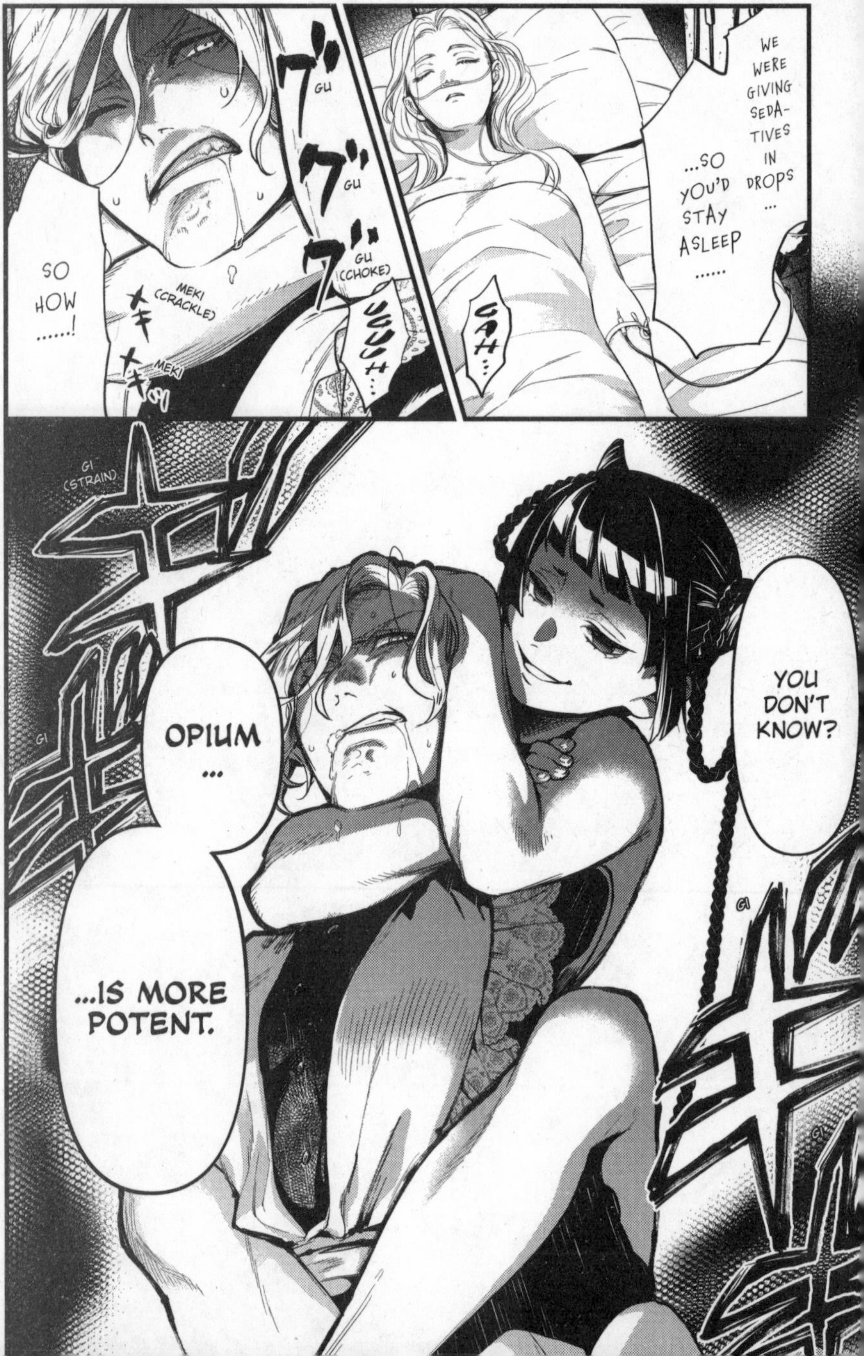
WE WERE GIVING SEDATIVES IN DROPS...
...SO YOU'D STAY ASLEEP......
GAH...
GU
GU
GU (CHOKE)
UGUUH...
SO HOW......!
MEKI (CRACKLE)
MEKI
YOU DON'T KNOW?
OPIUM...
...IS MORE POTENT.
GI (STRAIN)
GI
GI
GI

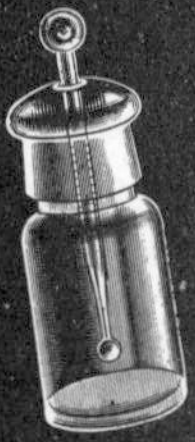

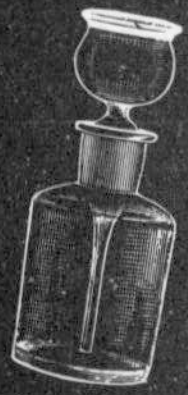

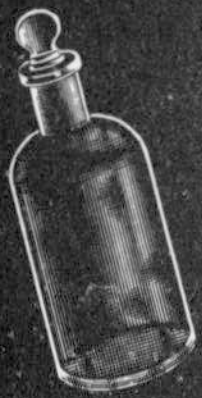

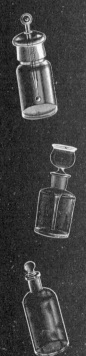

Black Butler

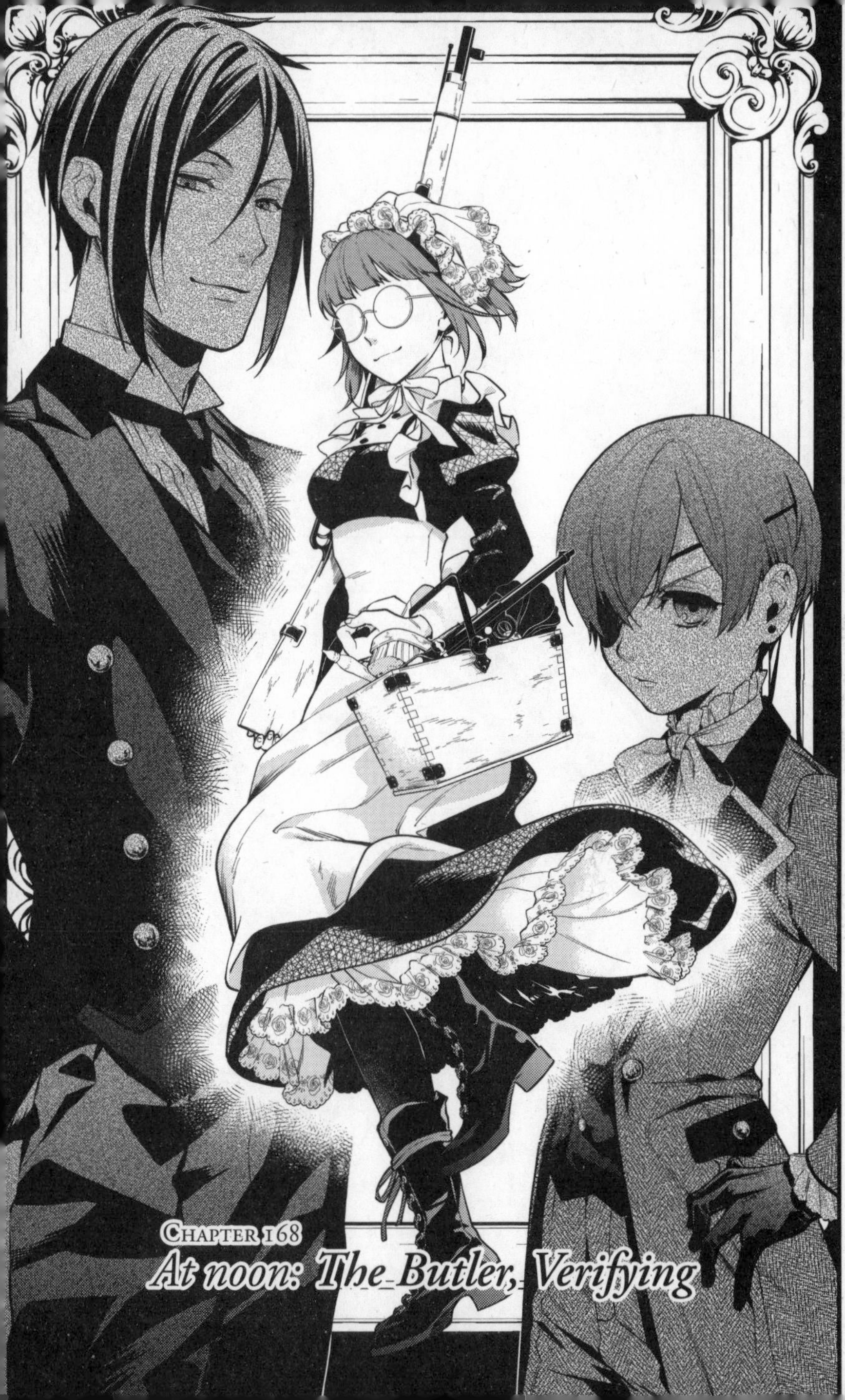
CHAPTER 168
At noon: The Butler, Verifying

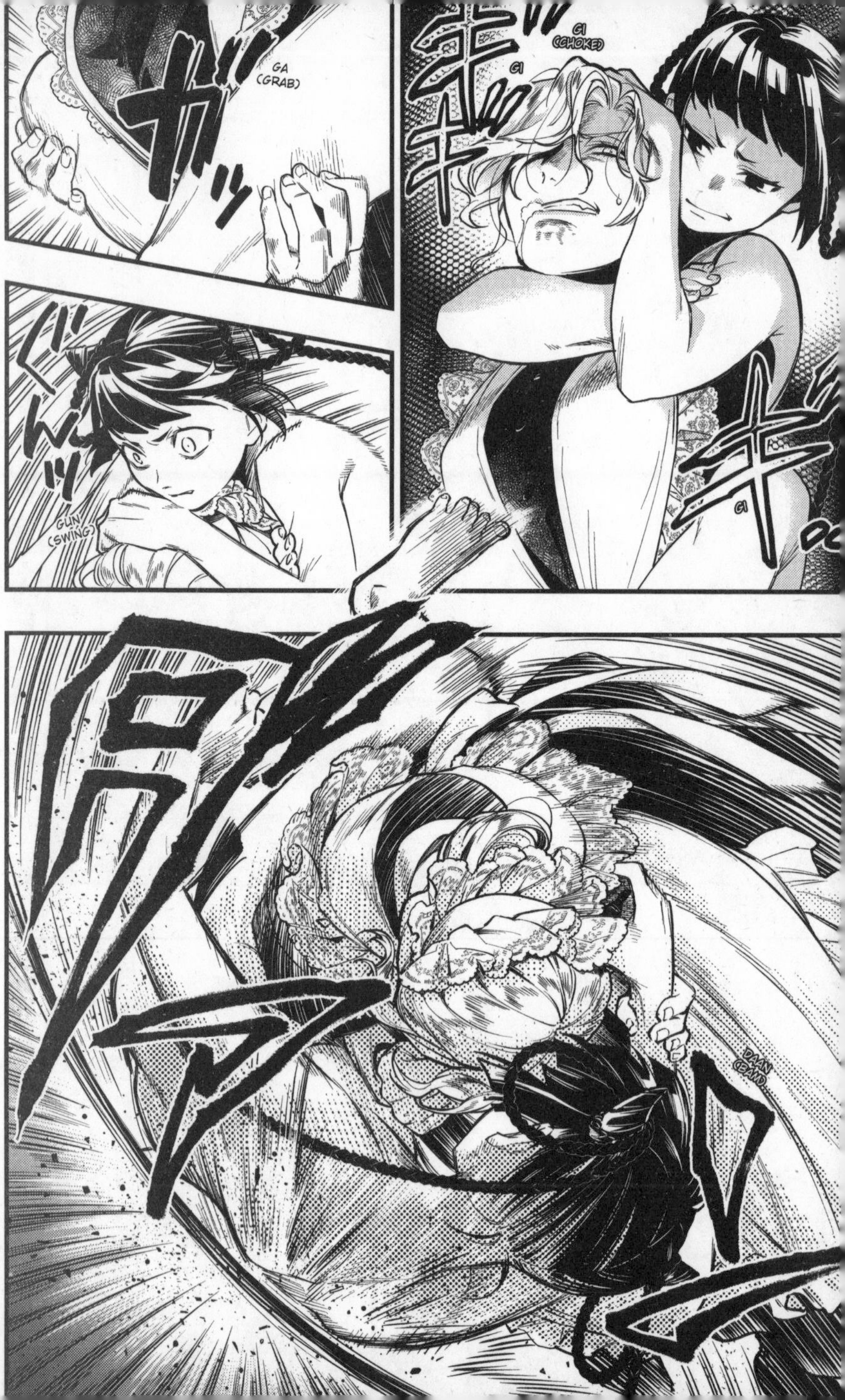
GI (CHOKED)
GI
GI
GA (GRAB)
GUN (SWING)
DAAN (BAM)

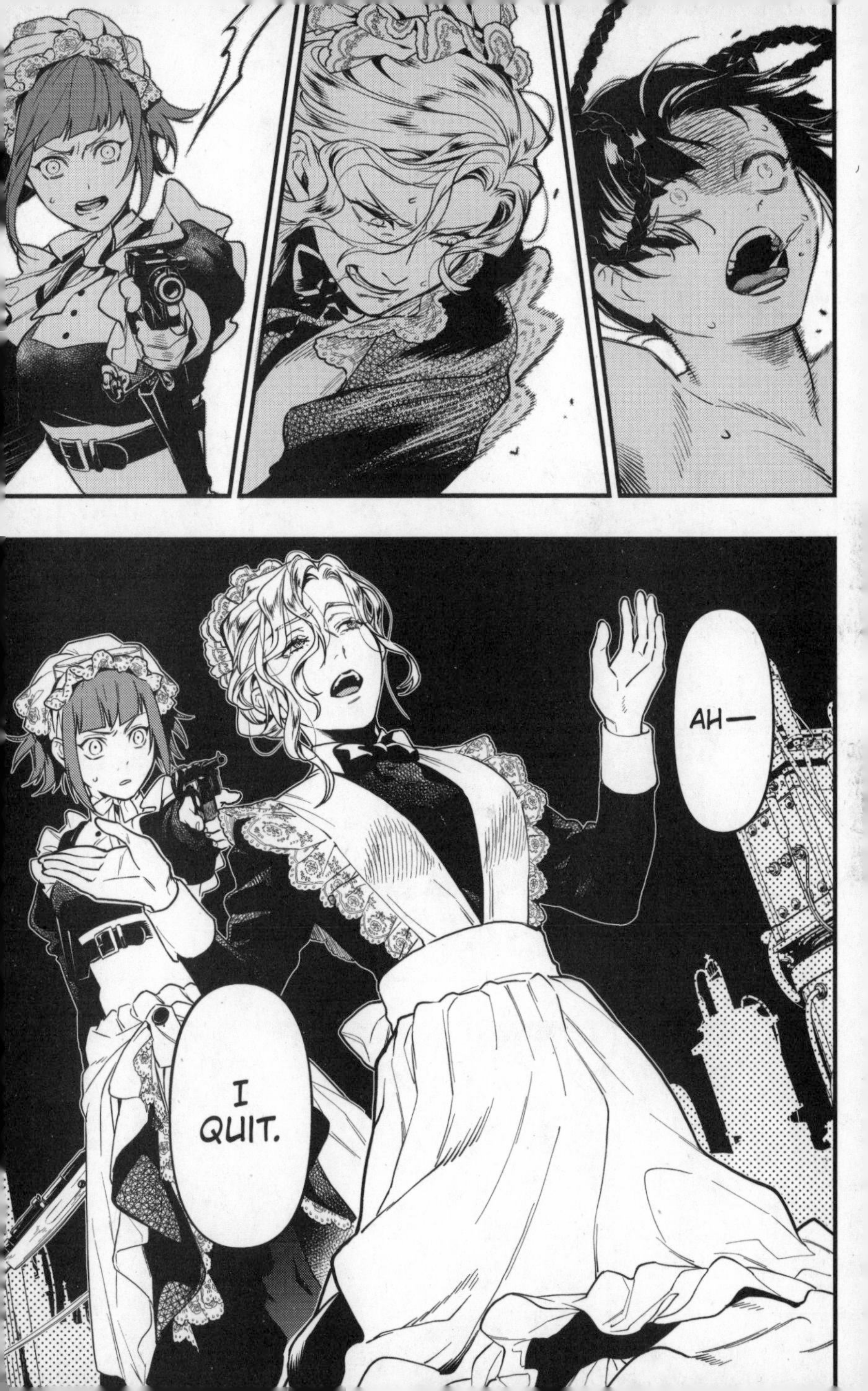
AH—
I QUIT.

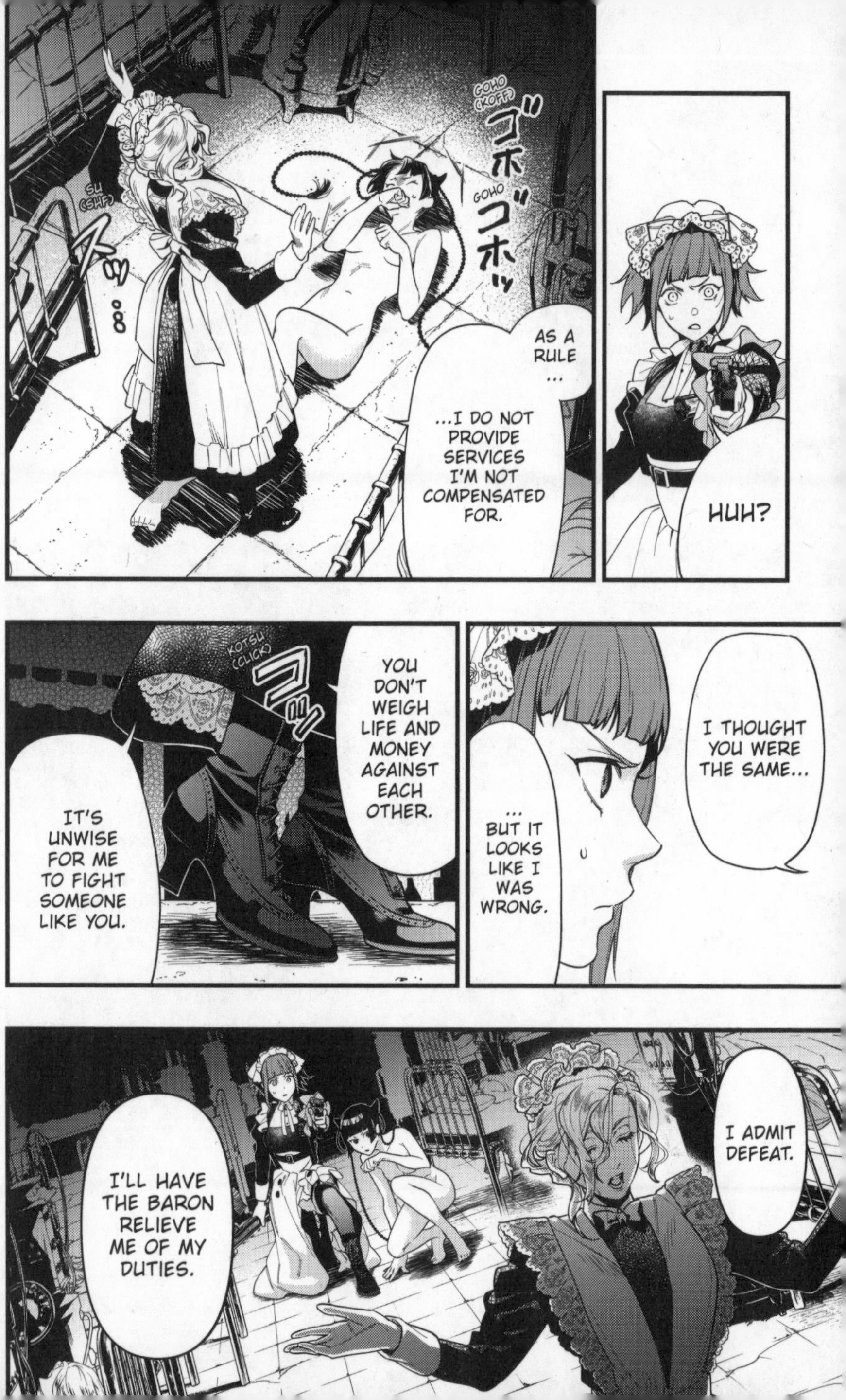
HUH?
GOHO (KOFF)
GOHO
SU (SHF)
AS A RULE ...
...I DO NOT PROVIDE SERVICES I'M NOT COMPENSATED FOR.
I THOUGHT YOU WERE THE SAME...
... BUT IT LOOKS LIKE I WAS WRONG.
KOTSU (CLICK)
YOU DON'T WEIGH LIFE AND MONEY AGAINST EACH OTHER.
IT'S UNWISE FOR ME TO FIGHT SOMEONE LIKE YOU.
I ADMIT DEFEAT.
I'LL HAVE THE BARON RELIEVE ME OF MY DUTIES.

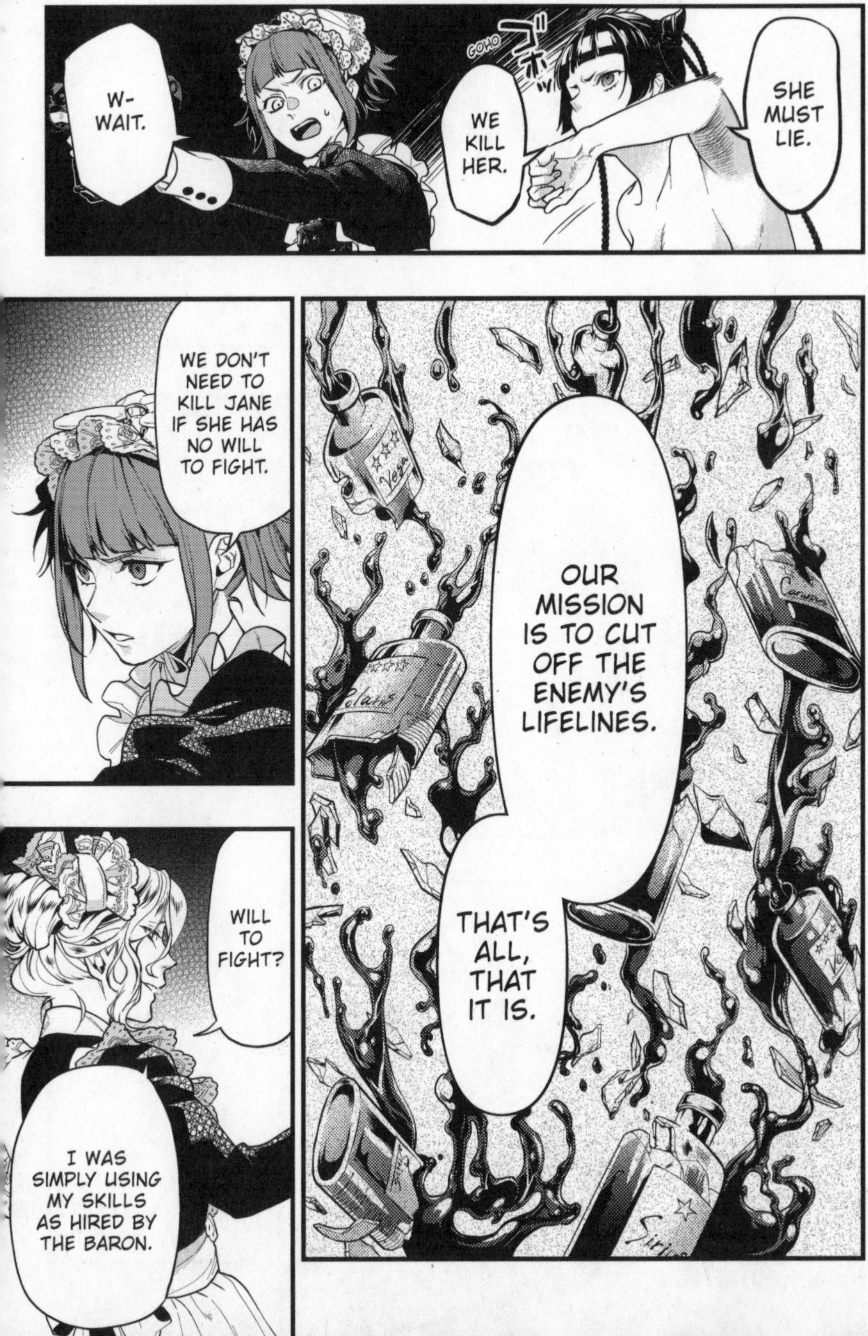
SHE MUST LIE.
GOHO
WE KILL HER.
W- WAIT.
OUR MISSION IS TO CUT OFF THE ENEMY'S LIFELINES.
THAT'S ALL, THAT IT IS.
WE DON'T NEED TO KILL JANE IF SHE HAS NO WILL TO FIGHT.
WILL TO FIGHT?
I WAS SIMPLY USING MY SKILLS AS HIRED BY THE BARON.

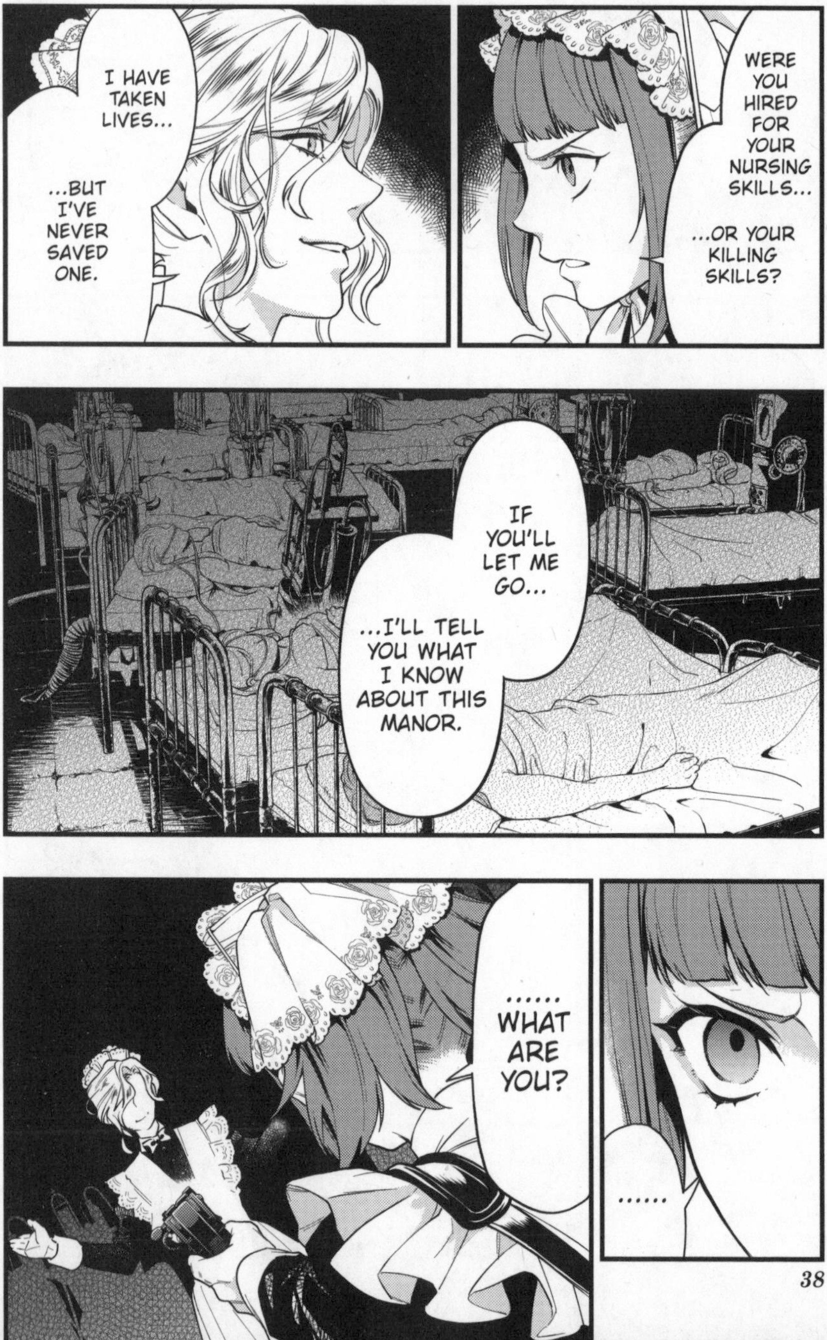
WERE YOU HIRED FOR YOUR NURSING SKILLS...
...OR YOUR KILLING SKILLS?
I HAVE TAKEN LIVES...
...BUT I'VE NEVER SAVED ONE.
IF YOU'LL LET ME GO...
...I'LL TELL YOU WHAT I KNOW ABOUT THIS MANOR.
......
...... WHAT ARE YOU?

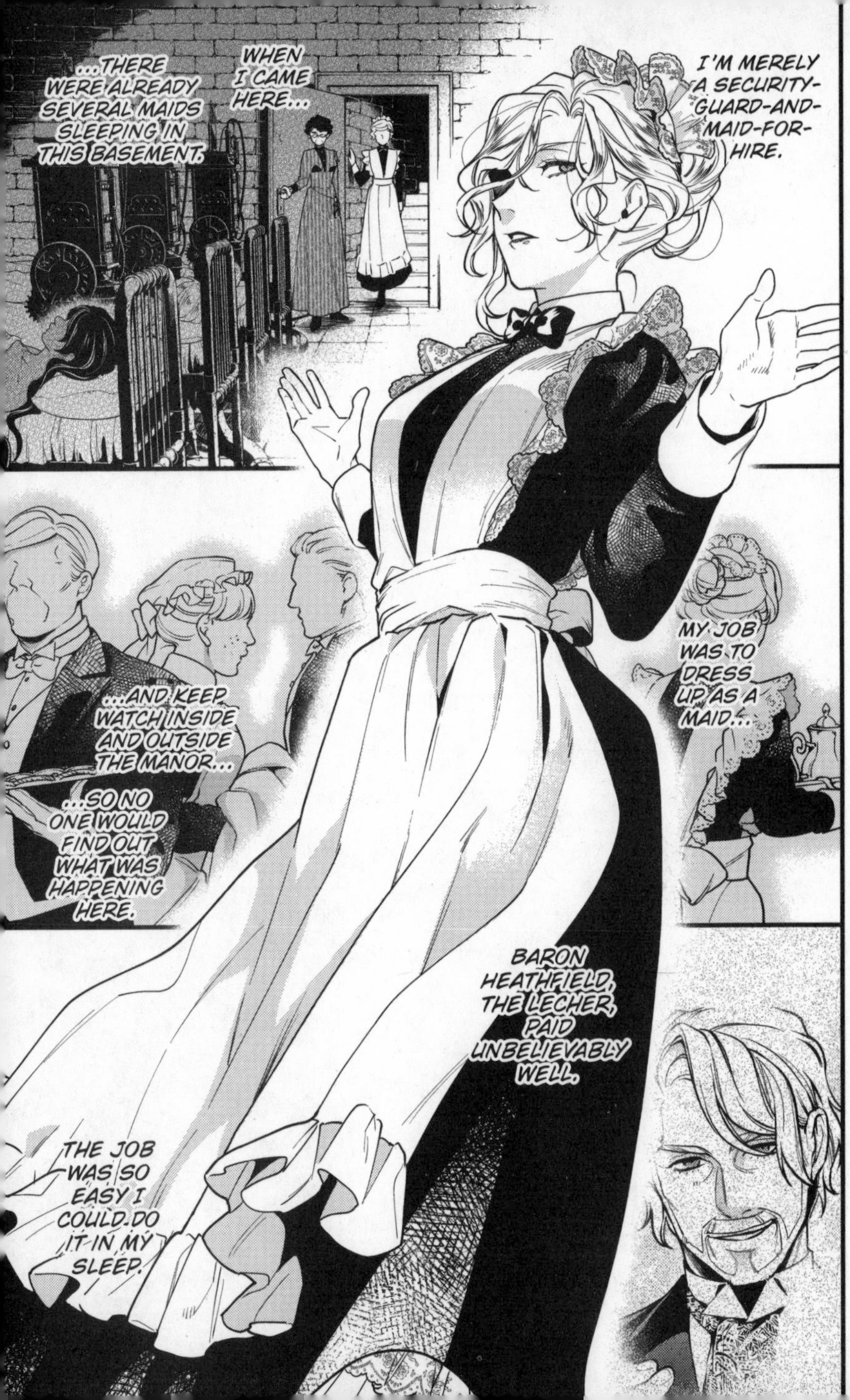
I'M MERELY A SECURITY-GUARD-AND-MAID-FOR-HIRE.
WHEN I CAME HERE...
...THERE WERE ALREADY SEVERAL MAIDS SLEEPING IN THIS BASEMENT.
MY JOB WAS TO DRESS UP AS A MAID...
...AND KEEP WATCH INSIDE AND OUTSIDE THE MANOR...
...SO NO ONE WOULD FIND OUT WHAT WAS HAPPENING HERE.
BARON HEATHFIELD, THE LECHER, PAID UNBELIEVABLY WELL.
THE JOB WAS SO EASY I COULD DO IT IN MY SLEEP.

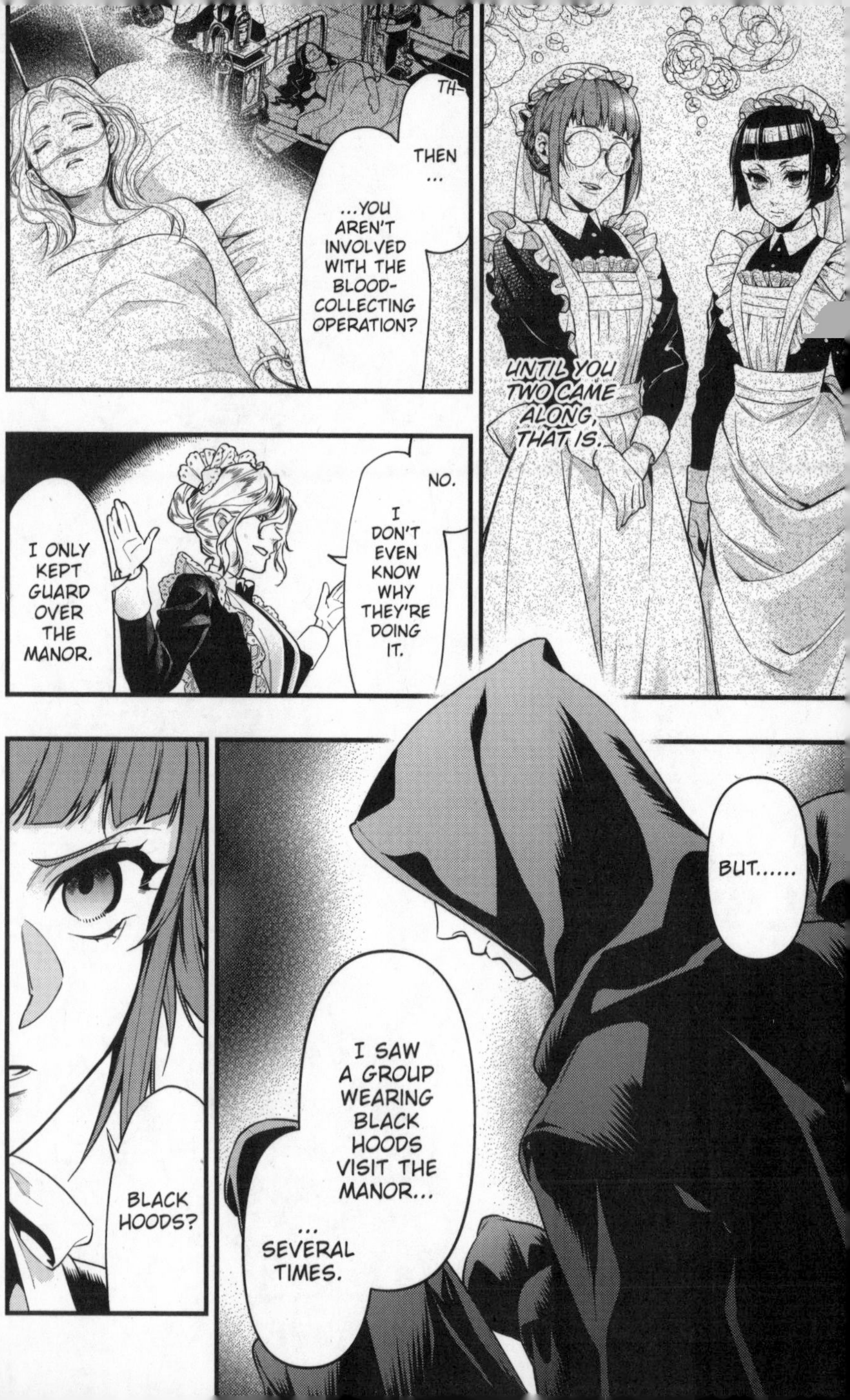
TH-
THEN ...
...YOU AREN'T INVOLVED WITH THE BLOOD-COLLECTING OPERATION?
NO.
I DON'T EVEN KNOW WHY THEY'RE DOING IT.
I ONLY KEPT GUARD OVER THE MANOR.
UNTIL YOU TWO CAME ALONG, THAT IS.
BUT......
I SAW A GROUP WEARING BLACK HOODS VISIT THE MANOR...
... SEVERAL TIMES.
BLACK HOODS?

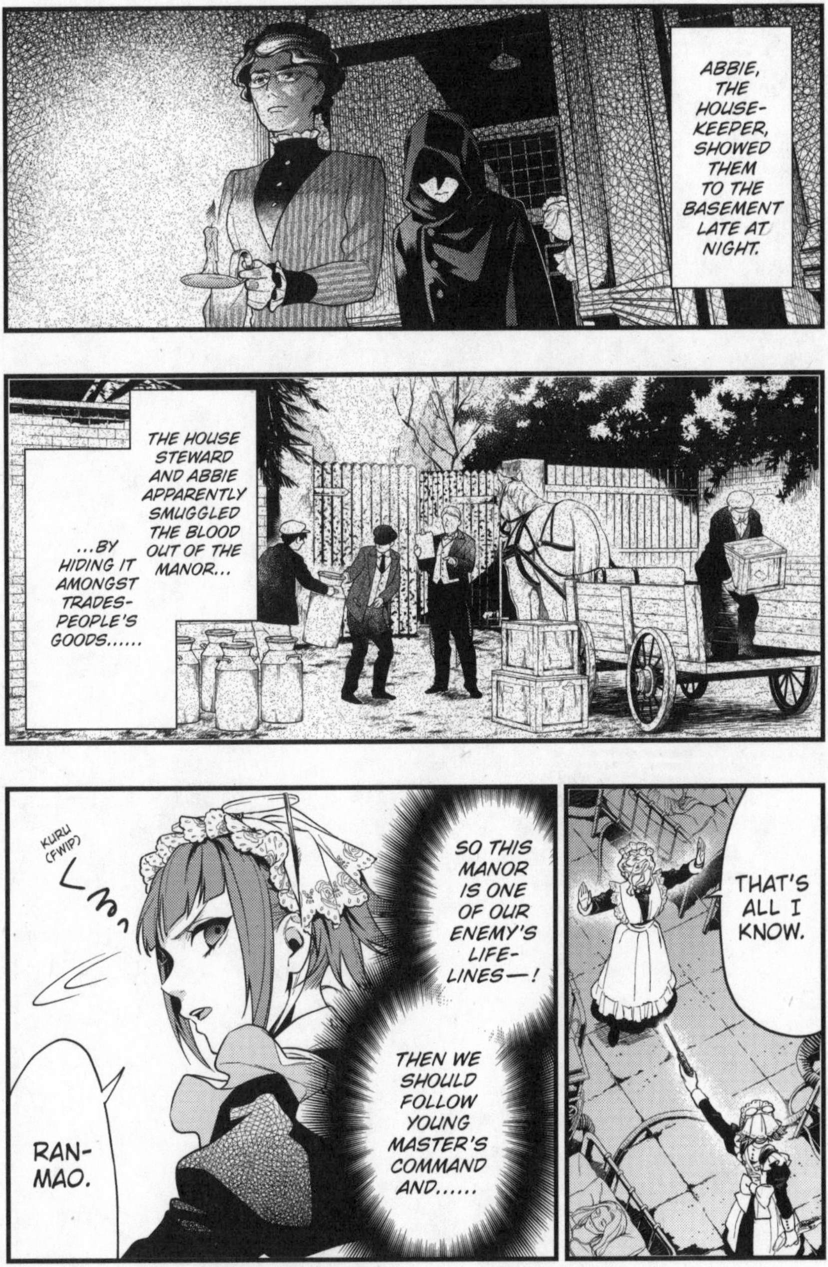
ABBIE, THE HOUSE-KEEPER, SHOWED THEM TO THE BASEMENT LATE AT NIGHT.
THE HOUSE STEWARD AND ABBIE APPARENTLY SMUGGLED THE BLOOD OUT OF THE MANOR...
...BY HIDING IT AMONGST TRADES-PEOPLE'S GOODS......
THAT'S ALL I KNOW.
SO THIS MANOR IS ONE OF OUR ENEMY'S LIFE-LINES—!
THEN WE SHOULD FOLLOW YOUNG MASTER'S COMMAND AND......
KURU (FWIP)
RAN-MAO.

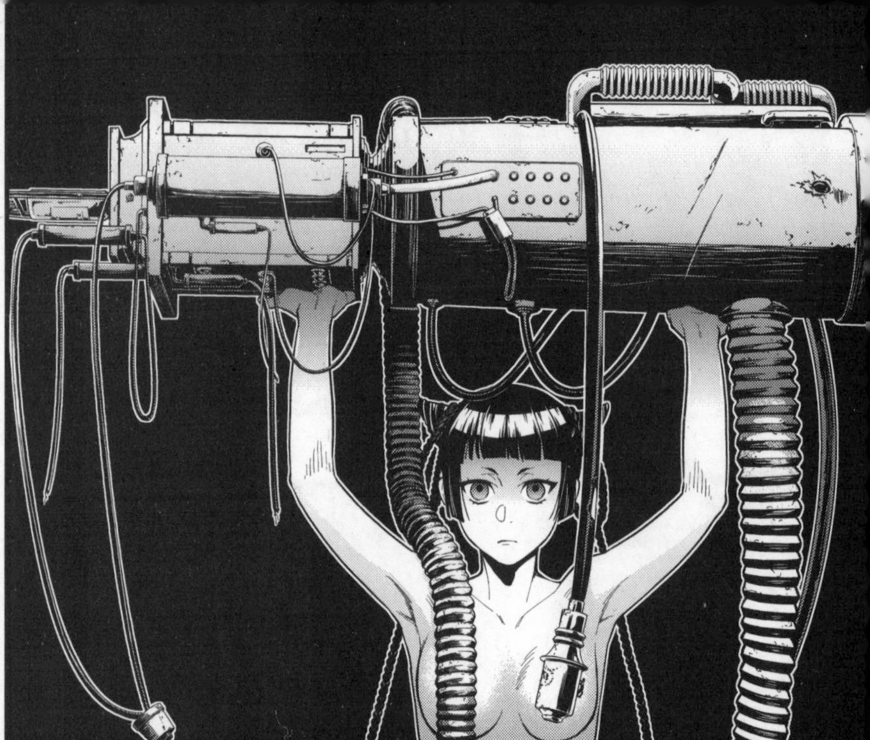

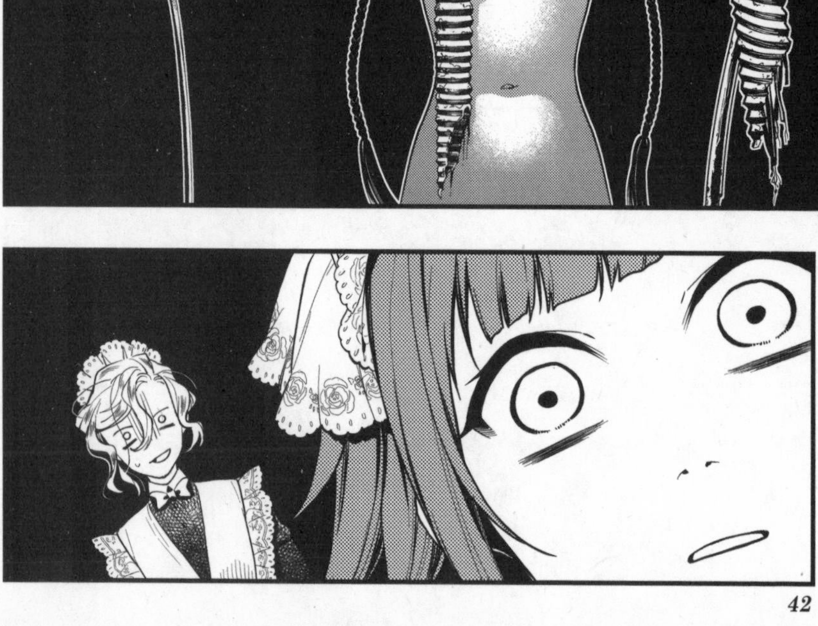

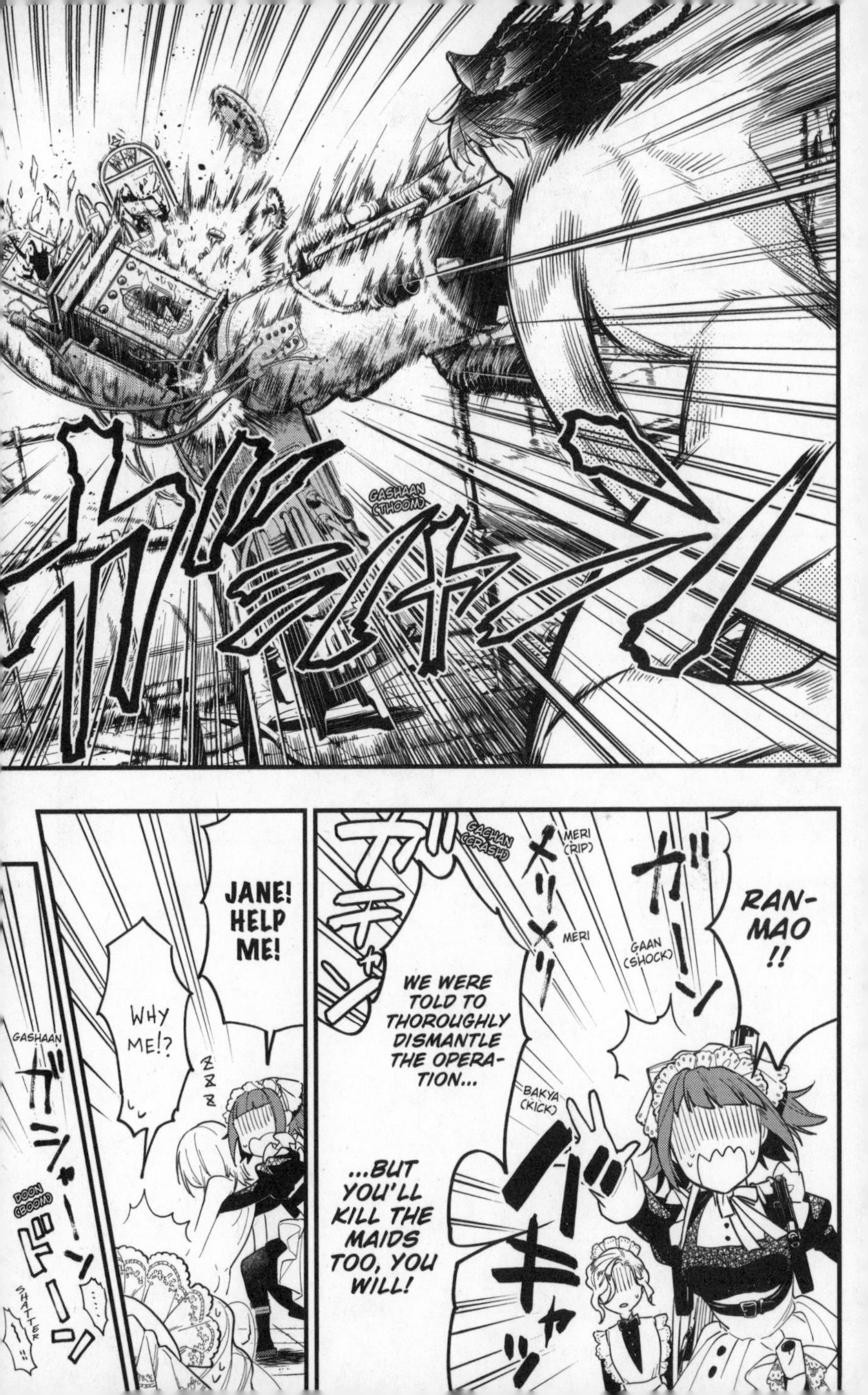
GASHAAN (THOOM)
RAN-MAO!!
GAAN (SHOCK)
MERI (RIP)
MERI
GAGHAN (CRASH)
WE WERE TOLD TO THOROUGHLY DISMANTLE THE OPERATION...
BAKYA (KICK)
...BUT YOU'LL KILL THE MAIDS TOO, YOU WILL!
JANE! HELP ME!
WHY ME!?
GASHAAN
DOON (BOOM)
SHATTER

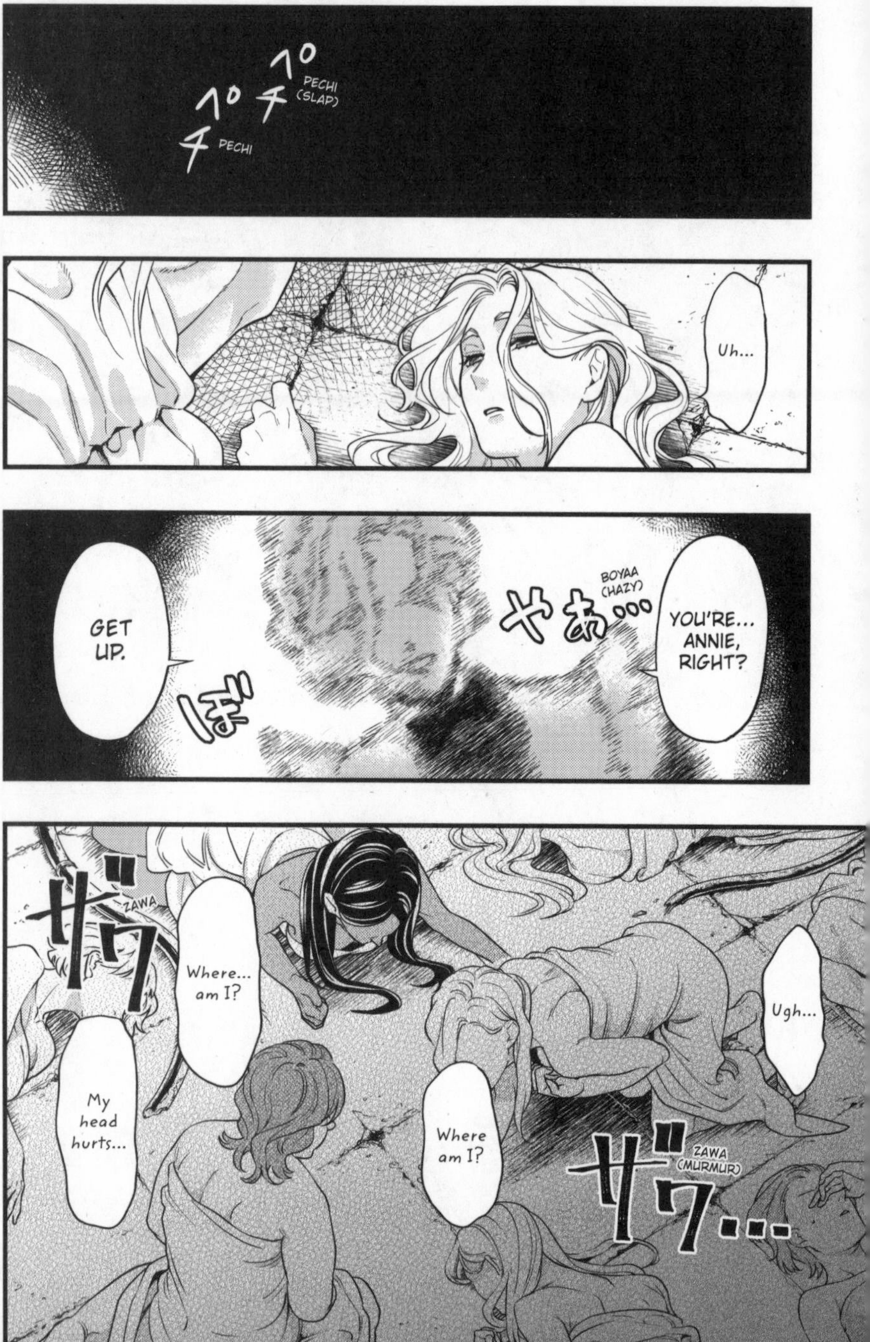
ペチ
PECHI (SLAP)
ペチ
PECHI
Uh...
YOU'RE... ANNIE, RIGHT?
ぼやあ...
BOYAA (HAZY)
GET UP.
Ugh...
Where... am I?
ザワ
ZAWA
Where am I?
My head hurts...
ザワ...
ZAWA (MURMUR)

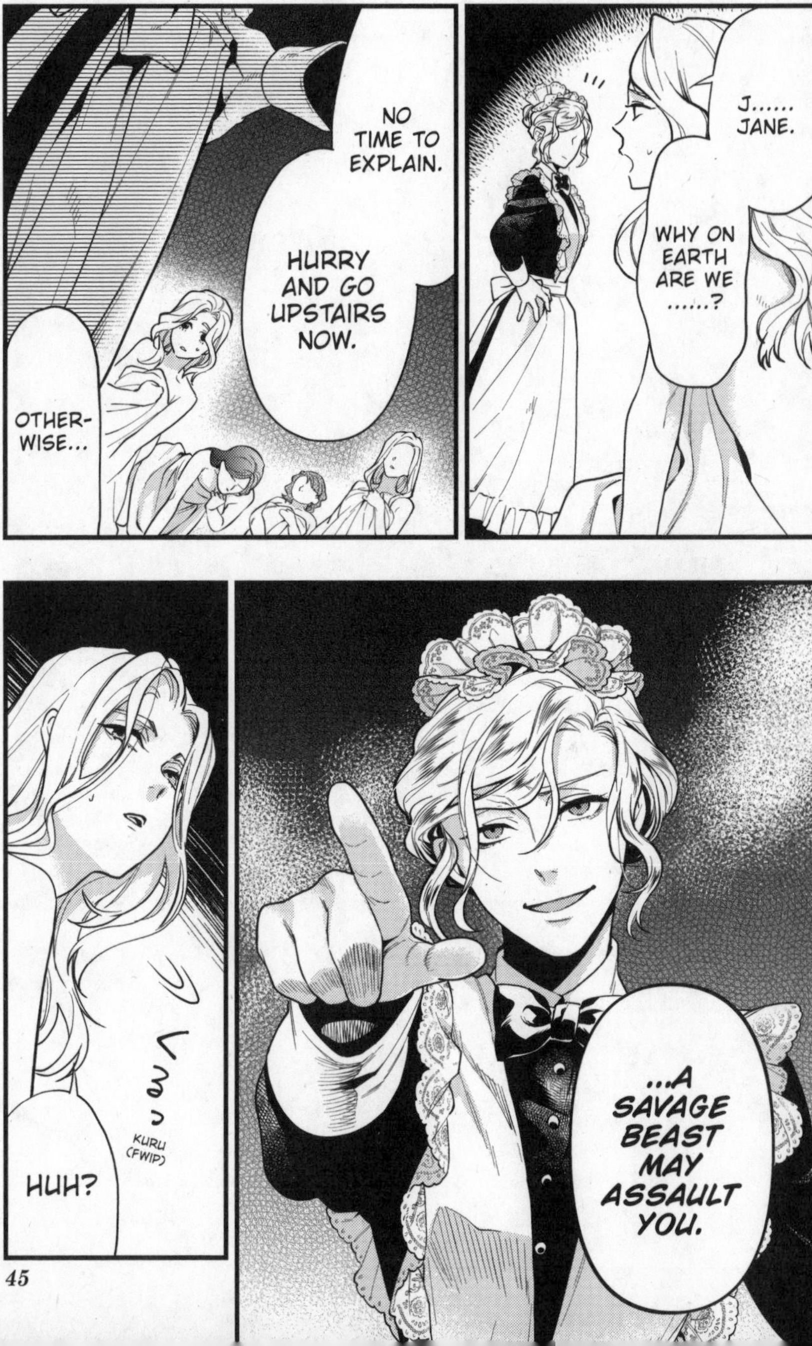
J...... JANE.
WHY ON EARTH ARE WE ......?
NO TIME TO EXPLAIN.
HURRY AND GO UPSTAIRS NOW.
OTHER-WISE...
...A SAVAGE BEAST MAY ASSAULT YOU.
KURU (FWIP)
HUH?

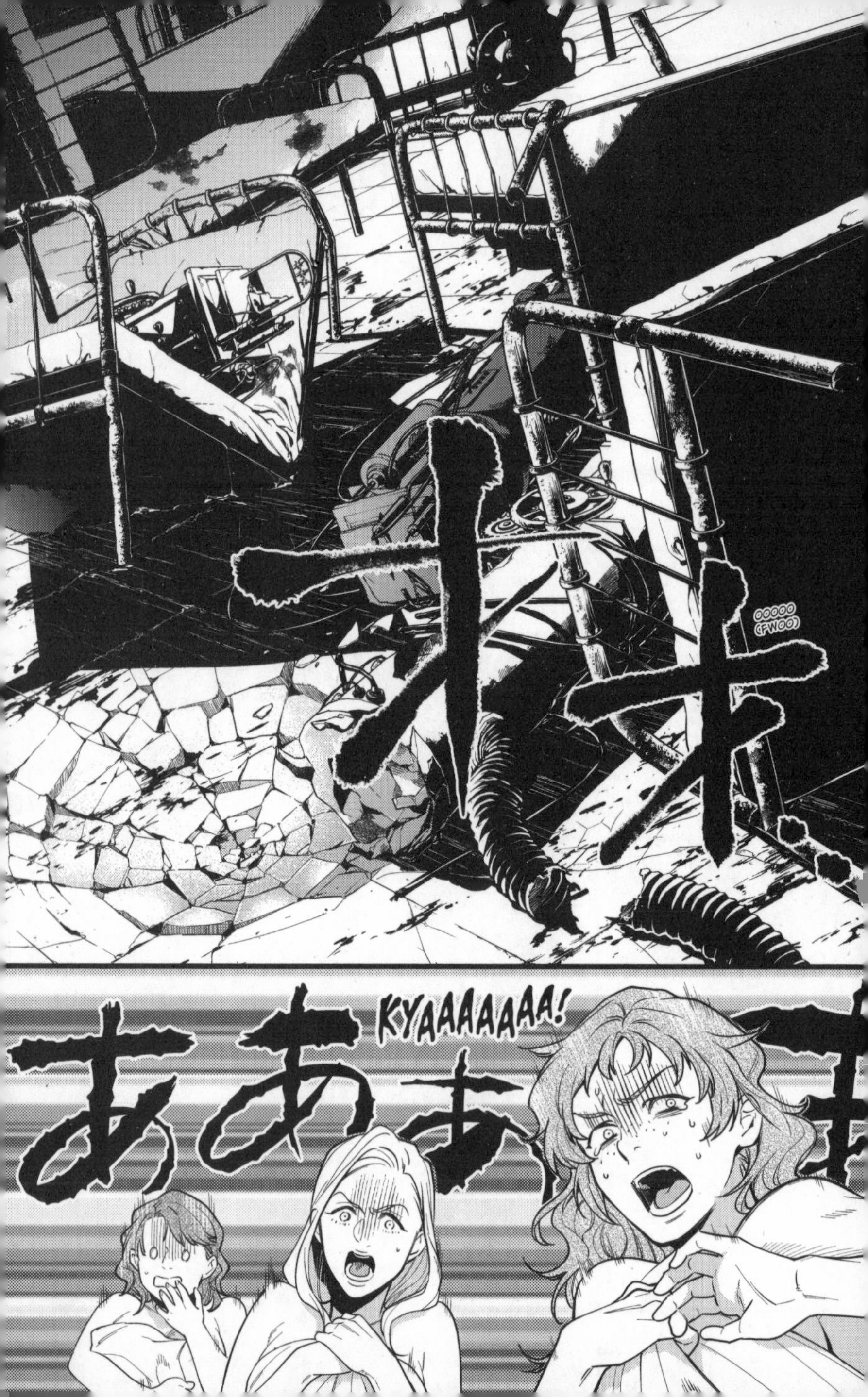
オォ…
OOOOO
(FWOO)
KYAAAAAAA!
あああ

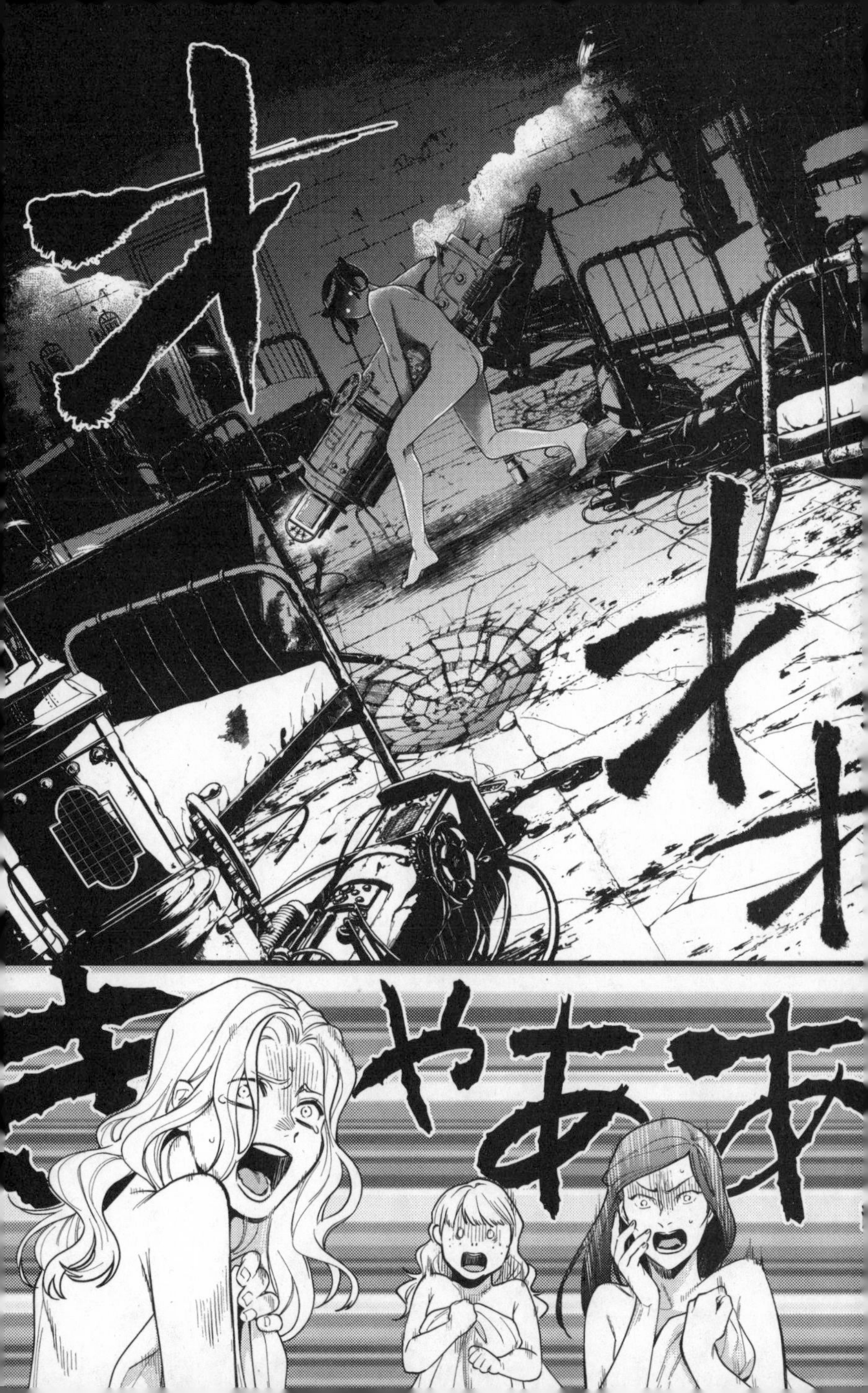

オオオ
きゃああ

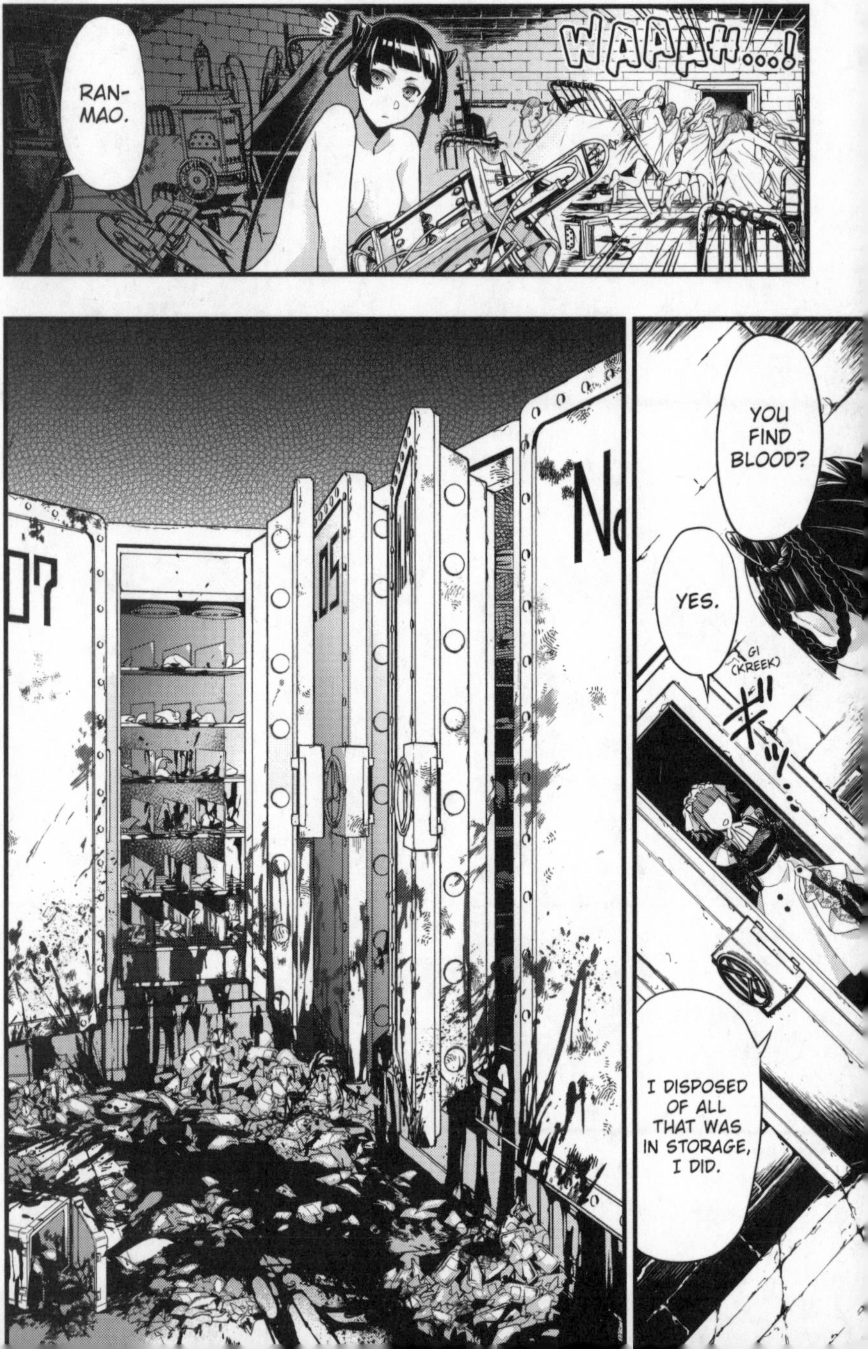
WAAAH...!
RAN-MAO.
YOU FIND BLOOD?
YES.
GI (KREEK)
I DISPOSED OF ALL THAT WAS IN STORAGE, I DID.

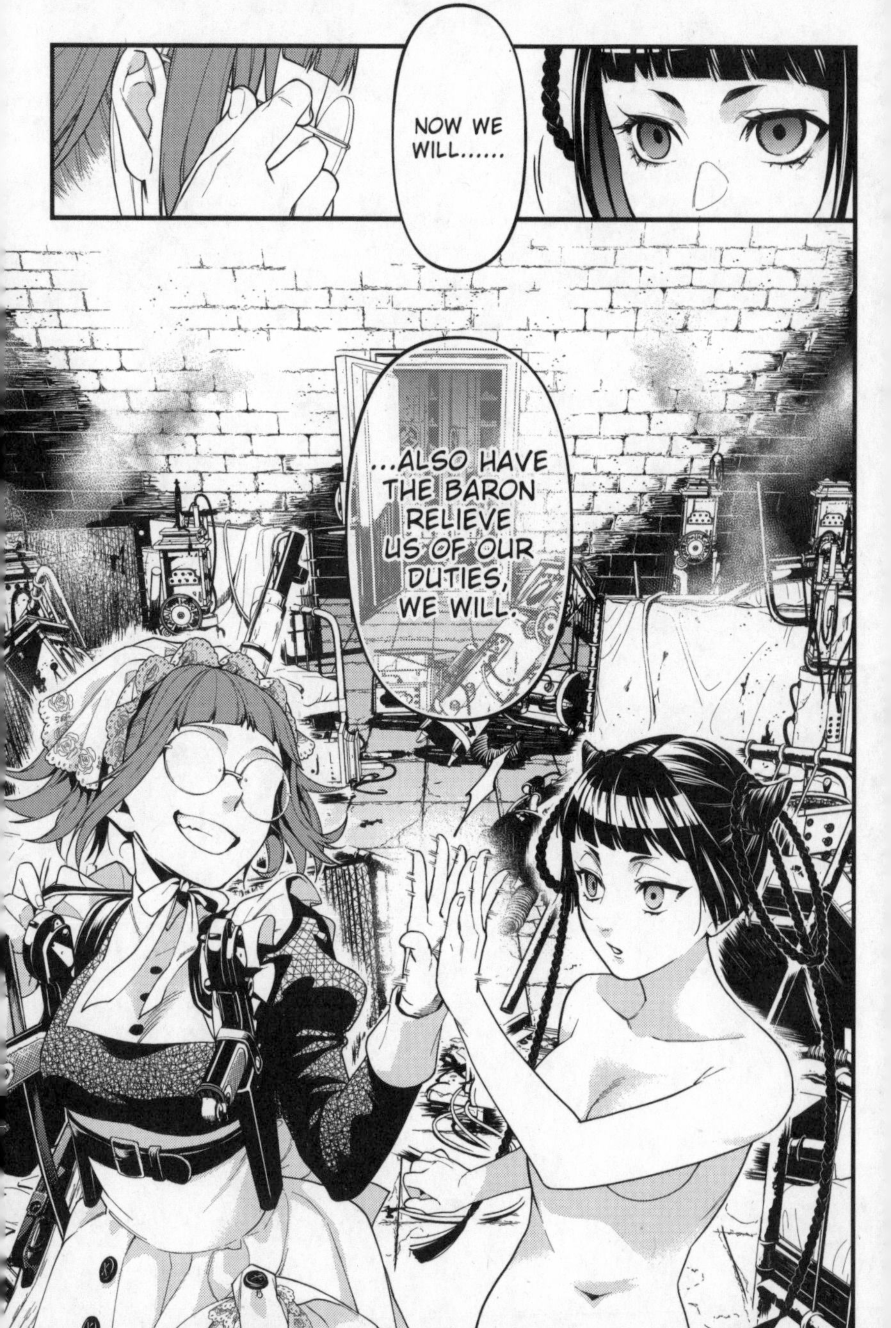
NOW WE WILL......
...ALSO HAVE THE BARON RELIEVE US OF OUR DUTIES, WE WILL.

Black Butler

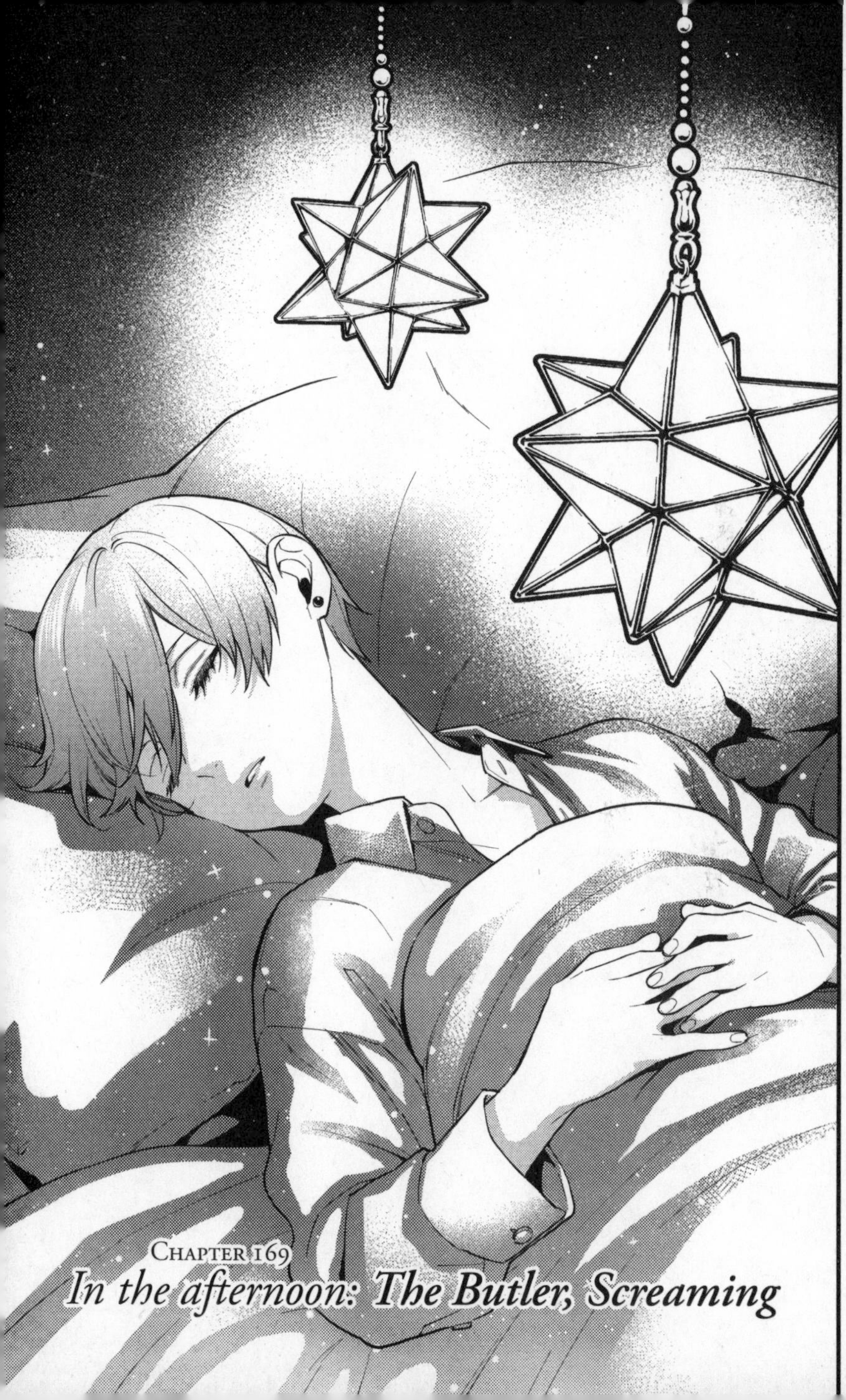
CHAPTER 169
In the afternoon: The Butler, Screaming

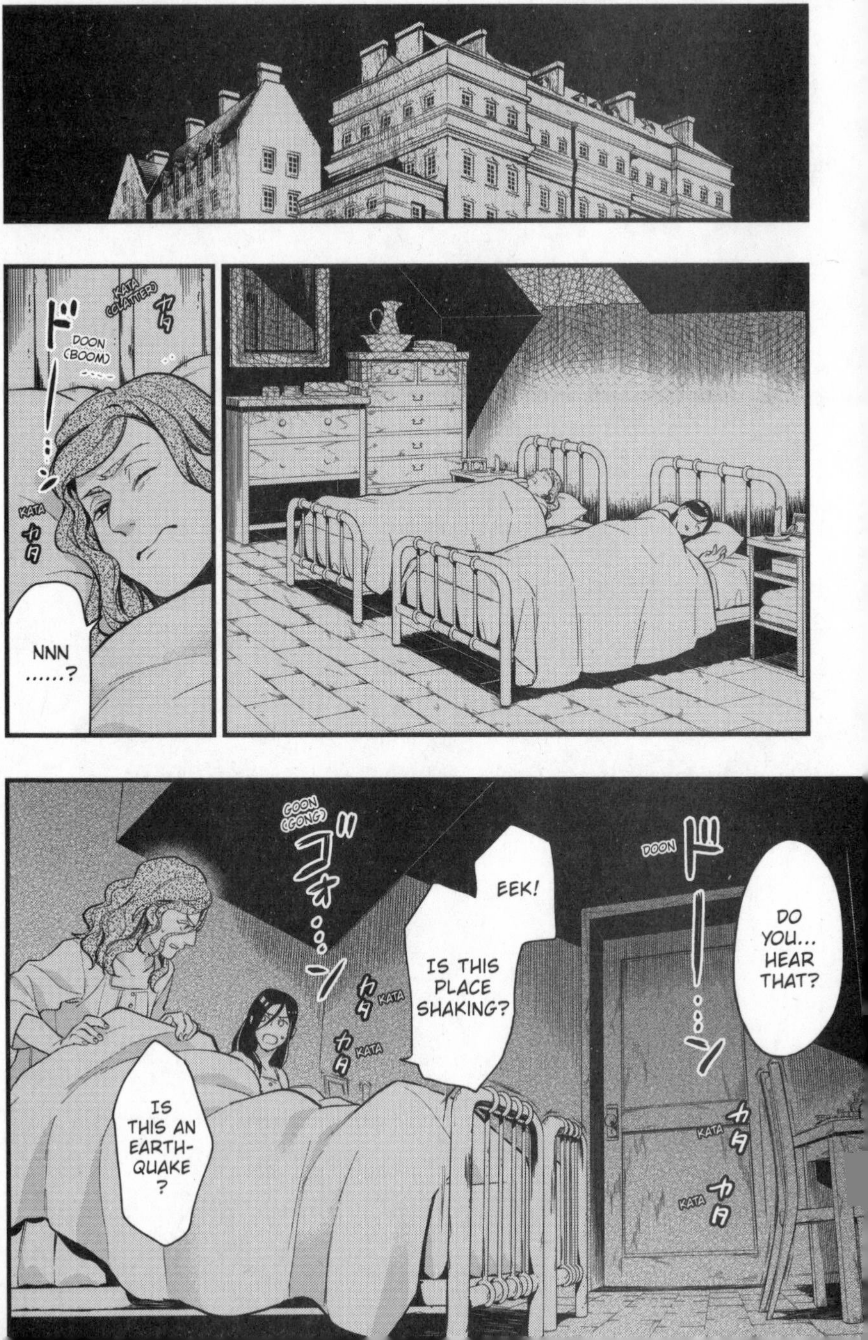
KATA (CLATTER)
DOON (BOOM)
KATA
NNN ......?
DO YOU... HEAR THAT?
DOON
KATA
KATA
EEK!
IS THIS PLACE SHAKING?
GOON (GONG)
KATA
KATA
IS THIS AN EARTH-QUAKE?

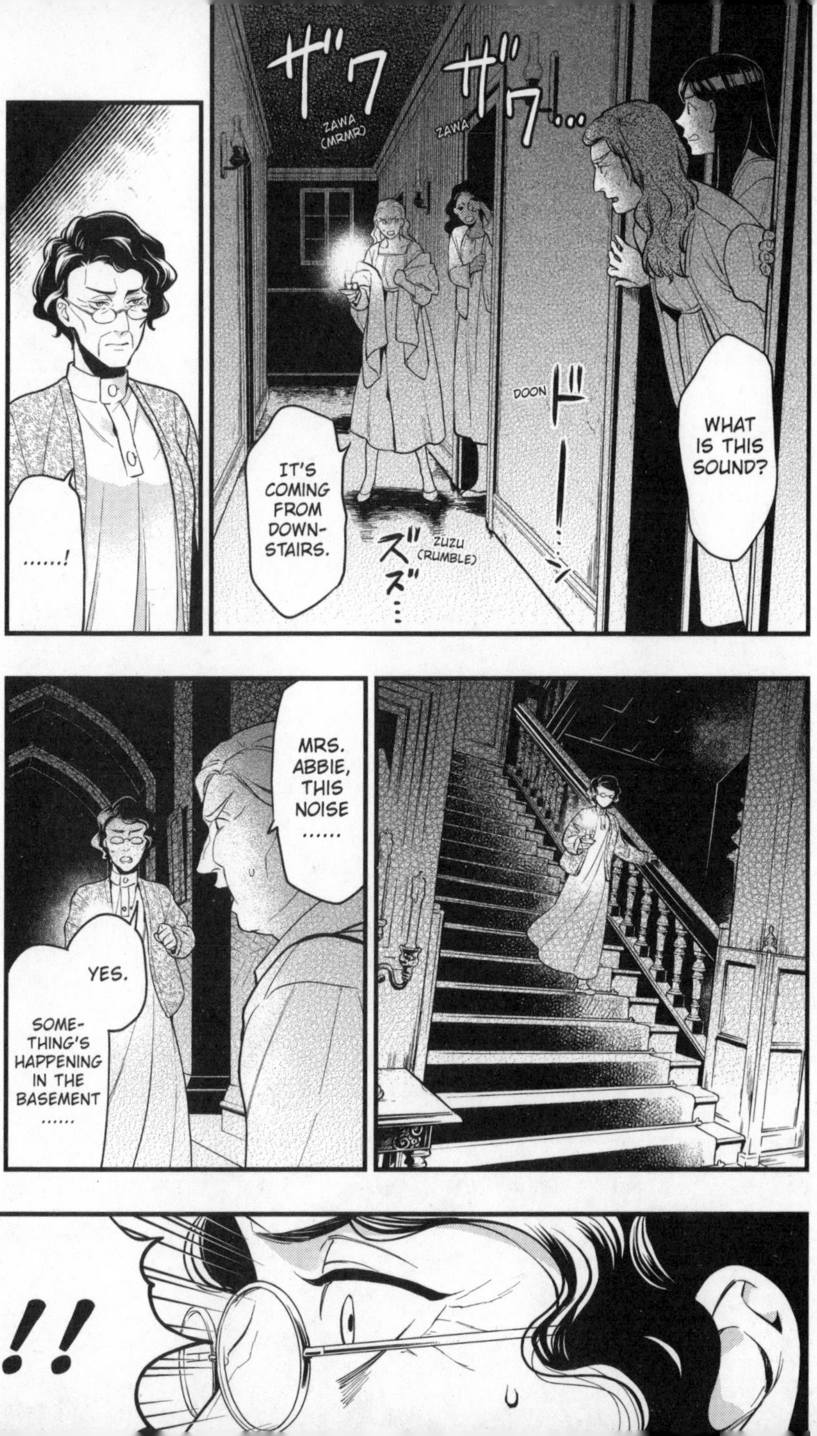
ZAWA (MRMR)
ZAWA
WHAT IS THIS SOUND?
DOON
IT'S COMING FROM DOWN-STAIRS.
ZUZU (RUMBLE)
......!
MRS. ABBIE, THIS NOISE ......
YES.
SOME-THING'S HAPPENING IN THE BASEMENT ......
!!

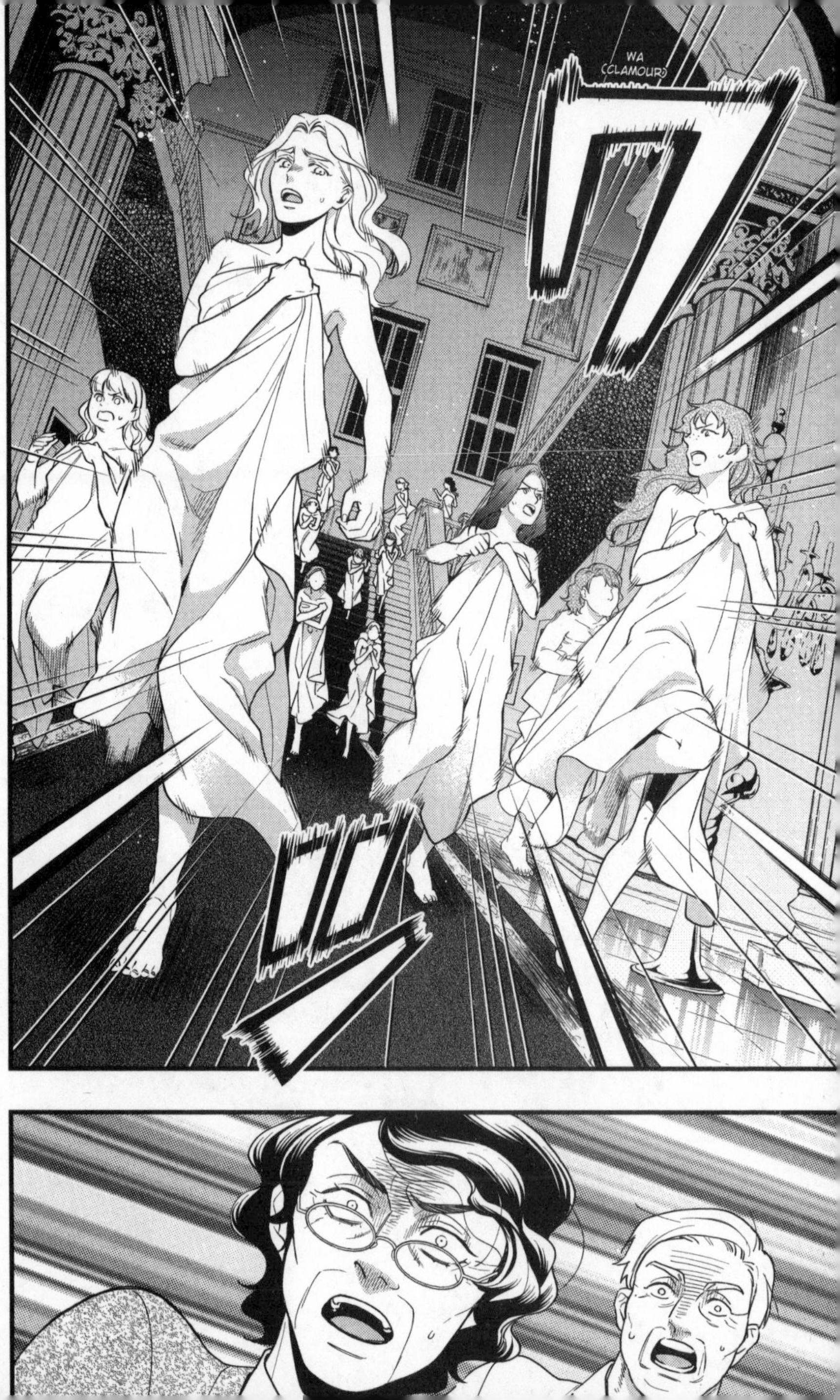
WA
(CLAMOUR)

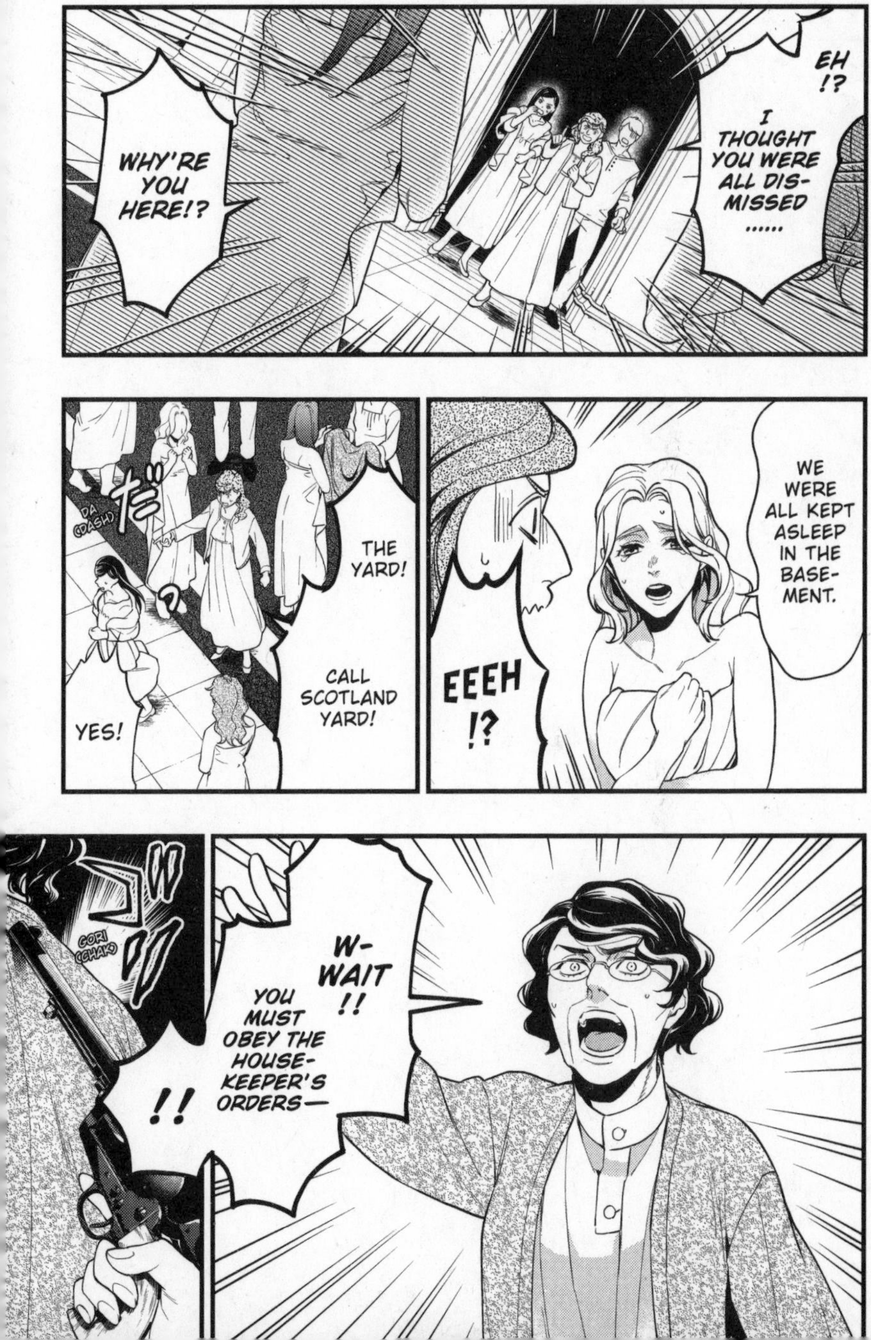

EH !?
I THOUGHT YOU WERE ALL DIS-MISSED ......
WHY'RE YOU HERE!?
WE WERE ALL KEPT ASLEEP IN THE BASE-MENT.
EEEH !?
THE YARD!
DA (DASH)
CALL SCOTLAND YARD!
YES!
W-WAIT !!
YOU MUST OBEY THE HOUSE-KEEPER'S ORDERS—
!!
GORI (CHAK)

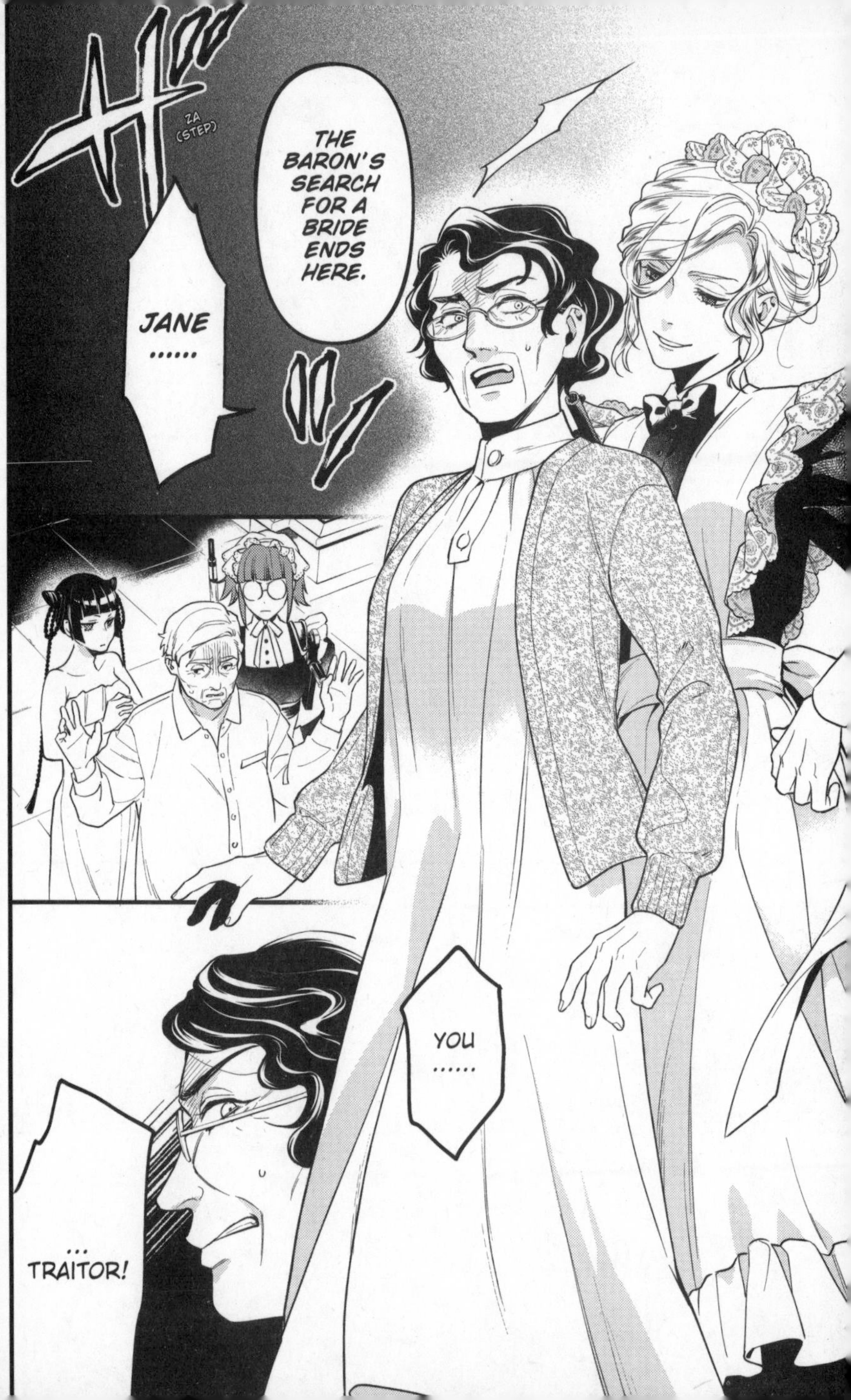
THE BARON'S SEARCH FOR A BRIDE ENDS HERE.
ZA (STEP)
JANE......
YOU......
...TRAITOR!

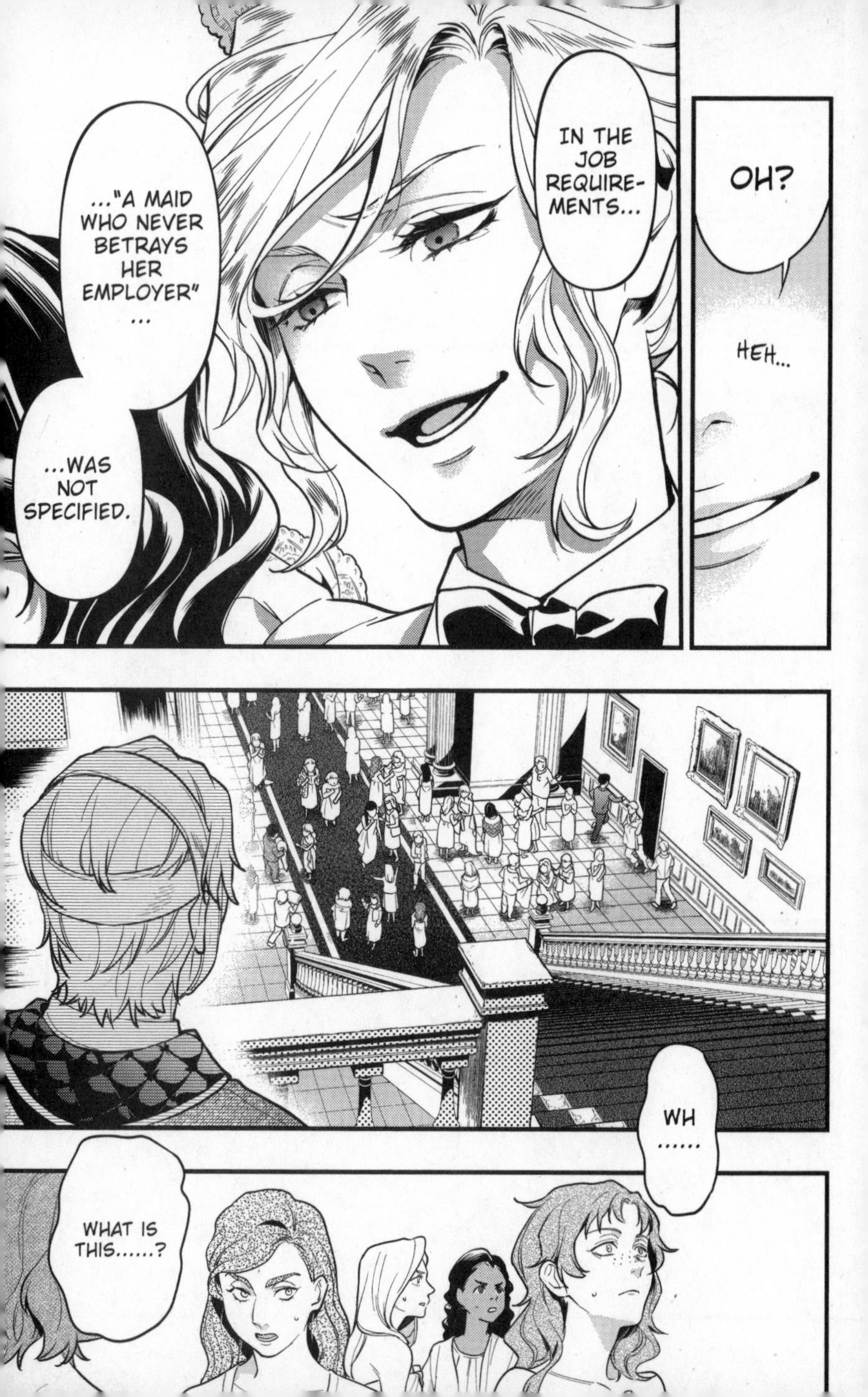
OH?
HEH...
IN THE JOB REQUIRE-MENTS...
..."A MAID WHO NEVER BETRAYS HER EMPLOYER"...
...WAS NOT SPECIFIED.
WH ......
WHAT IS THIS......?

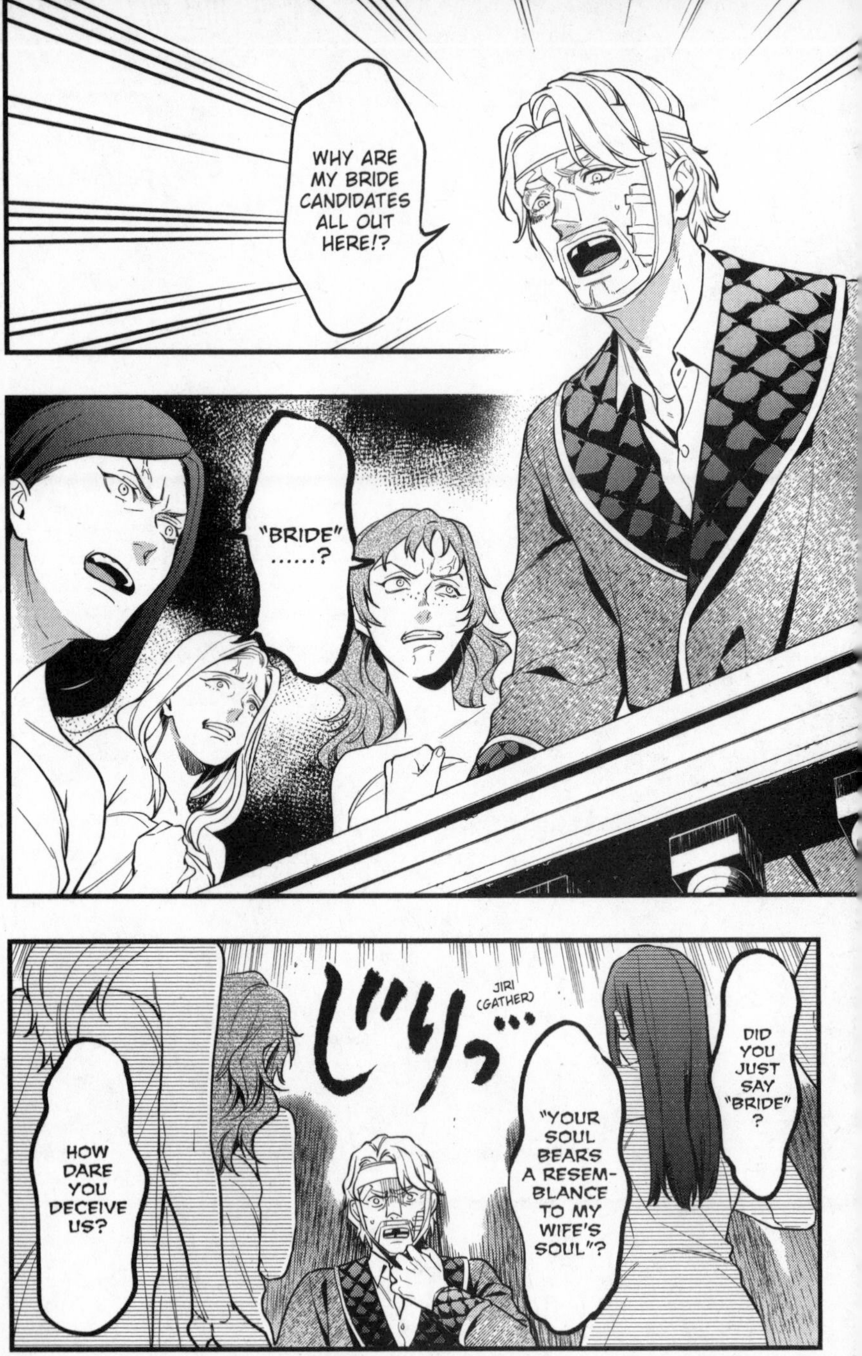
WHY ARE MY BRIDE CANDIDATES ALL OUT HERE!?
"BRIDE" ......?
DID YOU JUST SAY "BRIDE"?
JIRI (GATHER)
"YOUR SOUL BEARS A RESEM-BLANCE TO MY WIFE'S SOUL"?
HOW DARE YOU DECEIVE US?

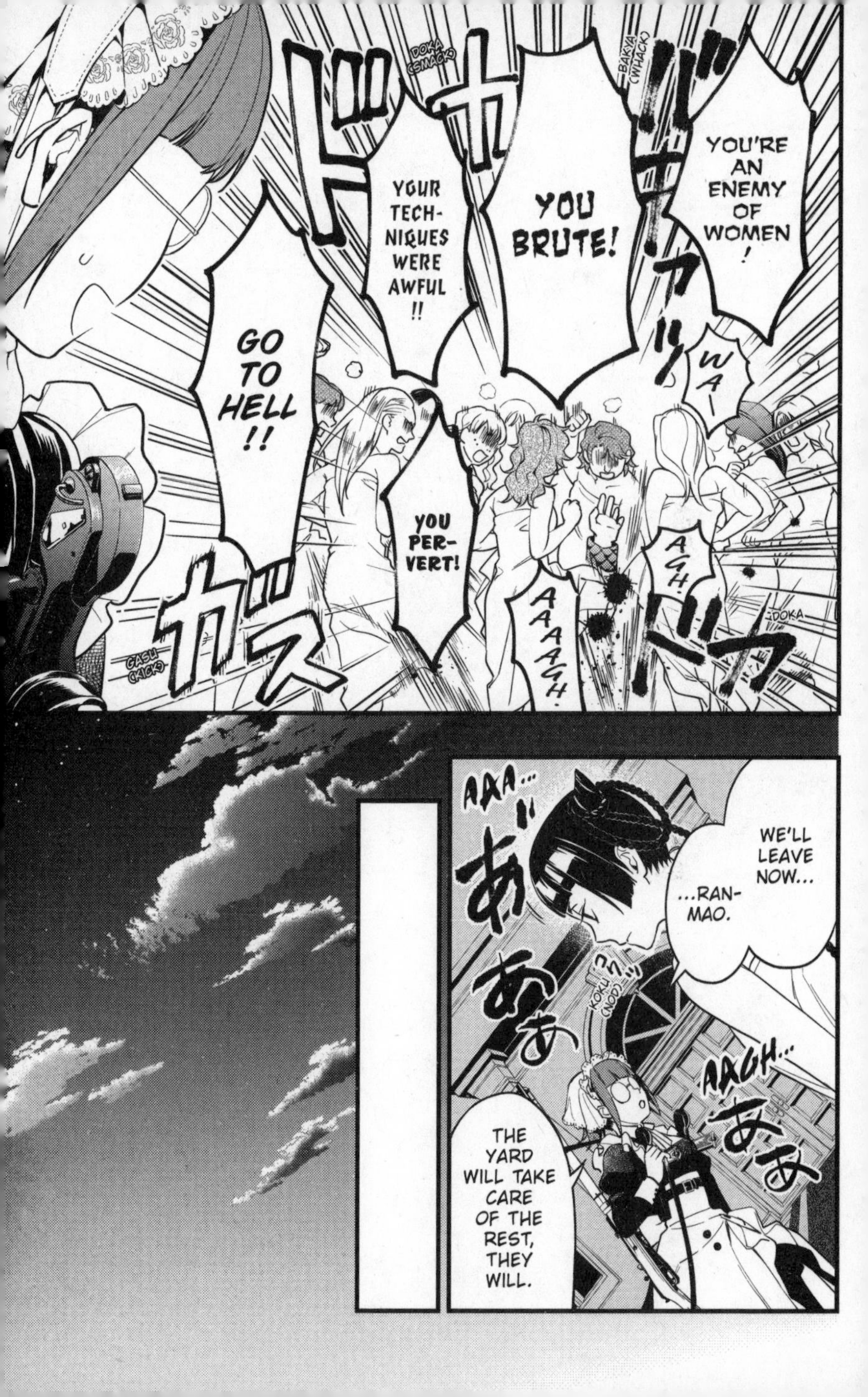
BAKYA (WHACK)
YOU'RE AN ENEMY OF WOMEN!
YOU BRUTE!
DOKA (SMACK)
YOUR TECHNIQUES WERE AWFUL!!
GO TO HELL!!
WA-
AGH!
DOKA
AAAAAGH!
YOU PERVERT!
GASU (KICK)
WE'LL LEAVE NOW...
...RANMAO.
AAA...
KOKU (NOD)
AAGH...
THE YARD WILL TAKE CARE OF THE REST, THEY WILL.

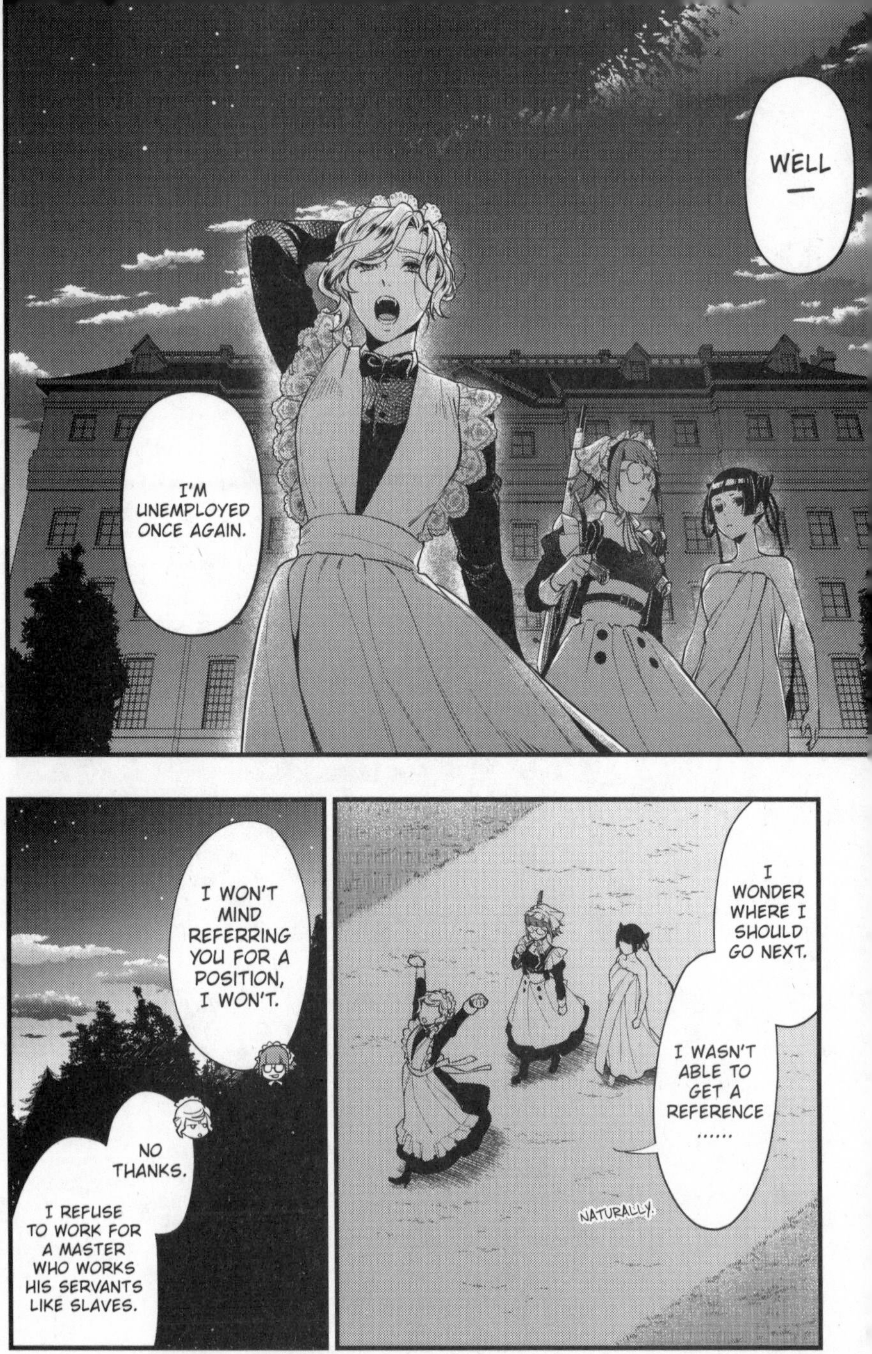
WELL —
I'M UNEMPLOYED ONCE AGAIN.
I WONDER WHERE I SHOULD GO NEXT.
I WASN'T ABLE TO GET A REFERENCE ......
NATURALLY.
I WON'T MIND REFERRING YOU FOR A POSITION, I WON'T.
NO THANKS.
I REFUSE TO WORK FOR A MASTER WHO WORKS HIS SERVANTS LIKE SLAVES.

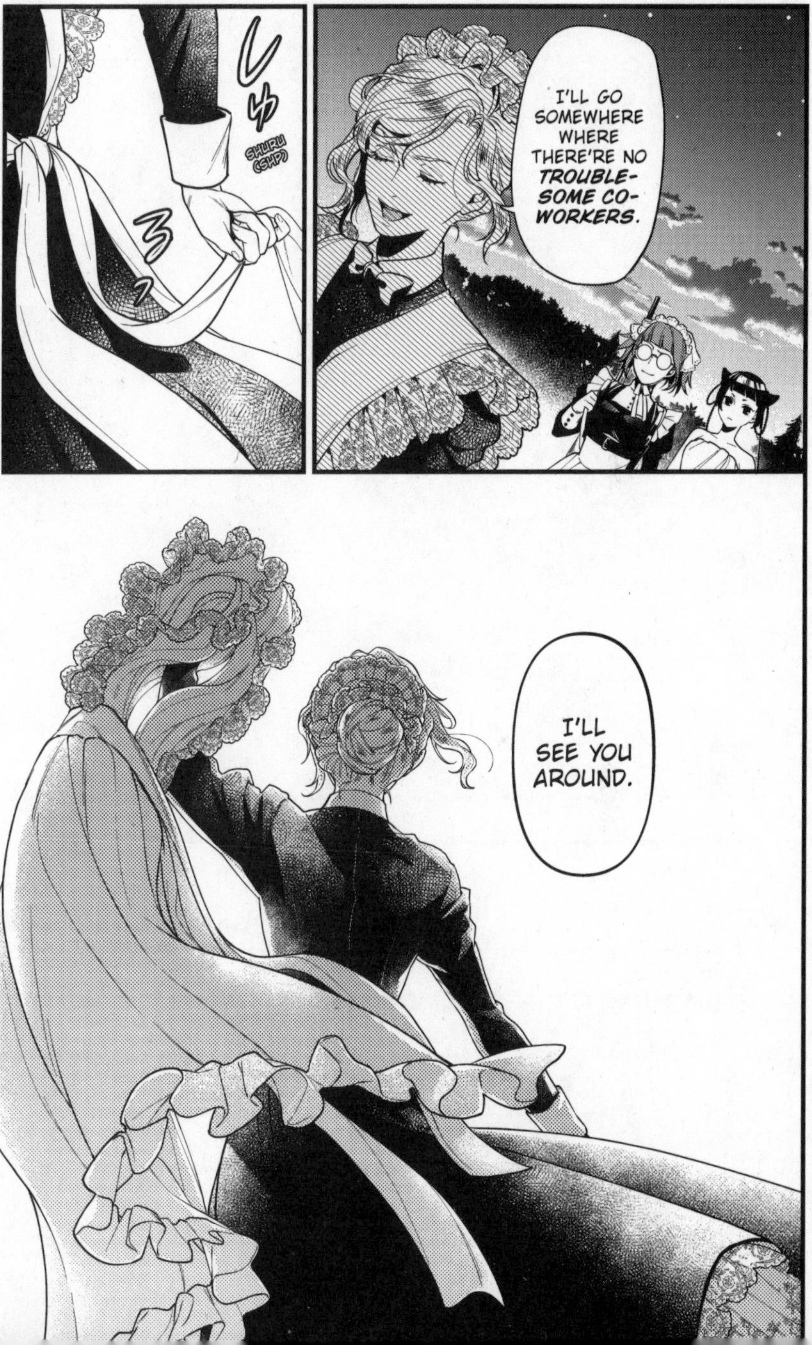
I'LL GO SOMEWHERE WHERE THERE'RE NO TROUBLE-SOME CO-WORKERS.
SHURU (SHP)
I'LL SEE YOU AROUND.

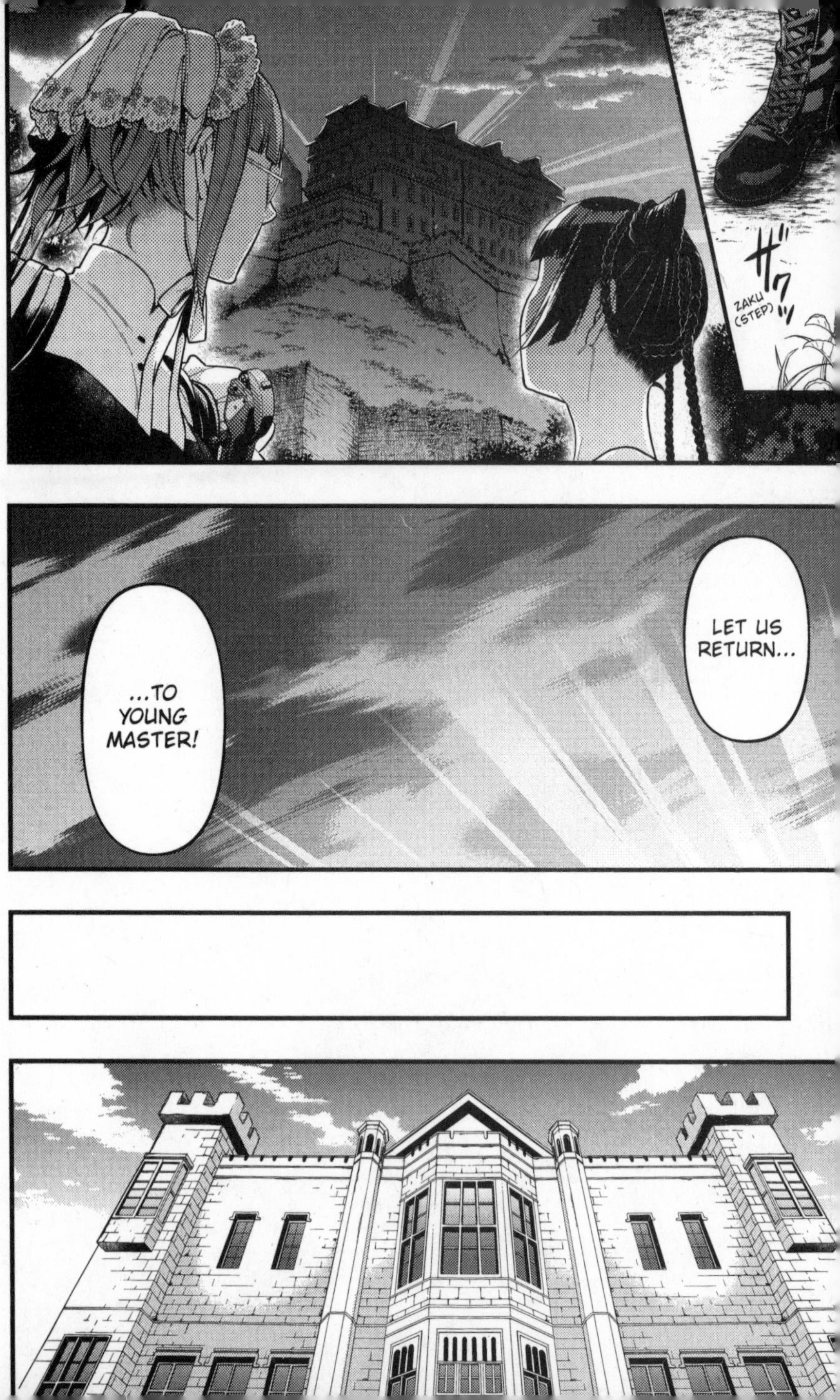
ZAKU (STEP)
LET US RETURN...
...TO YOUNG MASTER!

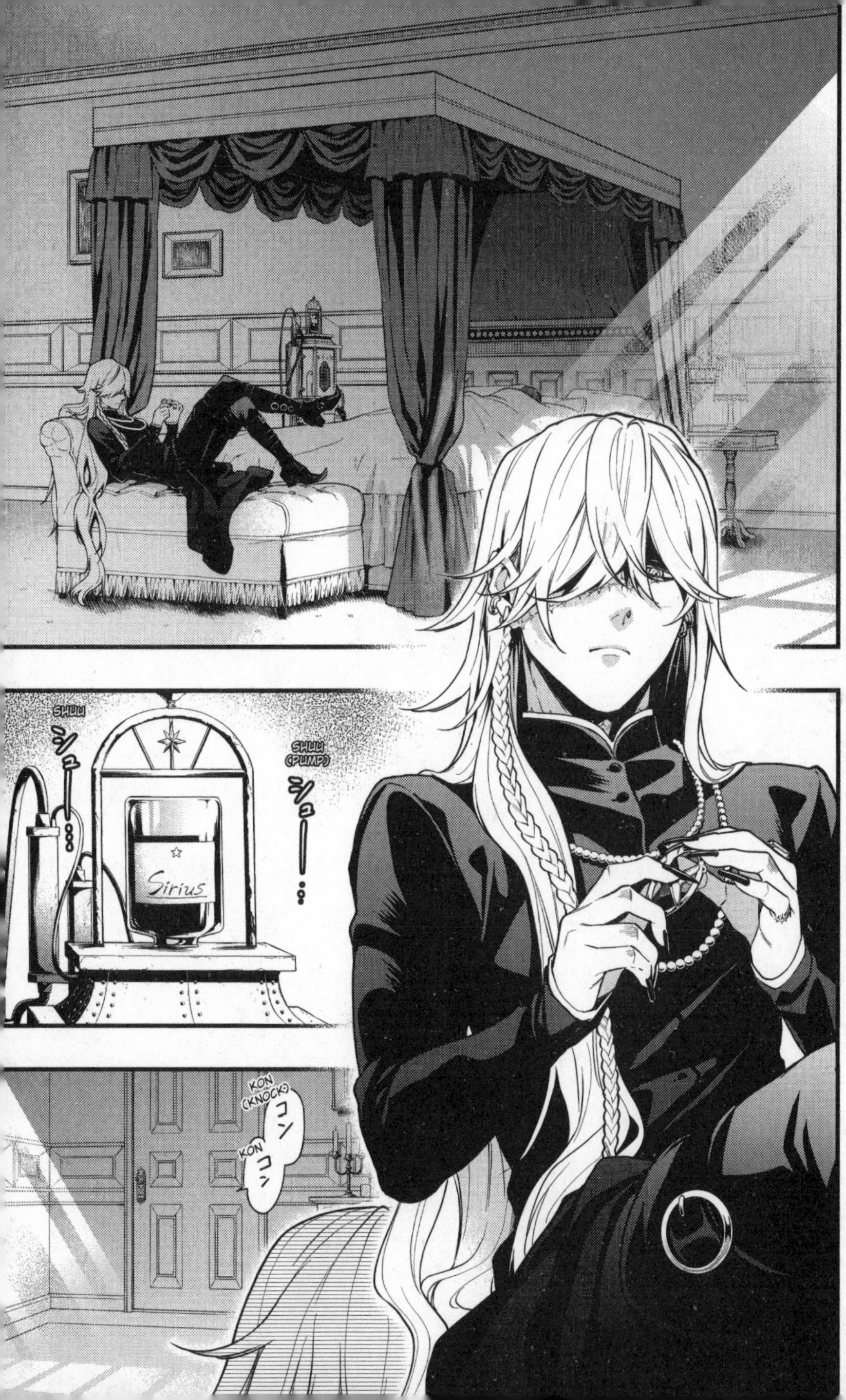
SHUU (PUMP)
シュー…
SHUU
シュー…
Sirius
KON (KNOCK)
コン
KON
コン

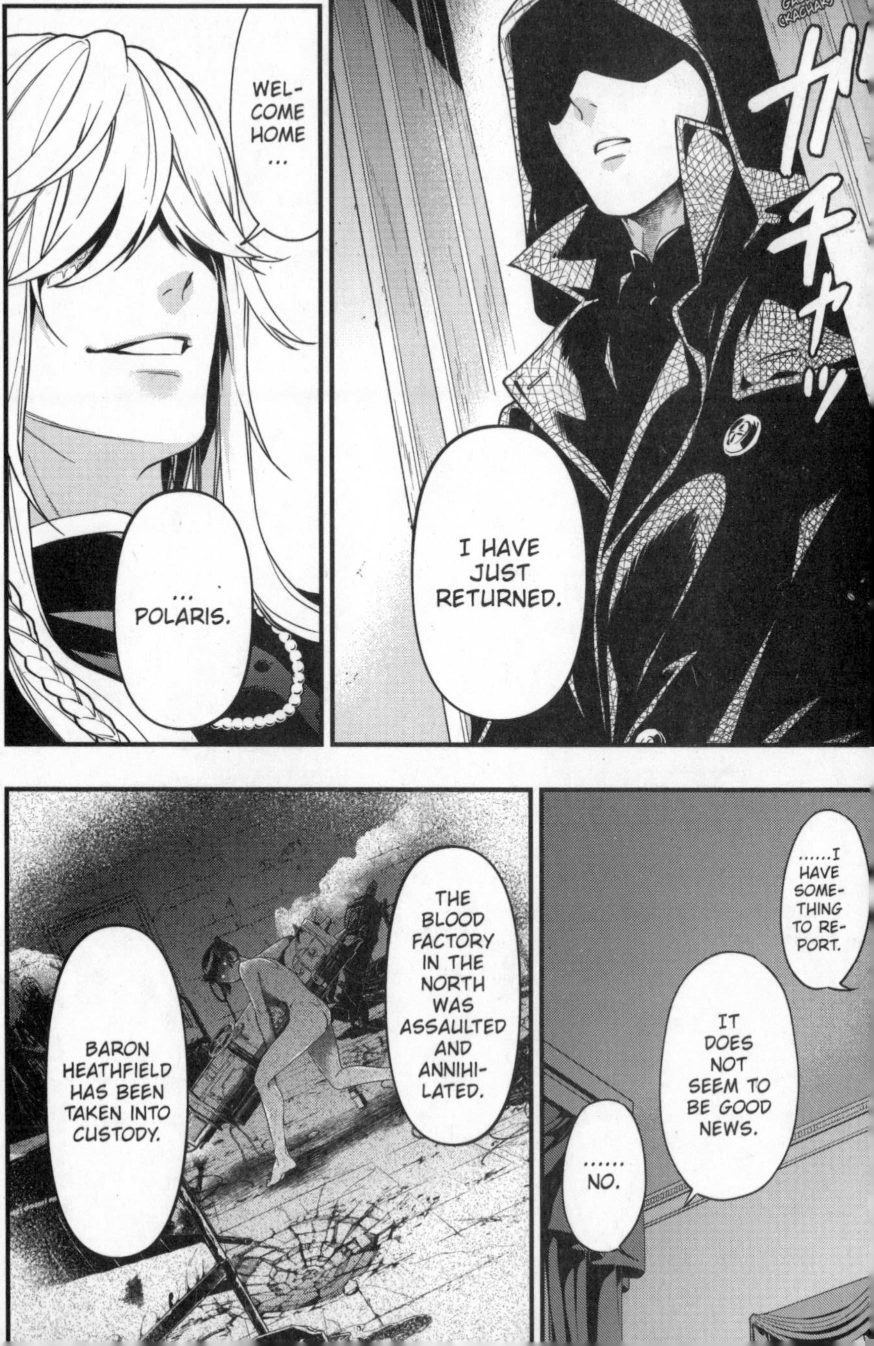
ガチャッ
GACHA (KACHAK)
I HAVE JUST RETURNED.
WEL-COME HOME ...
... POLARIS.
......I HAVE SOME-THING TO RE-PORT.
IT DOES NOT SEEM TO BE GOOD NEWS.
...... NO.
THE BLOOD FACTORY IN THE NORTH WAS ASSAULTED AND ANNIHI-LATED.
BARON HEATHFIELD HAS BEEN TAKEN INTO CUSTODY.

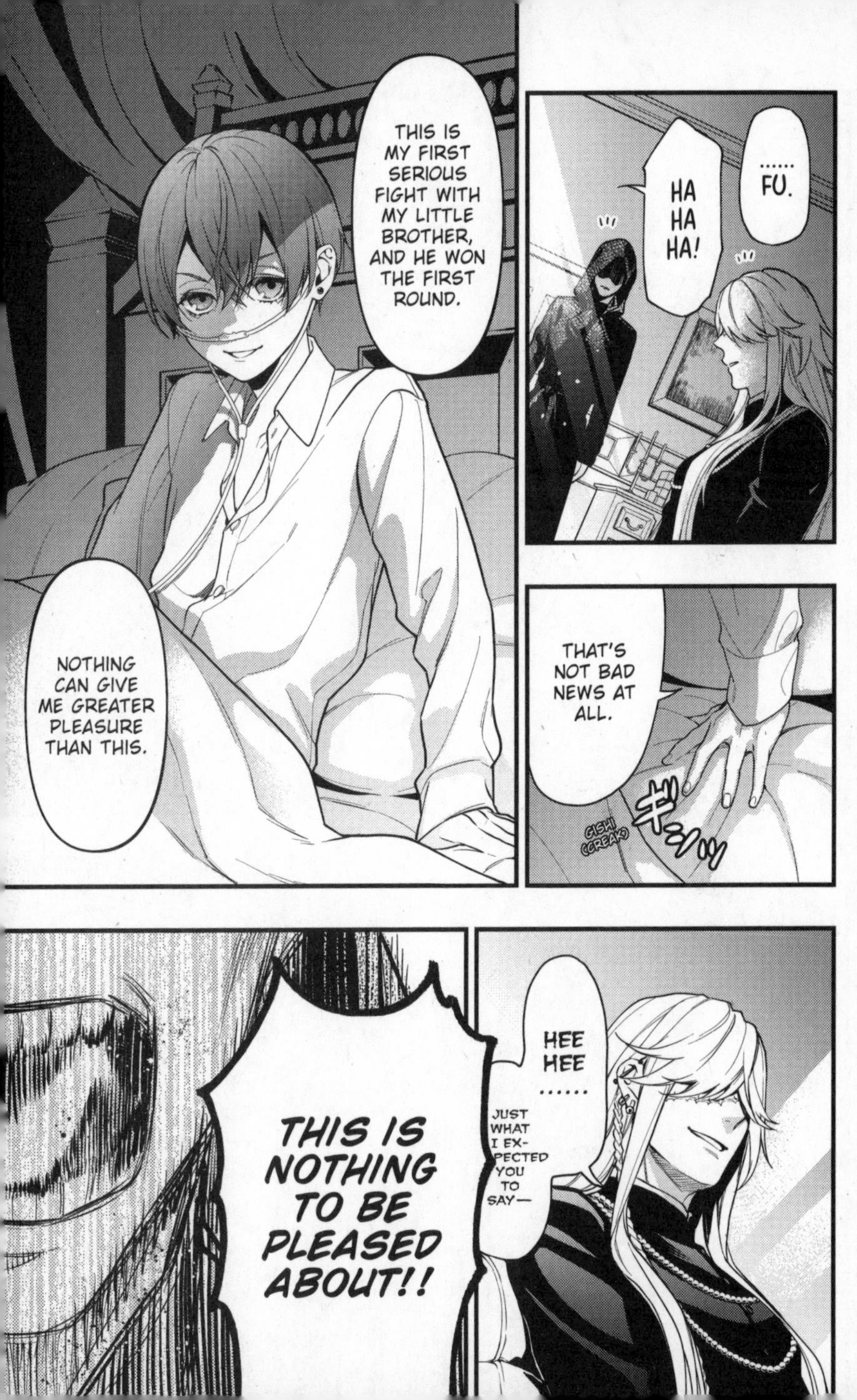
......FU.
HA HA HA!
THAT'S NOT BAD NEWS AT ALL.
GISHI (CREAK)
THIS IS MY FIRST SERIOUS FIGHT WITH MY LITTLE BROTHER, AND HE WON THE FIRST ROUND.
NOTHING CAN GIVE ME GREATER PLEASURE THAN THIS.
HEE HEE ......
JUST WHAT I EXPECTED YOU TO SAY—
THIS IS NOTHING TO BE PLEASED ABOUT!!

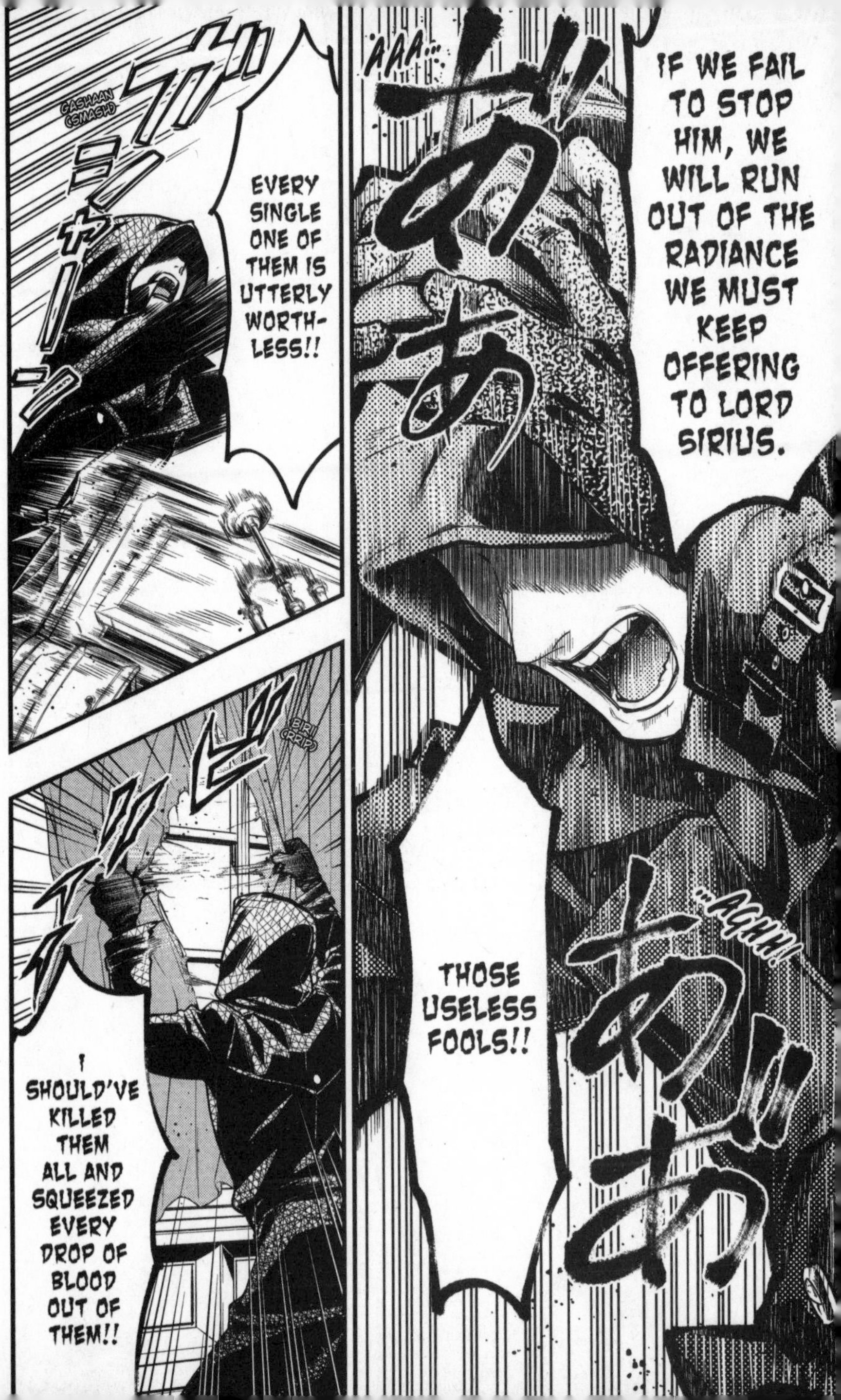
IF WE FAIL TO STOP HIM, WE WILL RUN OUT OF THE RADIANCE WE MUST KEEP OFFERING TO LORD SIRIUS.
AAA...
...AGHH!
THOSE USELESS FOOLS!!
EVERY SINGLE ONE OF THEM IS UTTERLY WORTH-LESS!!
GASHAAN (SMASH)
BIRI (RRIP)
I SHOULD'VE KILLED THEM ALL AND SQUEEZED EVERY DROP OF BLOOD OUT OF THEM!!

NO, IT'S NOT TOO LATE.

I'LL TURN THEM ALL INTO MINCE-MEAT!!

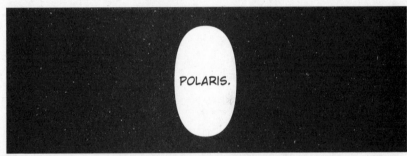

POLARIS.

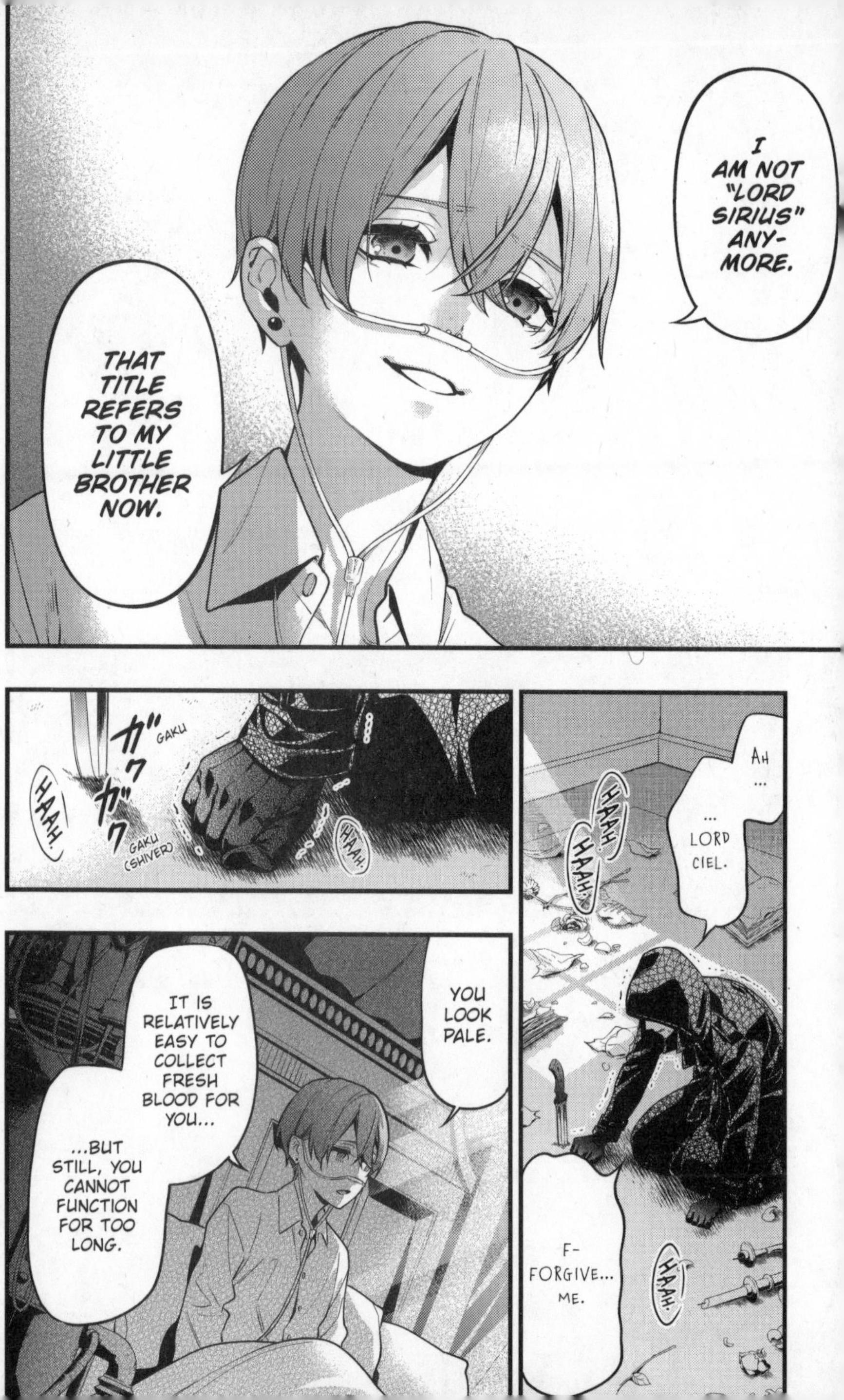
I AM NOT "LORD SIRIUS" ANYMORE.
THAT TITLE REFERS TO MY LITTLE BROTHER NOW.
AH ...
... LORD CIEL.
HAAH HAAH
HAAH
F- FORGIVE... ME.
HAAH.
HAAH.
ガク
GAKU
ガク
GAKU (SHIVER)
HAAH.
YOU LOOK PALE.
IT IS RELATIVELY EASY TO COLLECT FRESH BLOOD FOR YOU...
...BUT STILL, YOU CANNOT FUNCTION FOR TOO LONG.

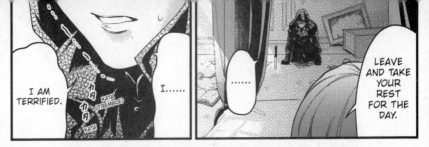

LEAVE AND TAKE YOUR REST FOR THE DAY.
......
I......
I AM TERRIFIED.
KATA (TREMBLE)
KATA
IF I SHOULD LOSE MY MASTER ONCE AGAIN...
...I WOULDN'T BE ABLE TO REST EVEN IF I DIED.
I CAN'T IMAGINE WHERE ELSE I COULD BE...

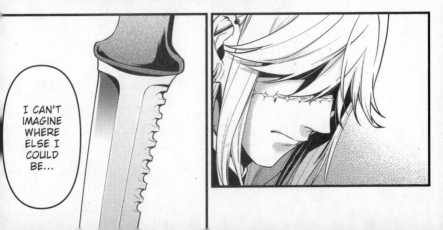

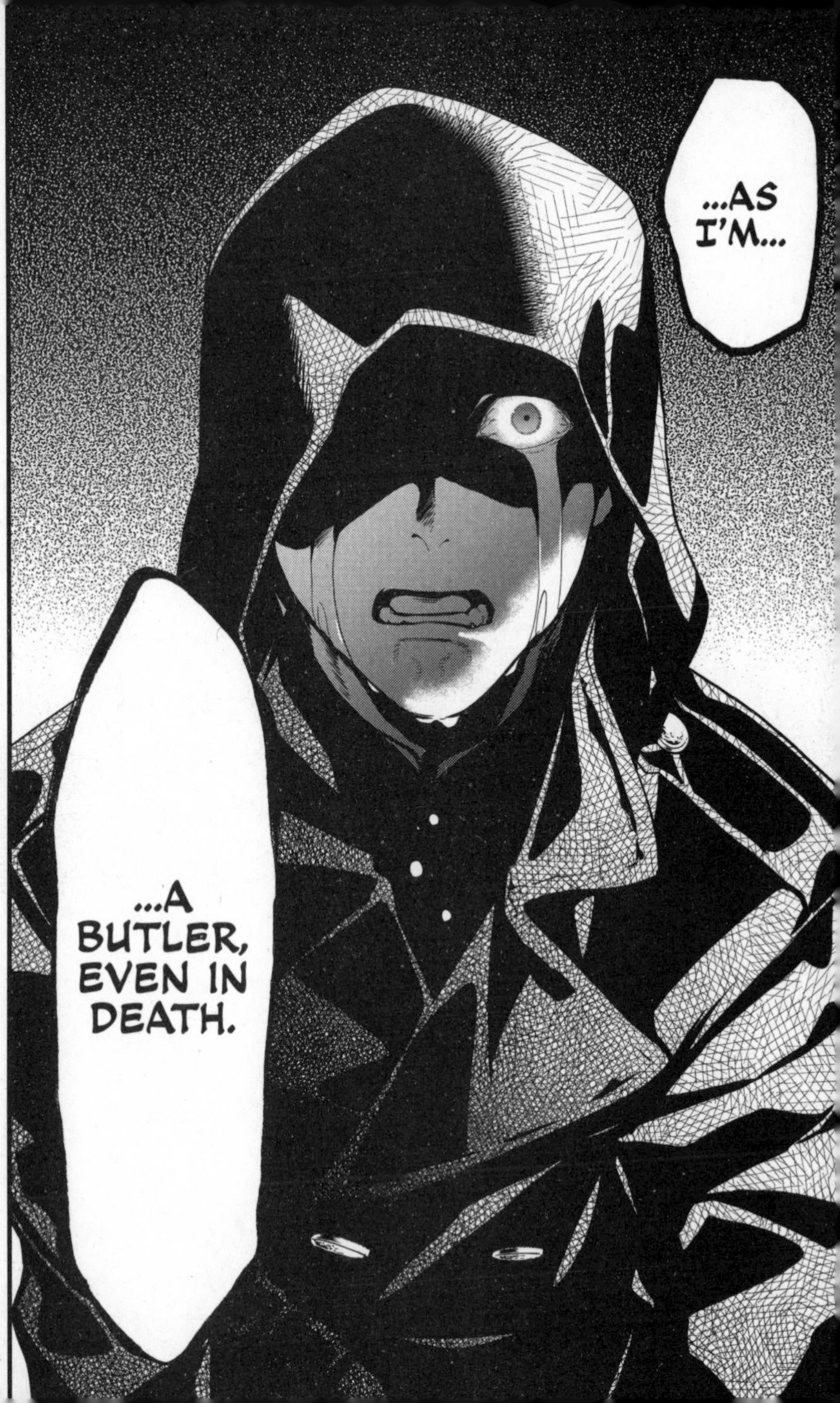
...AS I'M...
...A BUTLER, EVEN IN DEATH.

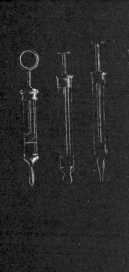

Black Butler

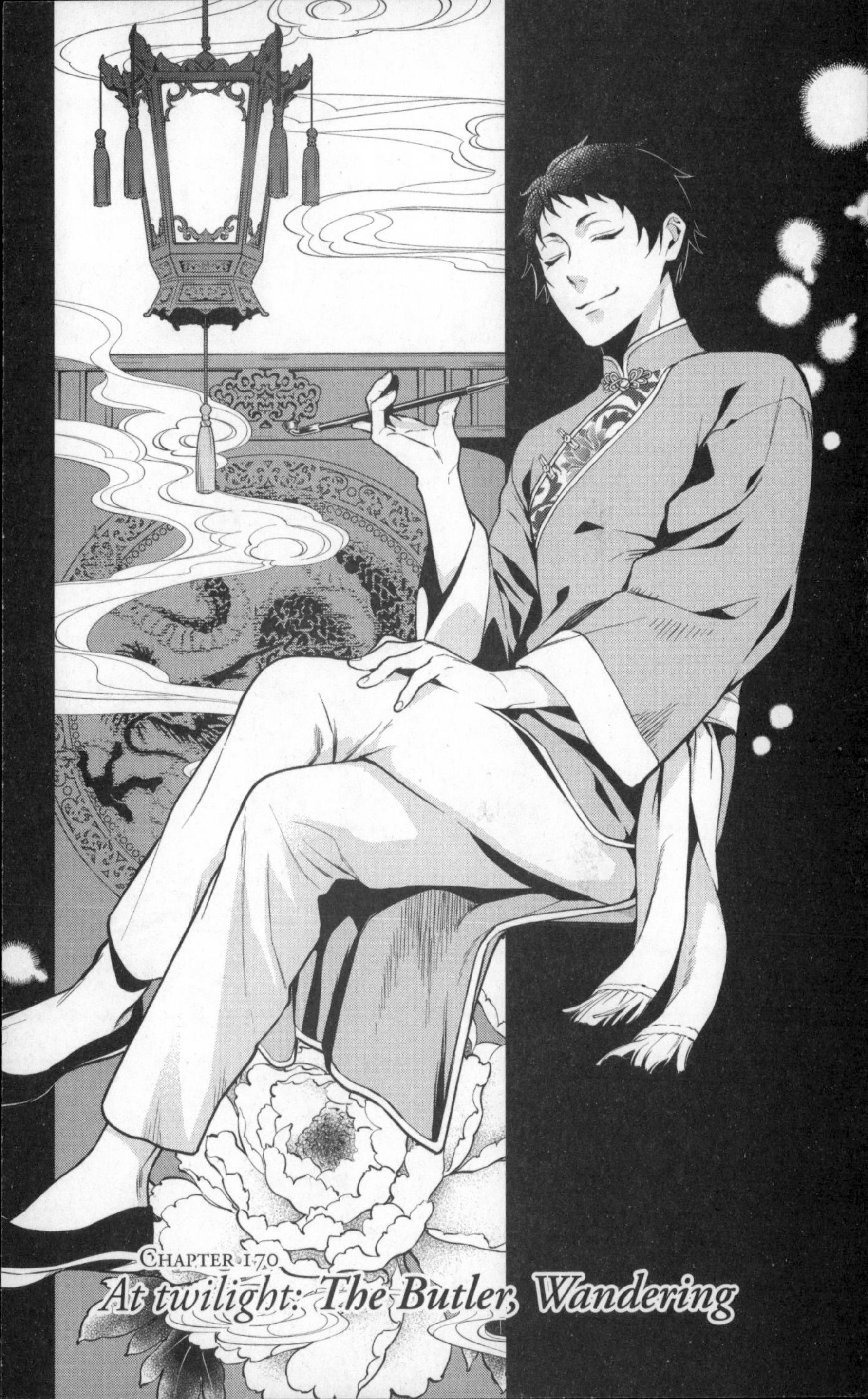
Chapter 170
At twilight: The Butler, Wandering

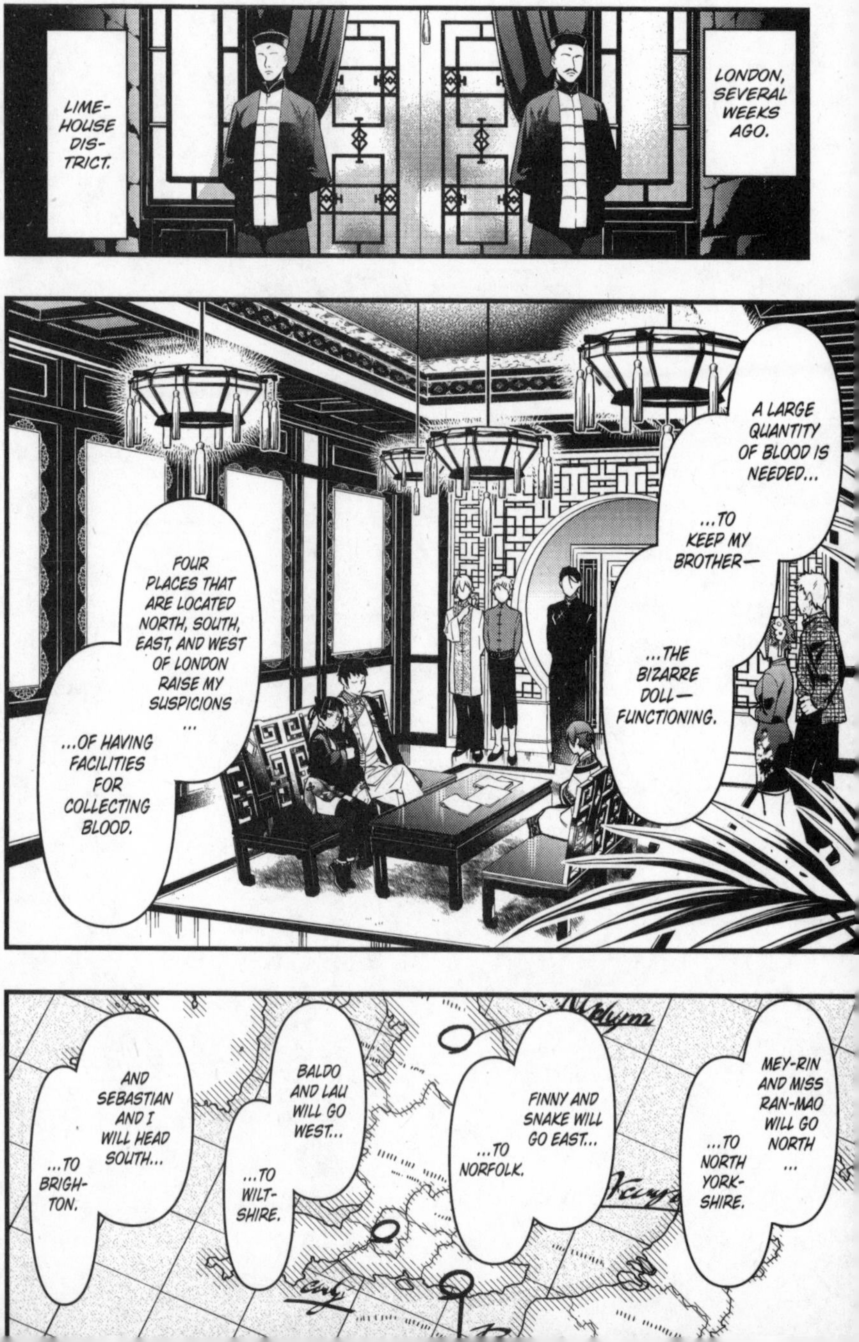
LONDON, SEVERAL WEEKS AGO.
LIME-HOUSE DISTRICT.
A LARGE QUANTITY OF BLOOD IS NEEDED...
...TO KEEP MY BROTHER—
...THE BIZARRE DOLL—FUNCTIONING.
FOUR PLACES THAT ARE LOCATED NORTH, SOUTH, EAST, AND WEST OF LONDON RAISE MY SUSPICIONS...
...OF HAVING FACILITIES FOR COLLECTING BLOOD.
MEY-RIN AND MISS RAN-MAO WILL GO NORTH...
...TO NORTH YORKSHIRE.
FINNY AND SNAKE WILL GO EAST...
...TO NORFOLK.
BALDO AND LAU WILL GO WEST...
...TO WILTSHIRE.
AND SEBASTIAN AND I WILL HEAD SOUTH...
...TO BRIGHTON.

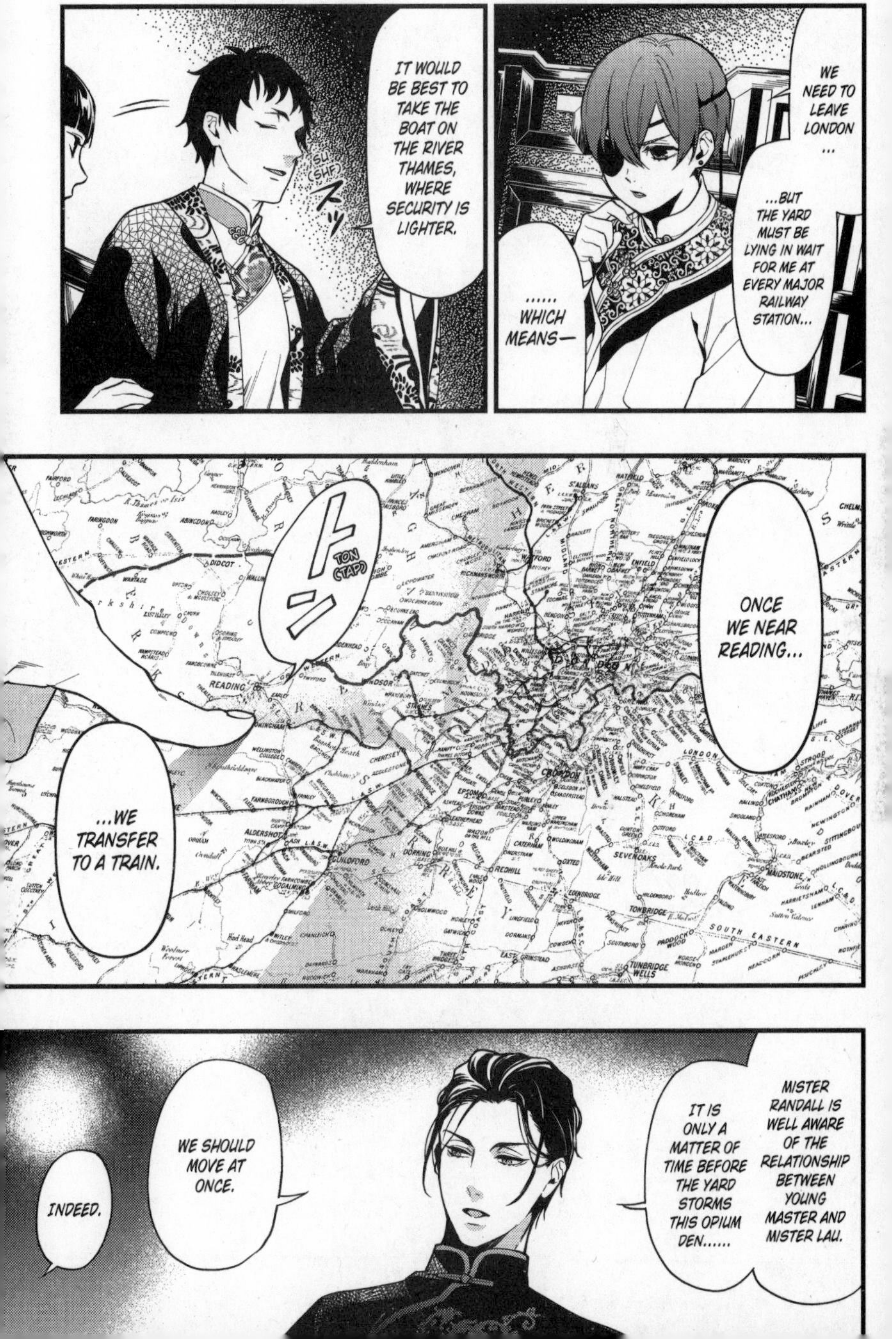
WE NEED TO LEAVE LONDON ...
...BUT THE YARD MUST BE LYING IN WAIT FOR ME AT EVERY MAJOR RAILWAY STATION...
......WHICH MEANS—
IT WOULD BE BEST TO TAKE THE BOAT ON THE RIVER THAMES, WHERE SECURITY IS LIGHTER.
スッ
SU (SHF)
ONCE WE NEAR READING...
トン
TON (TAP)
...WE TRANSFER TO A TRAIN.
READING
DIDCOT
WINDSOR
CROYDON
EPSOM
REDHILL
DORKING
GUILDFORD
ALDERSHOT
SEVENOAKS
MAIDSTONE
TONBRIDGE
TUNBRIDGE WELLS
SOUTH EASTERN
MISTER RANDALL IS WELL AWARE OF THE RELATIONSHIP BETWEEN YOUNG MASTER AND MISTER LAU.
IT IS ONLY A MATTER OF TIME BEFORE THE YARD STORMS THIS OPIUM DEN......
WE SHOULD MOVE AT ONCE.
INDEED.

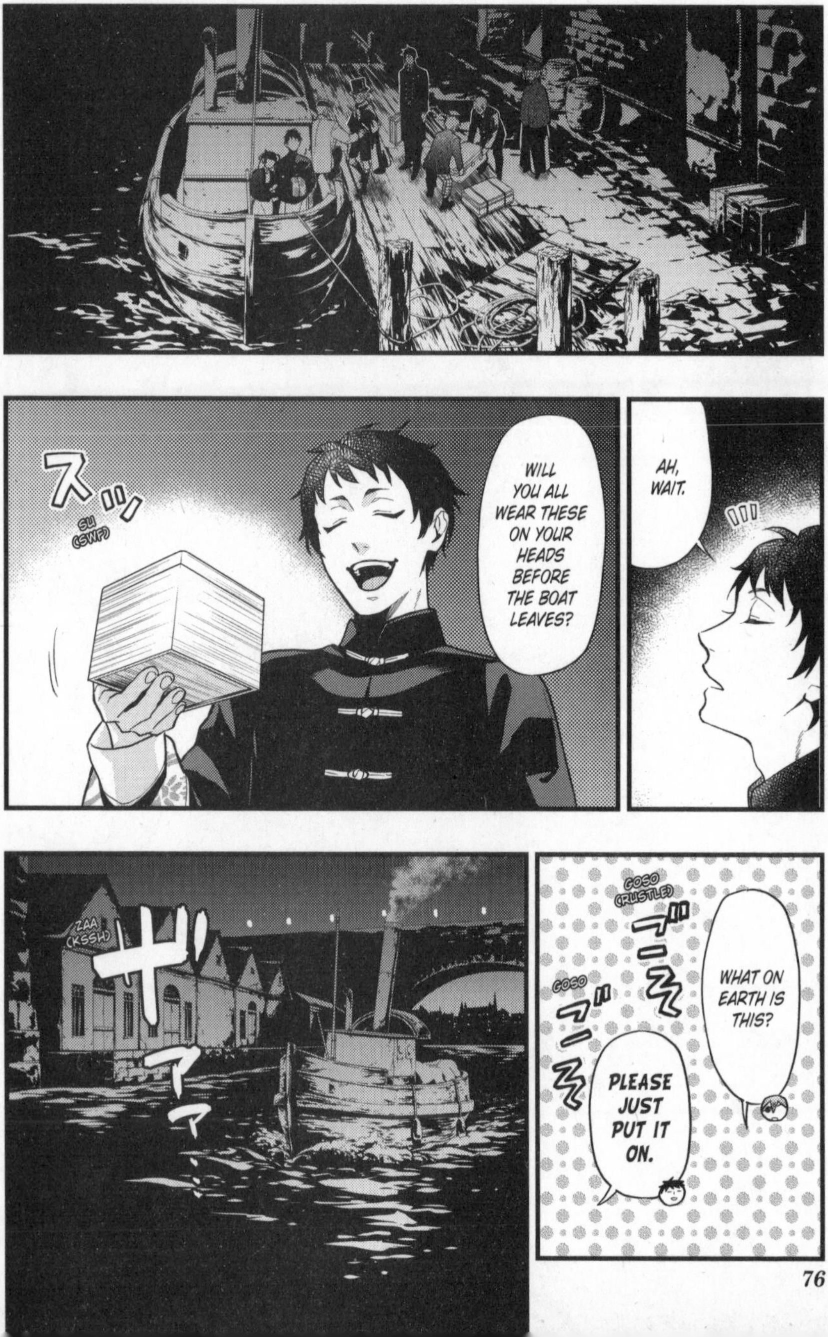
AH, WAIT.
WILL YOU ALL WEAR THESE ON YOUR HEADS BEFORE THE BOAT LEAVES?
SU (SWF)
GOSO (RUSTLE)
WHAT ON EARTH IS THIS?
GOSO
PLEASE JUST PUT IT ON.
ZAA (KSSH)

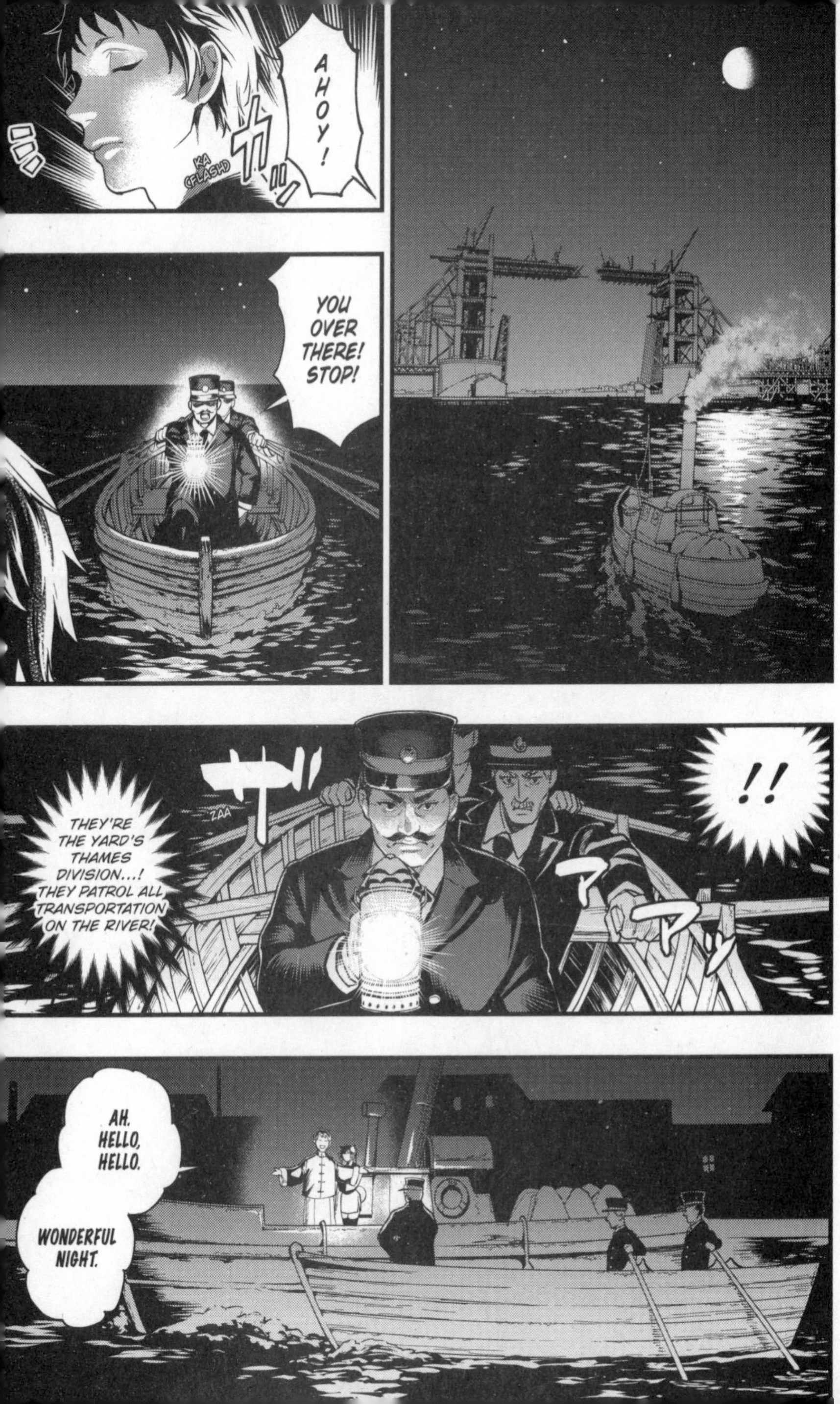
AHOY!
KA (FLASH)
YOU OVER THERE! STOP!
!!
THEY'RE THE YARD'S THAMES DIVISION...! THEY PATROL ALL TRANSPORTATION ON THE RIVER!
ZAA
AH. HELLO, HELLO.
WONDERFUL NIGHT.

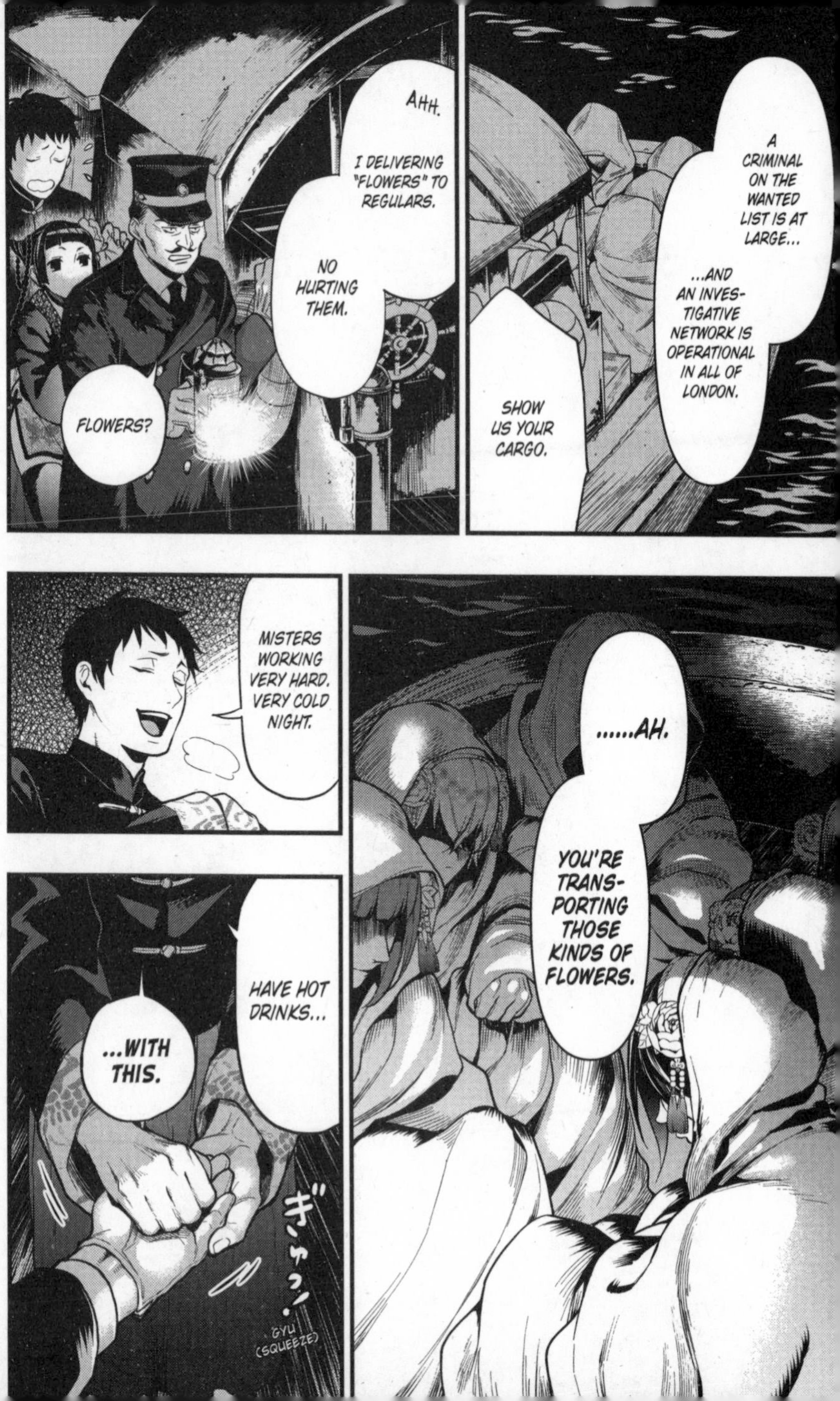
A CRIMINAL ON THE WANTED LIST IS AT LARGE...
...AND AN INVESTIGATIVE NETWORK IS OPERATIONAL IN ALL OF LONDON.
SHOW US YOUR CARGO.
AHH.
I DELIVERING "FLOWERS" TO REGULARS.
NO HURTING THEM.
FLOWERS?
......AH.
YOU'RE TRANSPORTING THOSE KINDS OF FLOWERS.
MISTERS WORKING VERY HARD. VERY COLD NIGHT.
HAVE HOT DRINKS...
...WITH THIS.
ぎゅっ!
GYU (SQUEEZE)

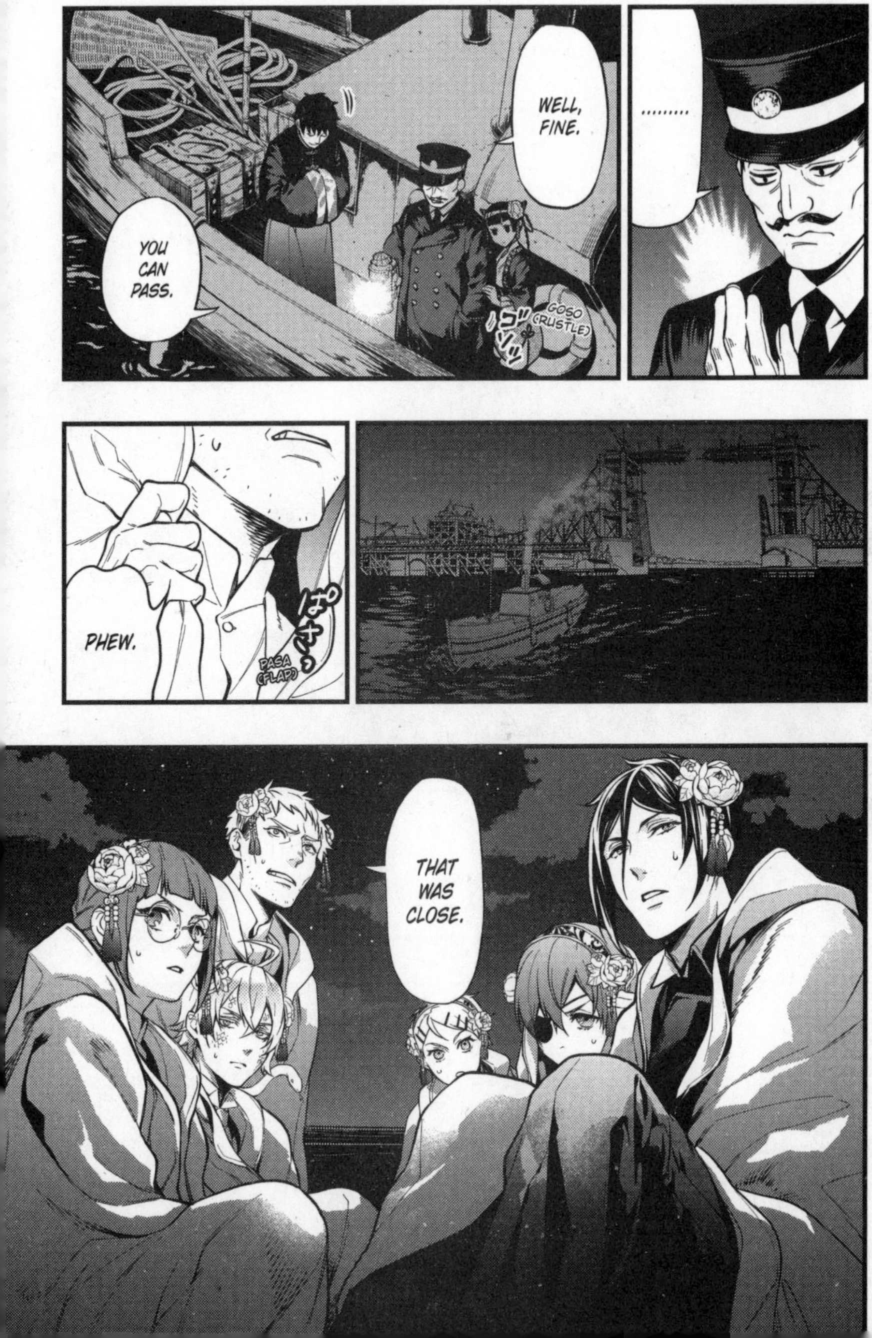

....
WELL, FINE.
YOU CAN PASS.
ゴソッ
GOSO (RUSTLE)
PHEW.
ぱさっ
PASA (FLAP)
THAT WAS CLOSE.

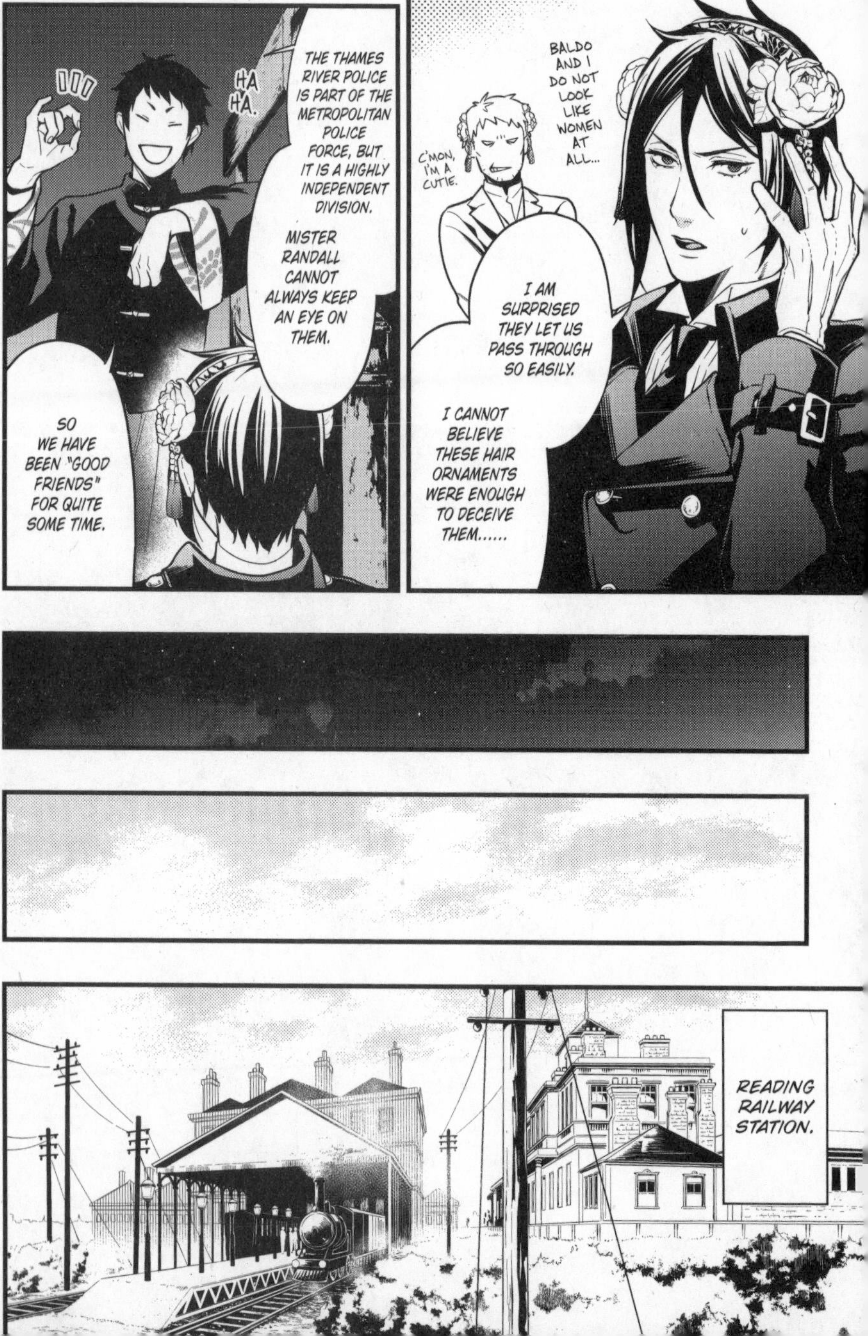
I AM SURPRISED THEY LET US PASS THROUGH SO EASILY.
I CANNOT BELIEVE THESE HAIR ORNAMENTS WERE ENOUGH TO DECEIVE THEM......
BALDO AND I DO NOT LOOK LIKE WOMEN AT ALL...
C'MON, I'M A CUTIE.
HA HA.
THE THAMES RIVER POLICE IS PART OF THE METROPOLITAN POLICE FORCE, BUT IT IS A HIGHLY INDEPENDENT DIVISION.
MISTER RANDALL CANNOT ALWAYS KEEP AN EYE ON THEM.
SO WE HAVE BEEN "GOOD FRIENDS" FOR QUITE SOME TIME.
READING RAILWAY STATION.

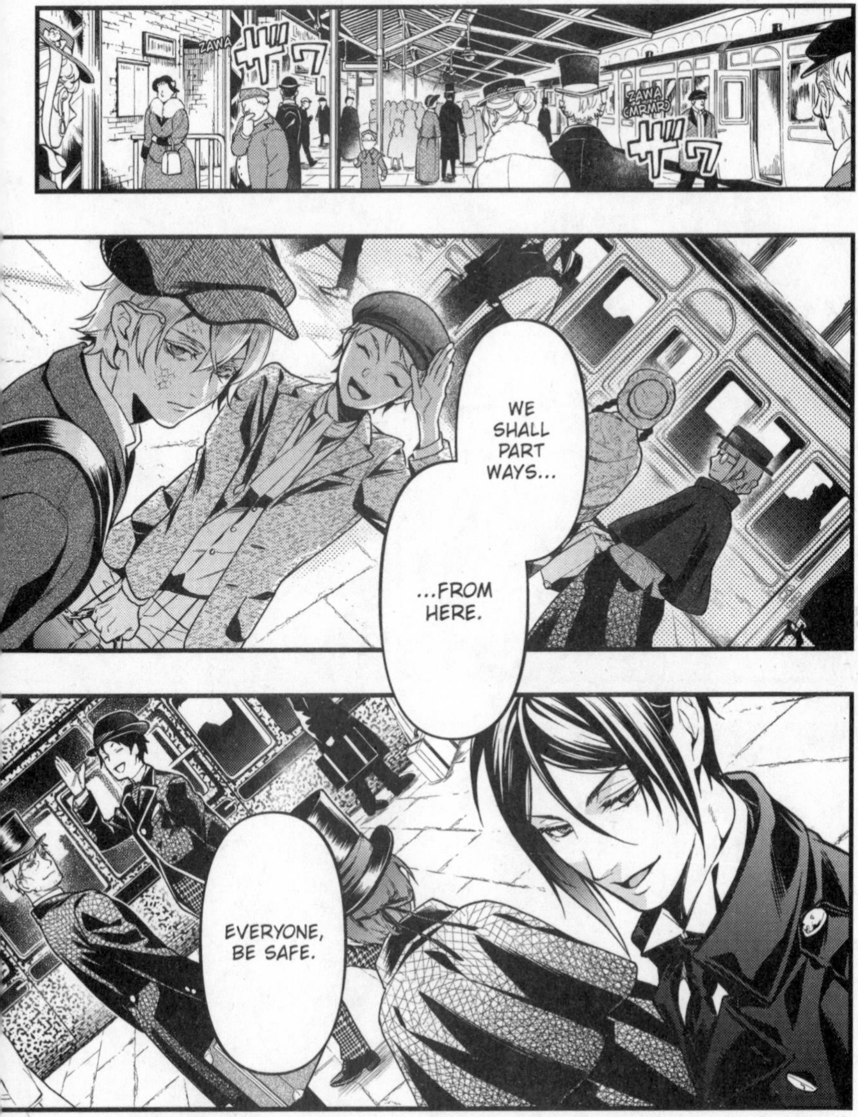
ZAWA (MRMR)
ザワ
ZAWA
ザワ
WE SHALL PART WAYS...
...FROM HERE.
EVERYONE, BE SAFE.

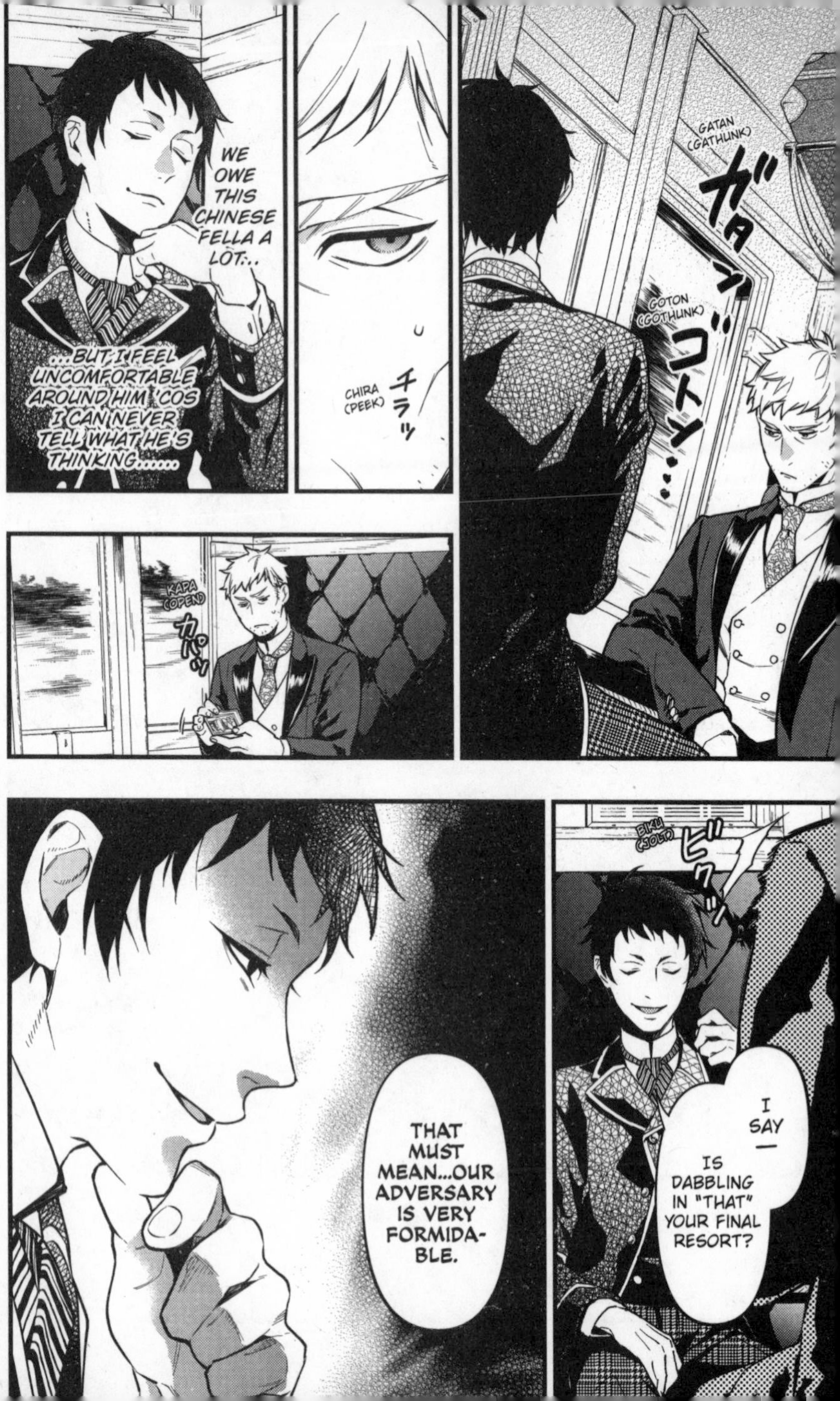
GATAN (GATHUNK)
ガタン
GOTON (GOTHUNK)
ゴトン…
CHIRA (PEEK)
チラッ
WE OWE THIS CHINESE FELLA A LOT...
...BUT I FEEL UNCOMFORTABLE AROUND HIM 'COS I CAN NEVER TELL WHAT HE'S THINKING......
KAPA (OPEN)
カパッ
BIKU (JOLT)
ビクッ
I SAY—
IS DABBLING IN "THAT" YOUR FINAL RESORT?
THAT MUST MEAN...OUR ADVERSARY IS VERY FORMIDA-BLE.

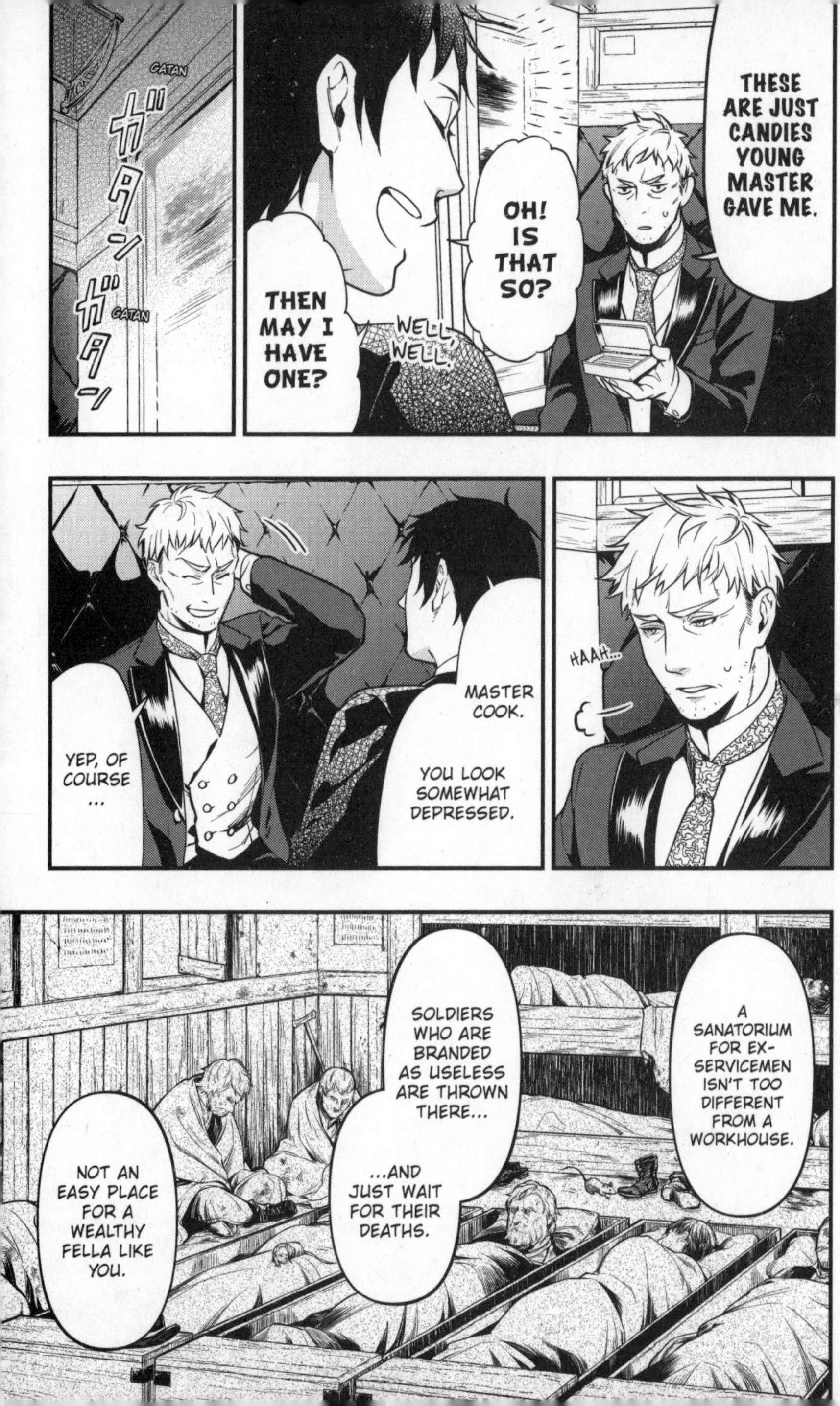
THESE ARE JUST CANDIES YOUNG MASTER GAVE ME.
OH! IS THAT SO?
WELL, WELL.
THEN MAY I HAVE ONE?
GATAN
GATAN
HAAH...
MASTER COOK.
YOU LOOK SOMEWHAT DEPRESSED.
YEP, OF COURSE...
A SANATORIUM FOR EX-SERVICEMEN ISN'T TOO DIFFERENT FROM A WORKHOUSE.
SOLDIERS WHO ARE BRANDED AS USELESS ARE THROWN THERE...
...AND JUST WAIT FOR THEIR DEATHS.
NOT AN EASY PLACE FOR A WEALTHY FELLA LIKE YOU.

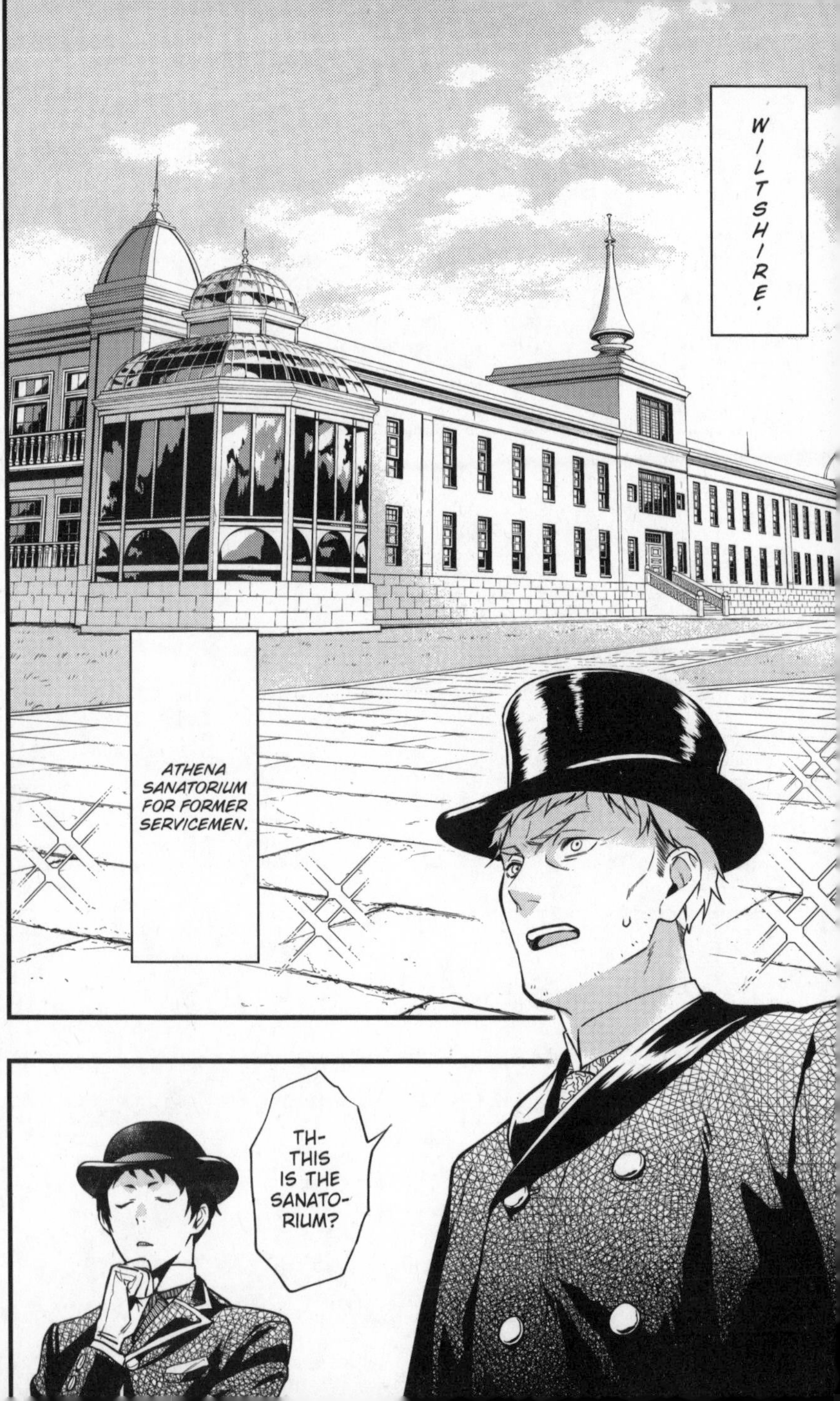
WILTSHIRE.
ATHENA SANATORIUM FOR FORMER SERVICEMEN.
TH- THIS IS THE SANATO- RIUM?

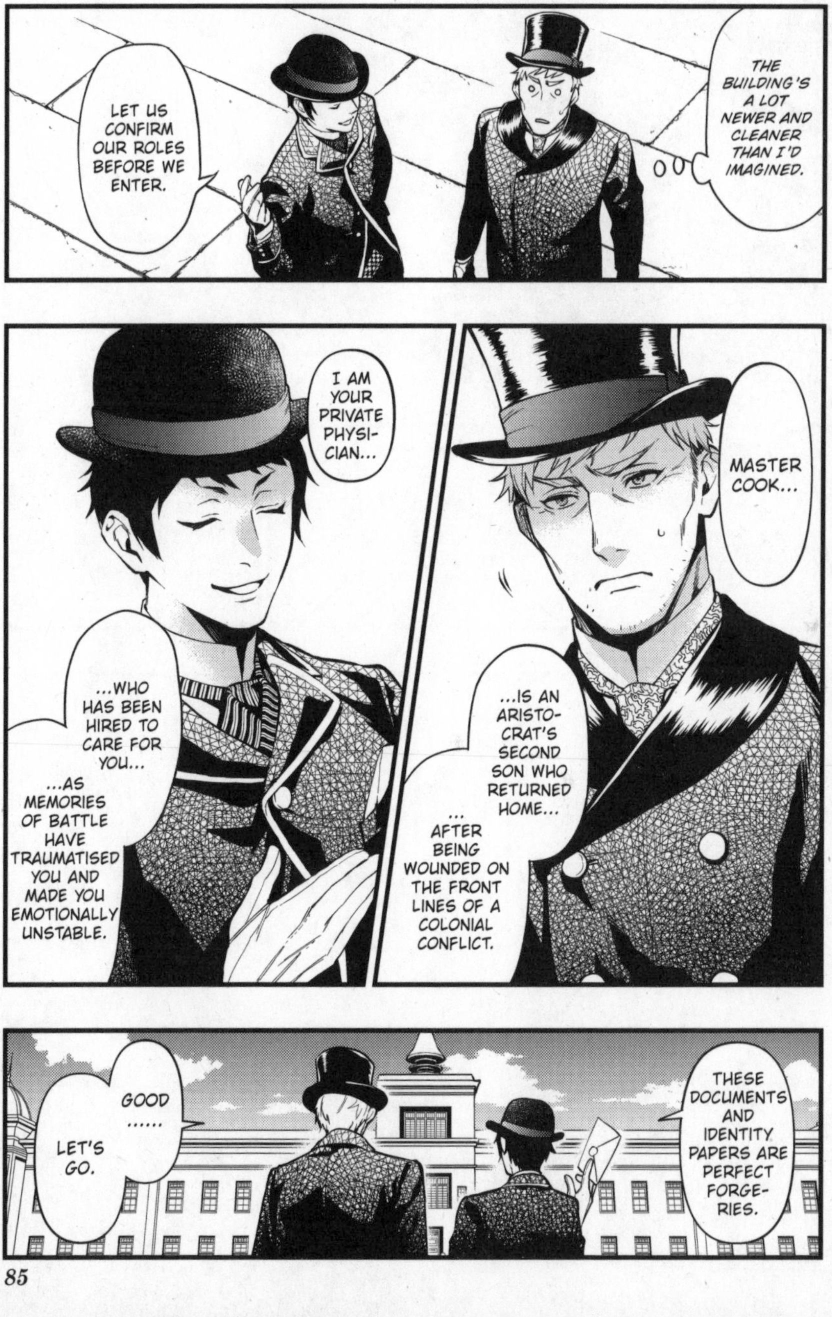
THE BUILDING'S A LOT NEWER AND CLEANER THAN I'D IMAGINED.
LET US CONFIRM OUR ROLES BEFORE WE ENTER.
MASTER COOK...
...IS AN ARISTOCRAT'S SECOND SON WHO RETURNED HOME...
...AFTER BEING WOUNDED ON THE FRONT LINES OF A COLONIAL CONFLICT.
I AM YOUR PRIVATE PHYSICIAN...
...WHO HAS BEEN HIRED TO CARE FOR YOU...
...AS MEMORIES OF BATTLE HAVE TRAUMATISED YOU AND MADE YOU EMOTIONALLY UNSTABLE.
THESE DOCUMENTS AND IDENTITY PAPERS ARE PERFECT FORGERIES.
GOOD ...... LET'S GO.

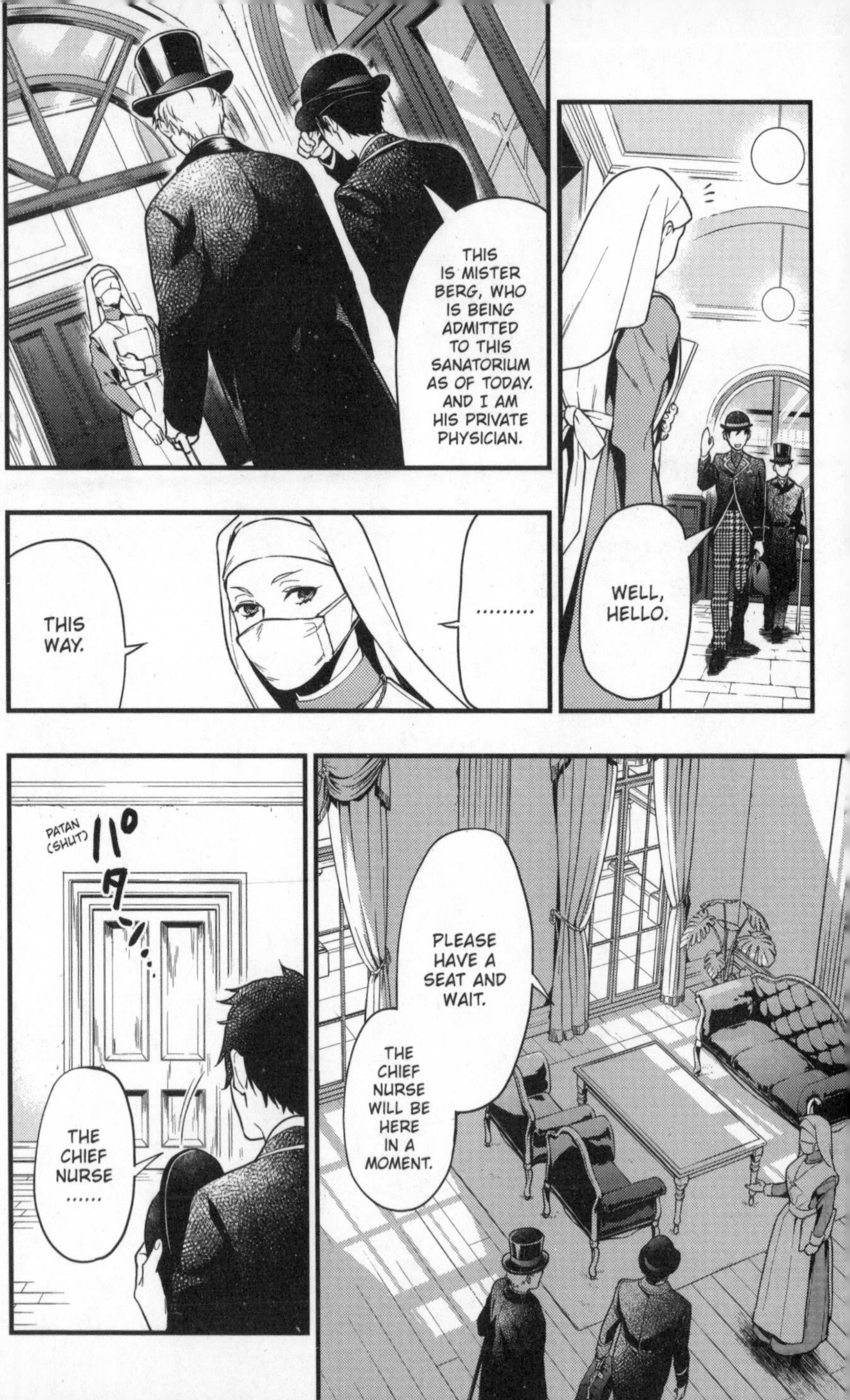
WELL, HELLO.
THIS IS MISTER BERG, WHO IS BEING ADMITTED TO THIS SANATORIUM AS OF TODAY. AND I AM HIS PRIVATE PHYSICIAN.
....
THIS WAY.
PLEASE HAVE A SEAT AND WAIT.
THE CHIEF NURSE WILL BE HERE IN A MOMENT.
PATAN (SHUT)
THE CHIEF NURSE ......

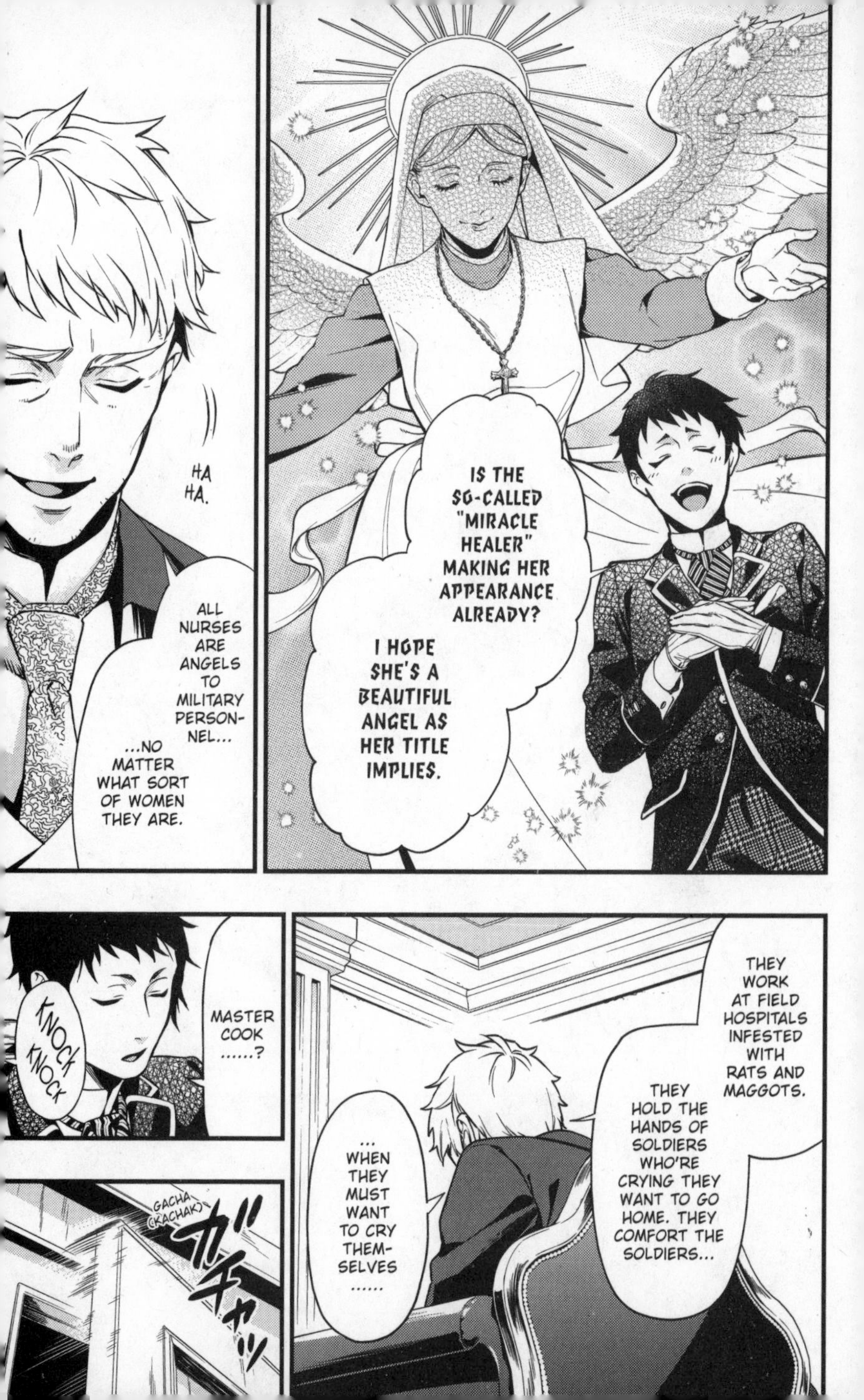
IS THE SO-CALLED "MIRACLE HEALER" MAKING HER APPEARANCE ALREADY?
I HOPE SHE'S A BEAUTIFUL ANGEL AS HER TITLE IMPLIES.
HA HA.
ALL NURSES ARE ANGELS TO MILITARY PERSONNEL...
...NO MATTER WHAT SORT OF WOMEN THEY ARE.
THEY WORK AT FIELD HOSPITALS INFESTED WITH RATS AND MAGGOTS.
THEY HOLD THE HANDS OF SOLDIERS WHO'RE CRYING THEY WANT TO GO HOME. THEY COMFORT THE SOLDIERS...
...WHEN THEY MUST WANT TO CRY THEMSELVES......
MASTER COOK ......?
KNOCK KNOCK
GACHA (KACHAK)
ガチャッ

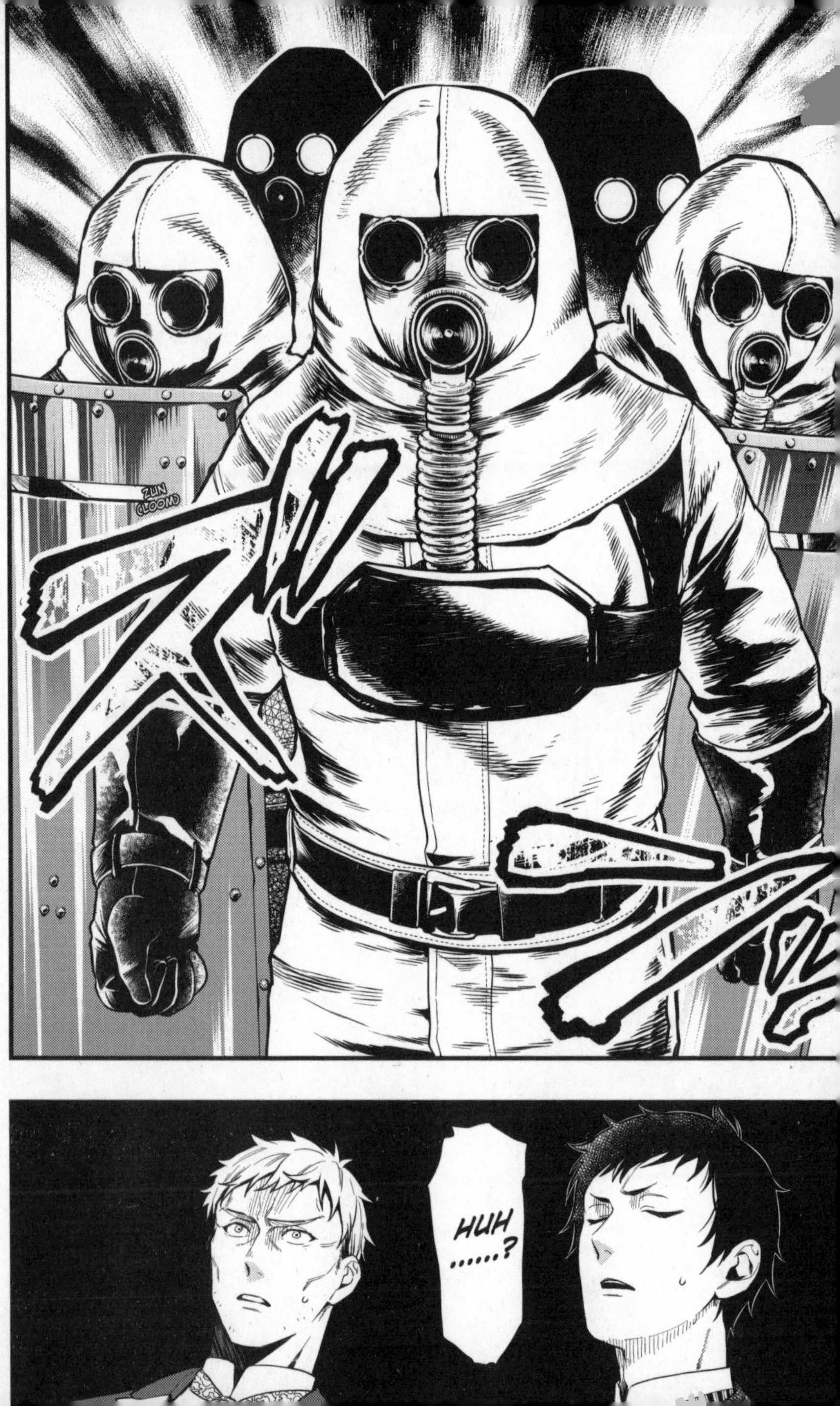
ZUN
(LOOM)
HUH ......?

Black Butler

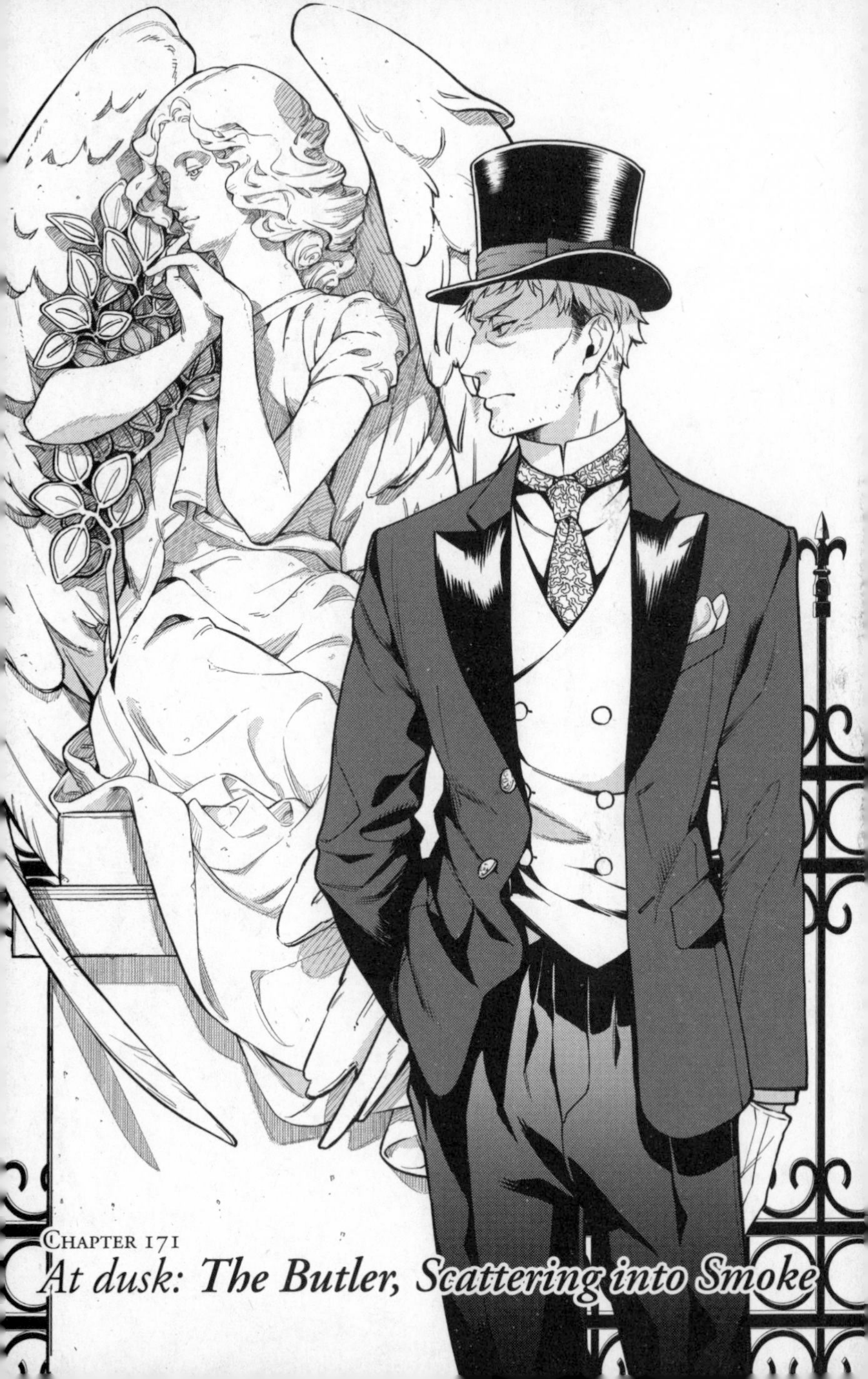

Chapter 171

At dusk: The Butler, Scattering into Smoke

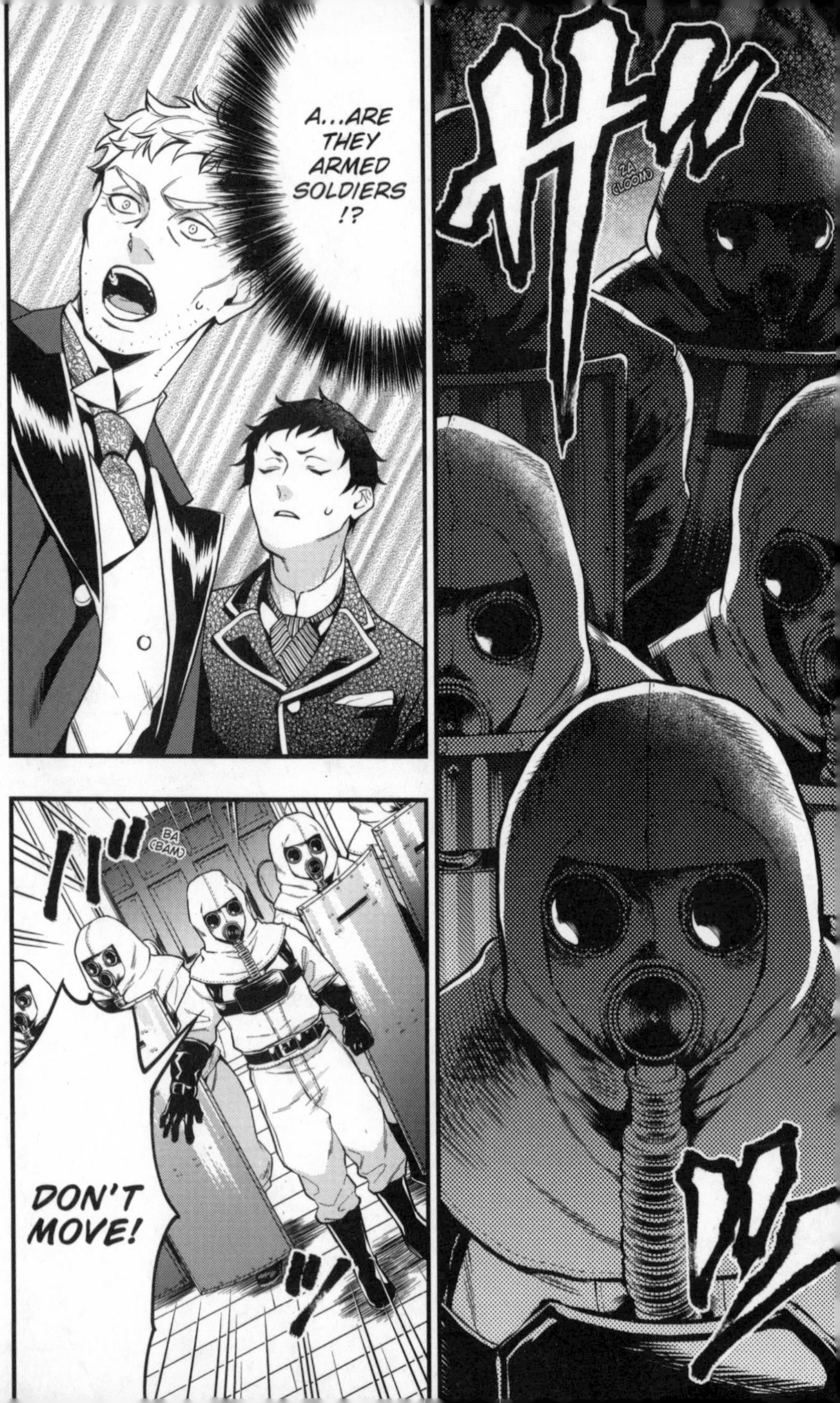
ZA (LOOM)
A...ARE THEY ARMED SOLDIERS!?
BA (BAM)
DON'T MOVE!

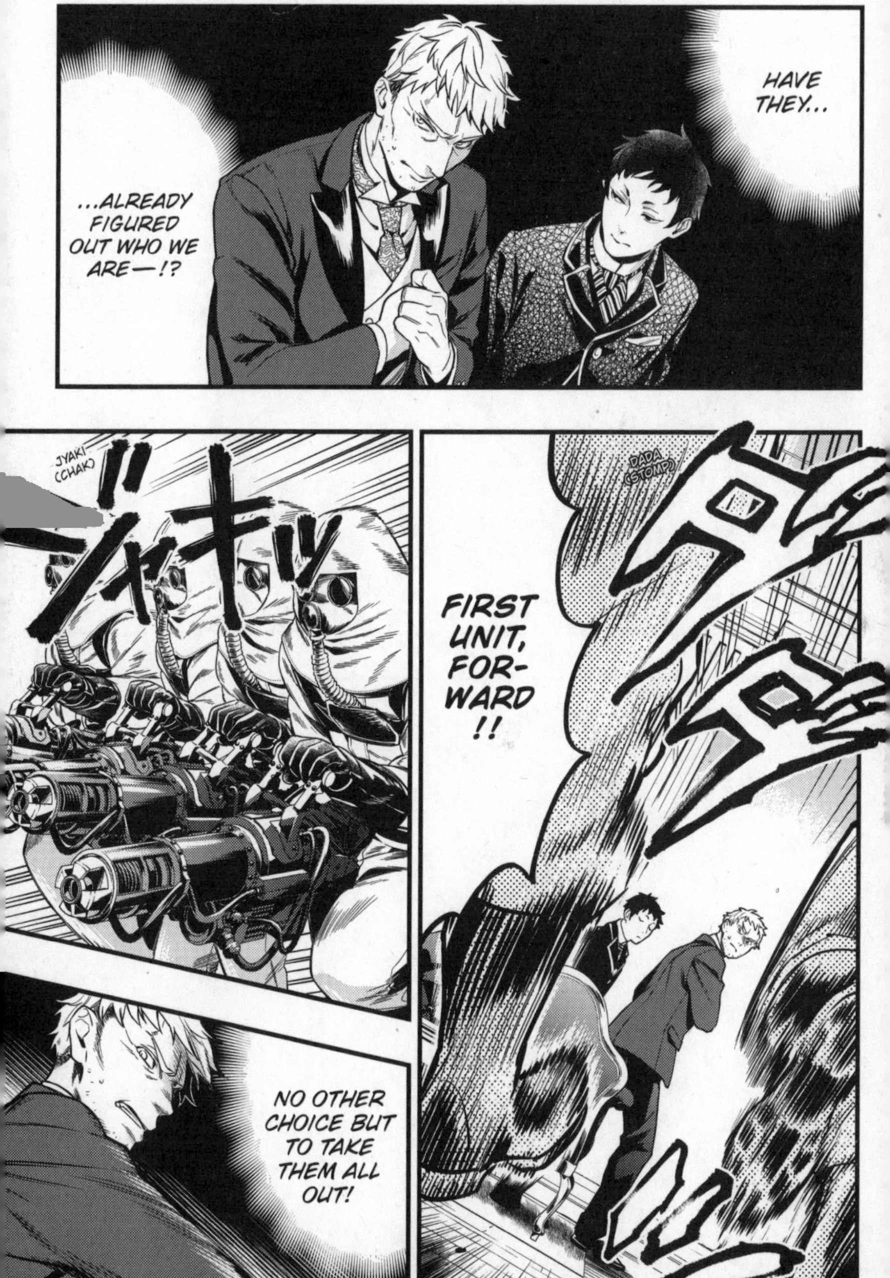
HAVE THEY...
...ALREADY FIGURED OUT WHO WE ARE—!?
DADA (STOMP)
FIRST UNIT, FOR-WARD!!
JYAKI (CHAK)
NO OTHER CHOICE BUT TO TAKE THEM ALL OUT!

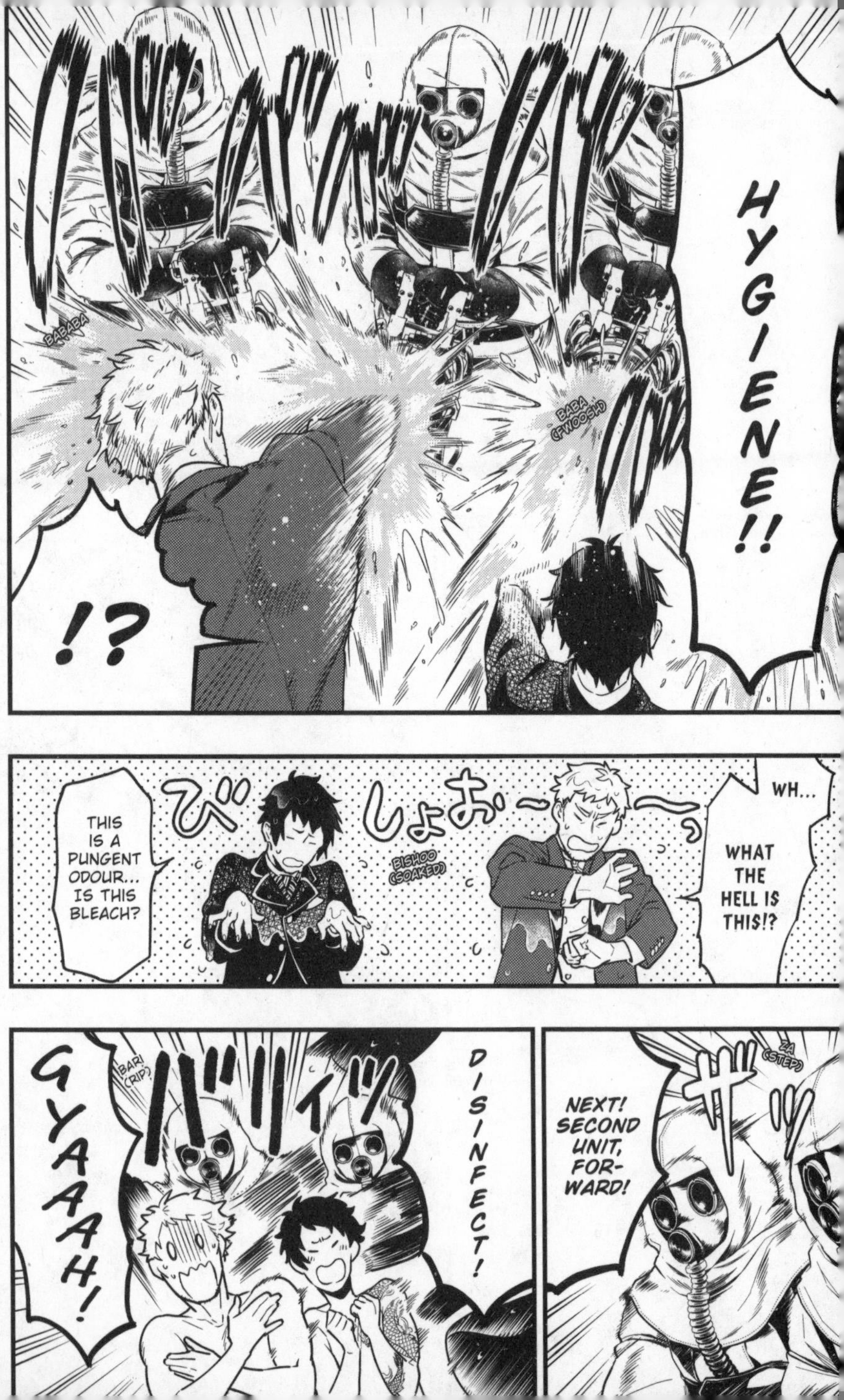
HYGIENE!!
BABA (FWOOSH)
BABABA
!?
WH...
WHAT THE HELL IS THIS!?
BISHOO (SOAKED)
THIS IS A PUNGENT ODOUR... IS THIS BLEACH?
ZA (STEP)
NEXT! SECOND UNIT, FOR-WARD!
DISINFECT!
BARI (RIP)
GYAAAAH!

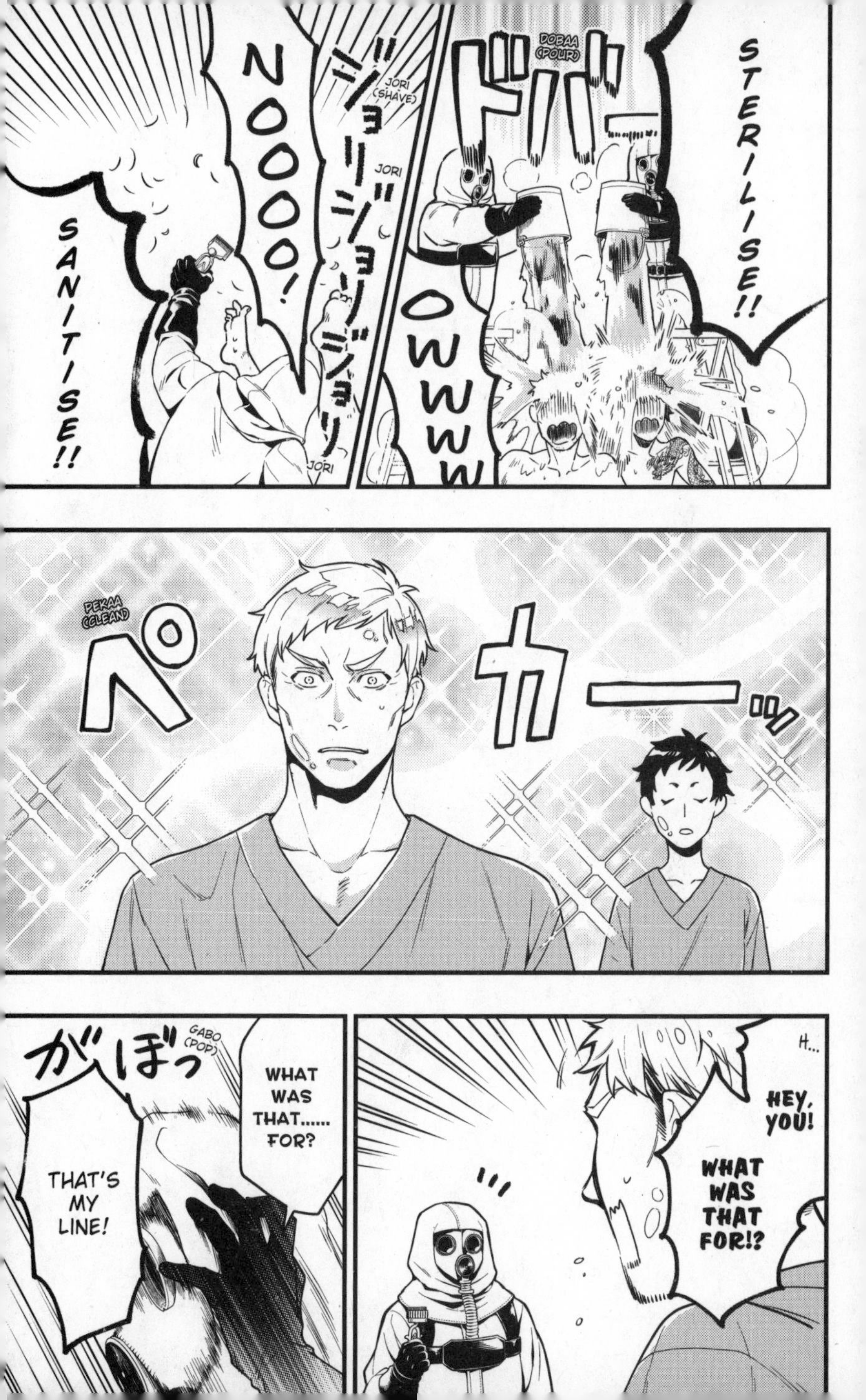
STERILISE!!
ドバー
DOBAA (POUR)
OWWWW
ジョリジョリジョリ
JORI (SHAVE)
JORI
JORI
NOOOOO!
SANITISE!!
ペカー
PEKAA (CLEAN)
H...
HEY, YOU!
WHAT WAS THAT FOR!?
がぼっ
GABO (POP)
WHAT WAS THAT...... FOR?
THAT'S MY LINE!

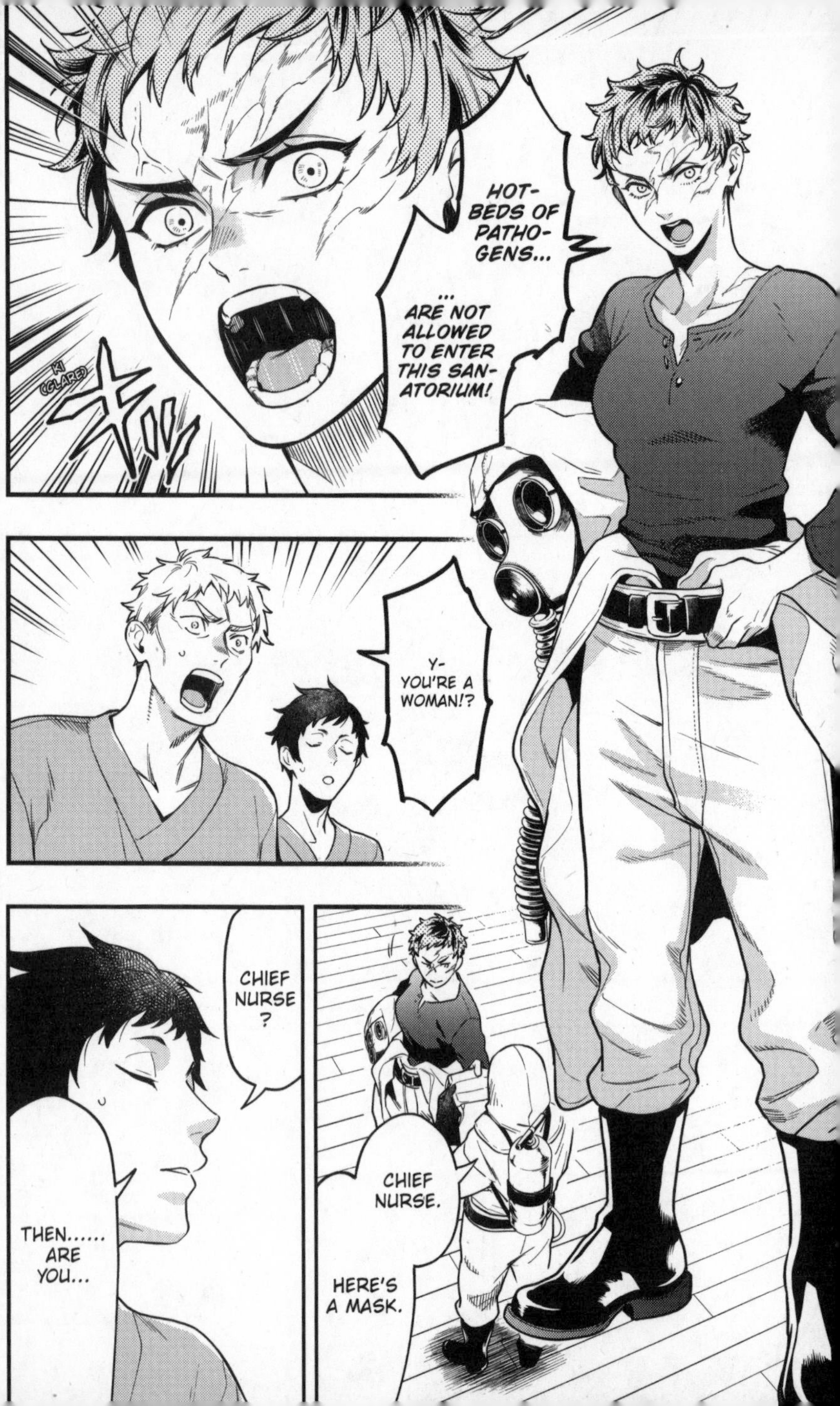
HOT-BEDS OF PATHO-GENS...
... ARE NOT ALLOWED TO ENTER THIS SAN-ATORIUM!
KI (GLARE)
Y-YOU'RE A WOMAN!?
CHIEF NURSE.
HERE'S A MASK.
CHIEF NURSE?
THEN...... ARE YOU...

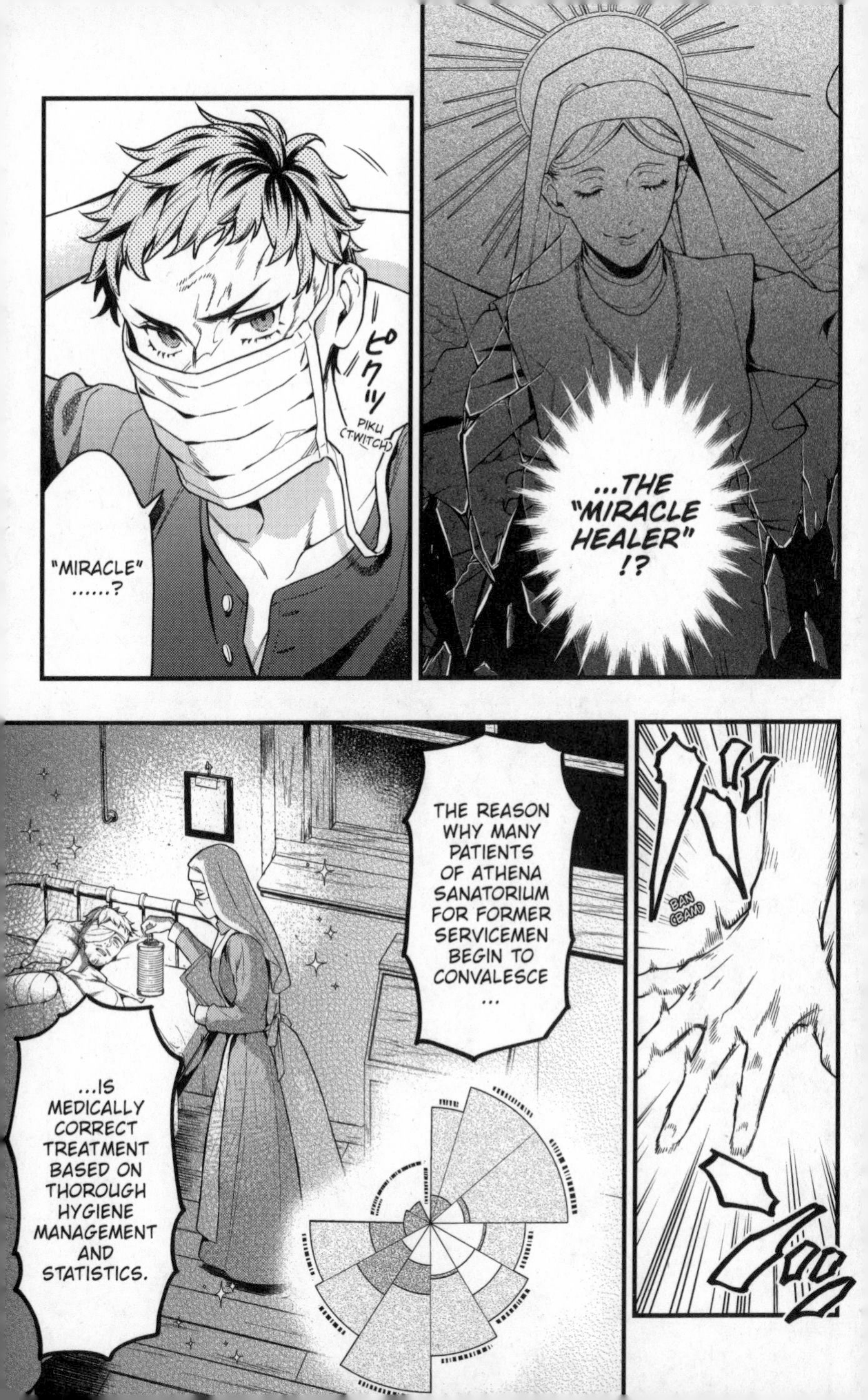
...THE "MIRACLE HEALER" !?
ピクッ
PIKU (TWITCH)
"MIRACLE" ......?
BAN (BAM)
THE REASON WHY MANY PATIENTS OF ATHENA SANATORIUM FOR FORMER SERVICEMEN BEGIN TO CONVALESCE ...
...IS MEDICALLY CORRECT TREATMENT BASED ON THOROUGH HYGIENE MANAGEMENT AND STATISTICS.

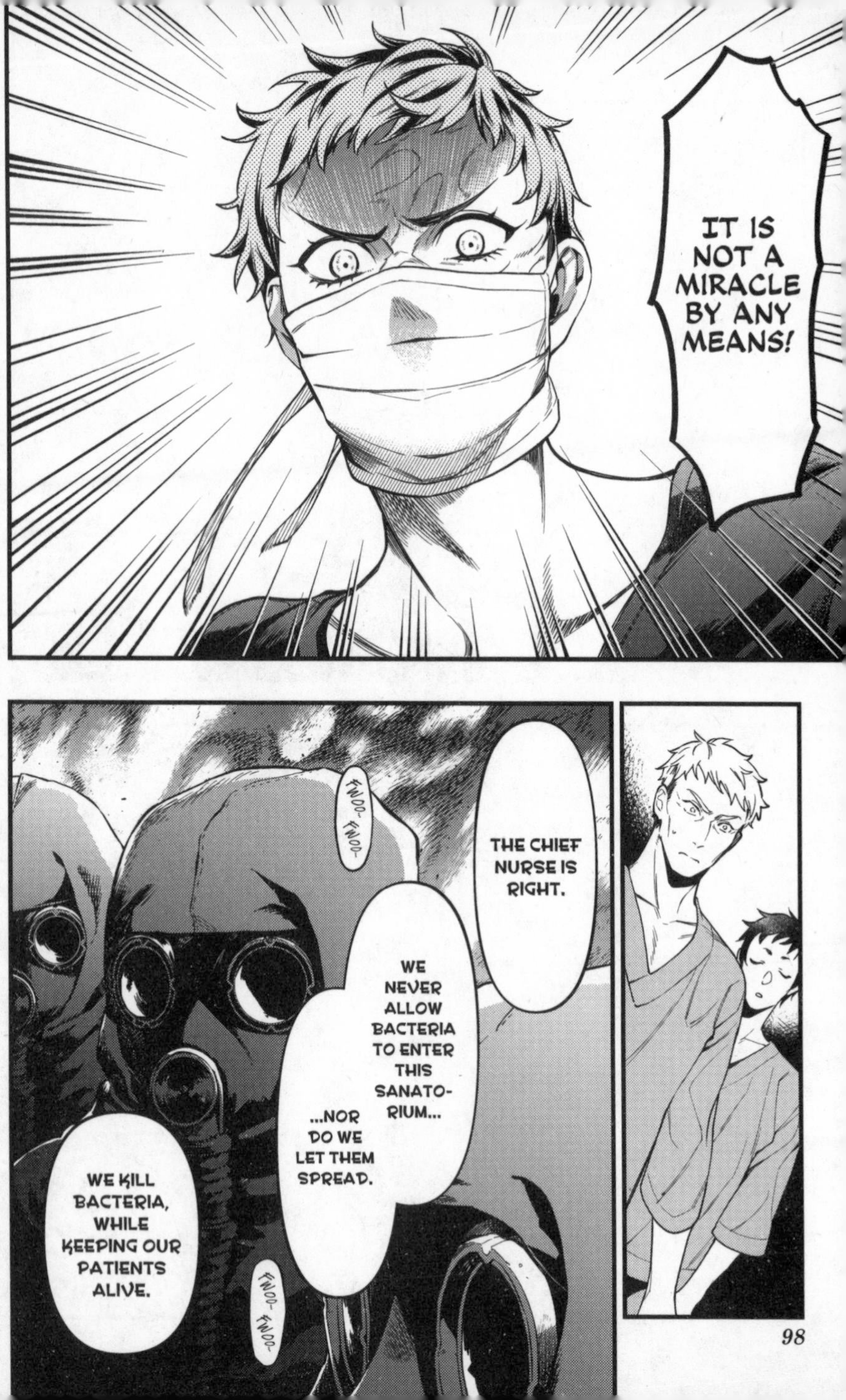
IT IS NOT A MIRACLE BY ANY MEANS!
THE CHIEF NURSE IS RIGHT.
FWOO- FWOO-
WE NEVER ALLOW BACTERIA TO ENTER THIS SANATO-RIUM...
...NOR DO WE LET THEM SPREAD.
WE KILL BACTERIA, WHILE KEEPING OUR PATIENTS ALIVE.
FWOO- FWOO-

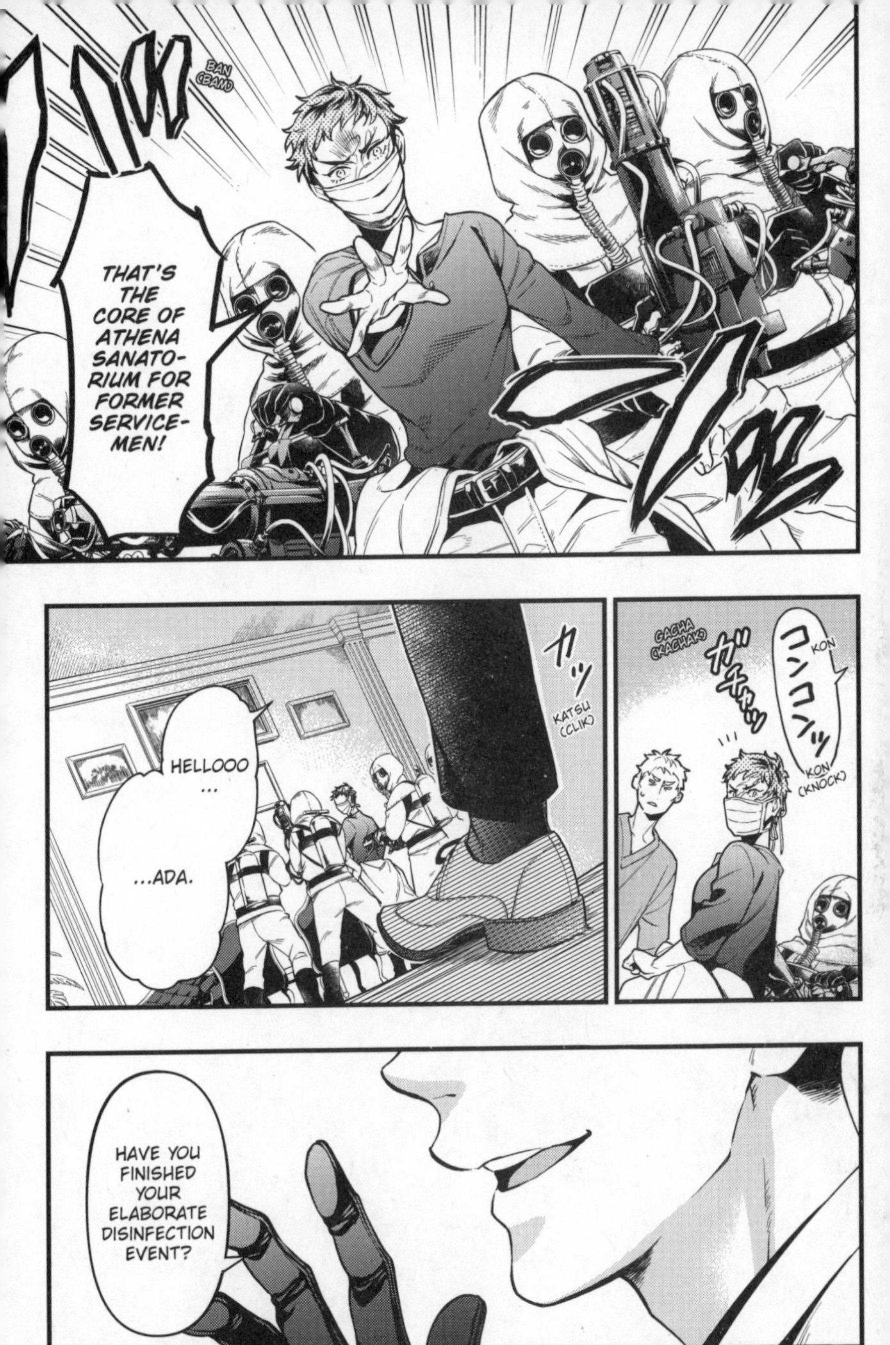
BAN (BAM)
THAT'S THE CORE OF ATHENA SANATORIUM FOR FORMER SERVICEMEN!
ガチャッ
GACHA (KACHAK)
コンコンッ
KON KON (KNOCK)
カッ
KATSU (CLIK)
HELLOOO ...
...ADA.
HAVE YOU FINISHED YOUR ELABORATE DISINFECTION EVENT?

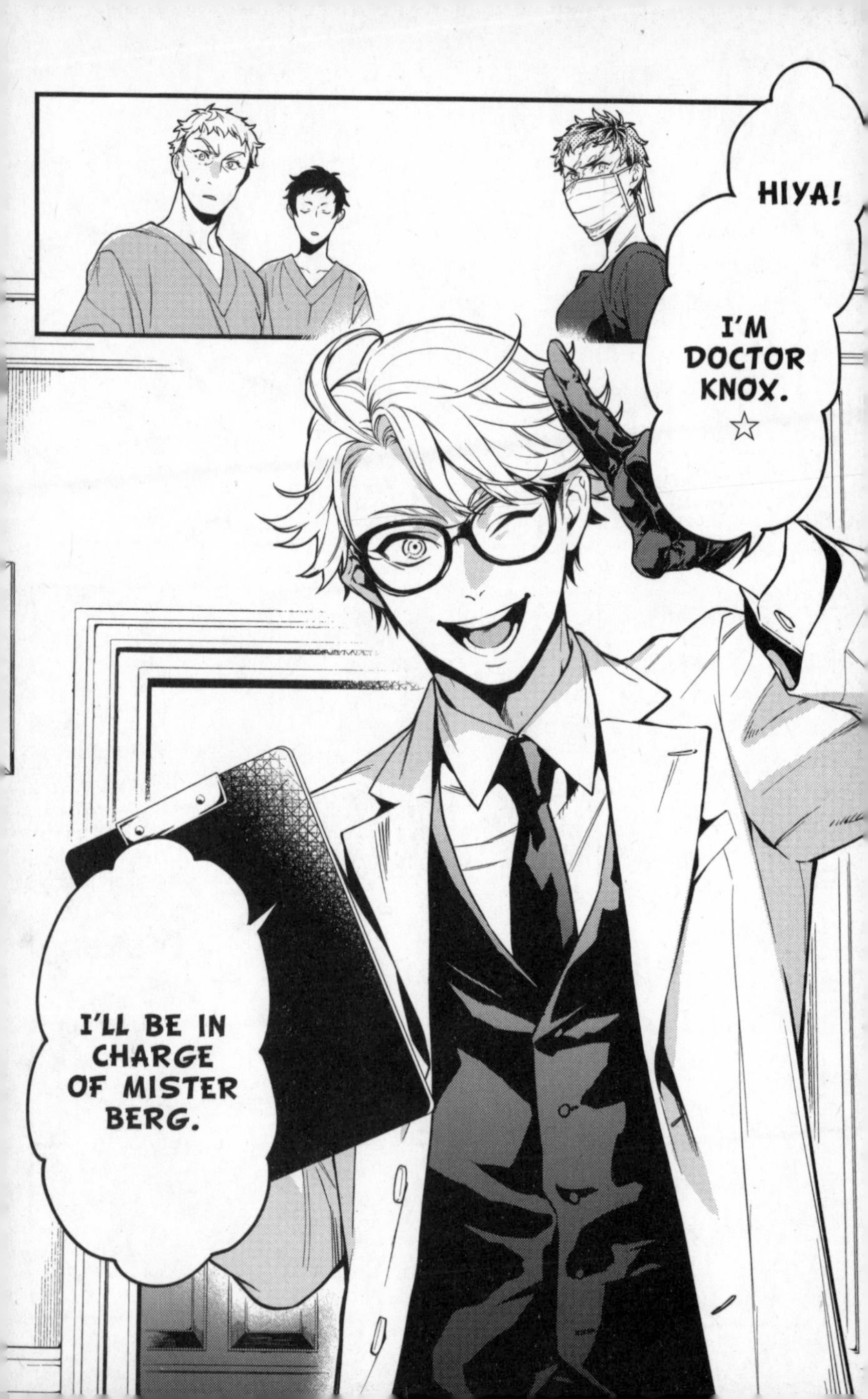
HIYA!
I'M DOCTOR KNOX. ☆
I'LL BE IN CHARGE OF MISTER BERG.

Black Butler

Chapter 172

In the evening: The Butler, Psychosomatic Treatment

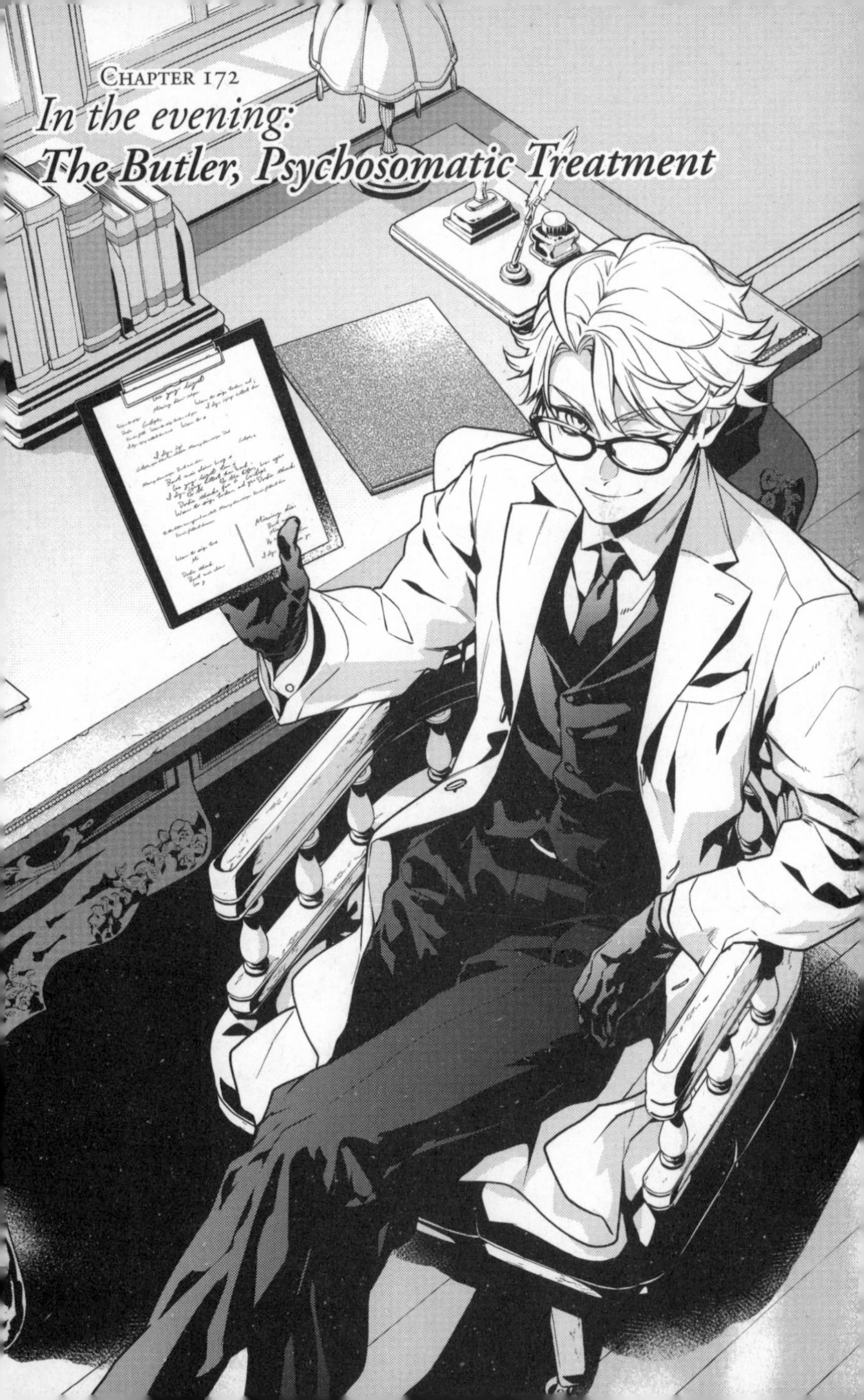

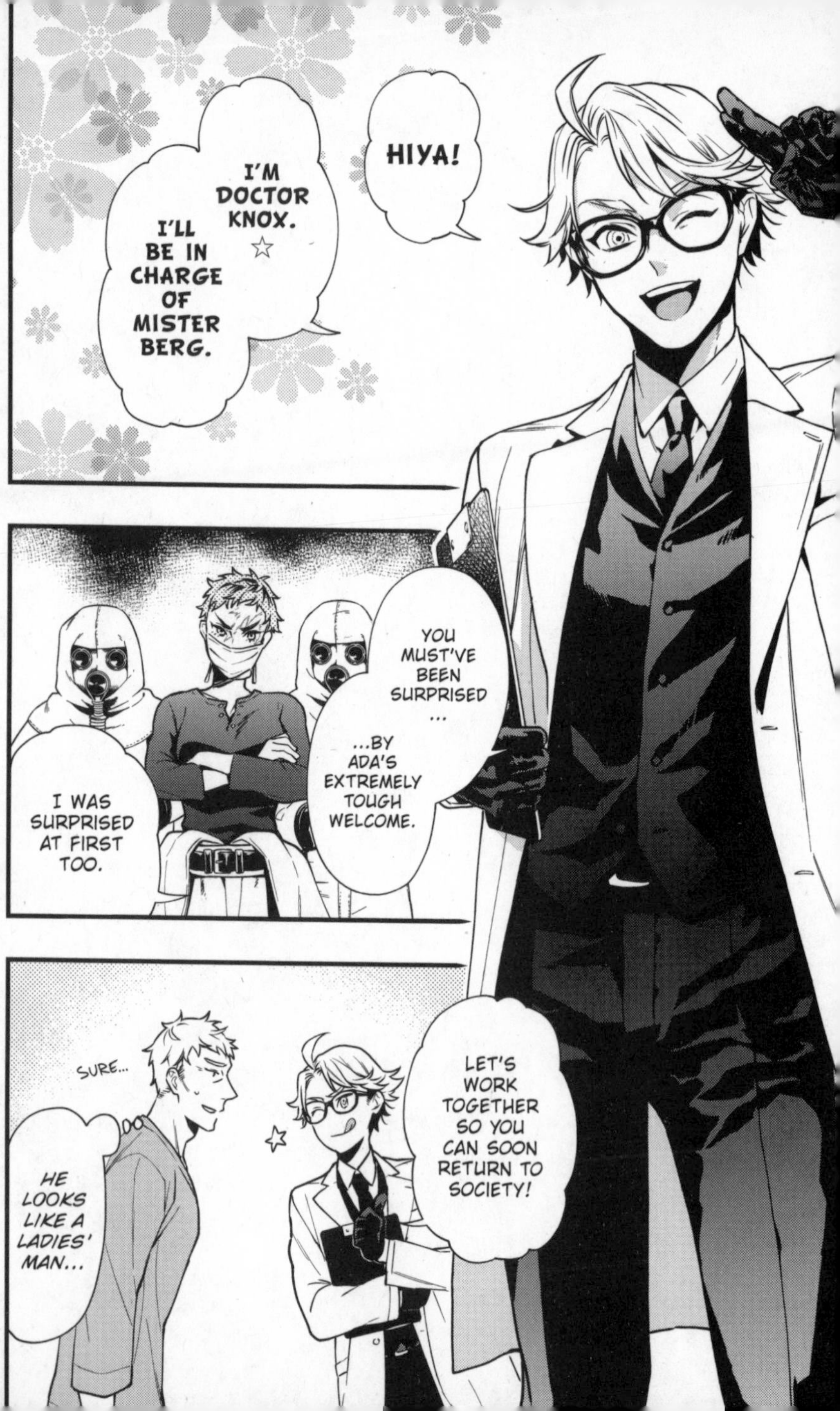
HIYA!
I'M DOCTOR KNOX. ☆ I'LL BE IN CHARGE OF MISTER BERG.
YOU MUST'VE BEEN SURPRISED...
...BY ADA'S EXTREMELY TOUGH WELCOME.
I WAS SURPRISED AT FIRST TOO.
LET'S WORK TOGETHER SO YOU CAN SOON RETURN TO SOCIETY!
SURE...
HE LOOKS LIKE A LADIES' MAN...

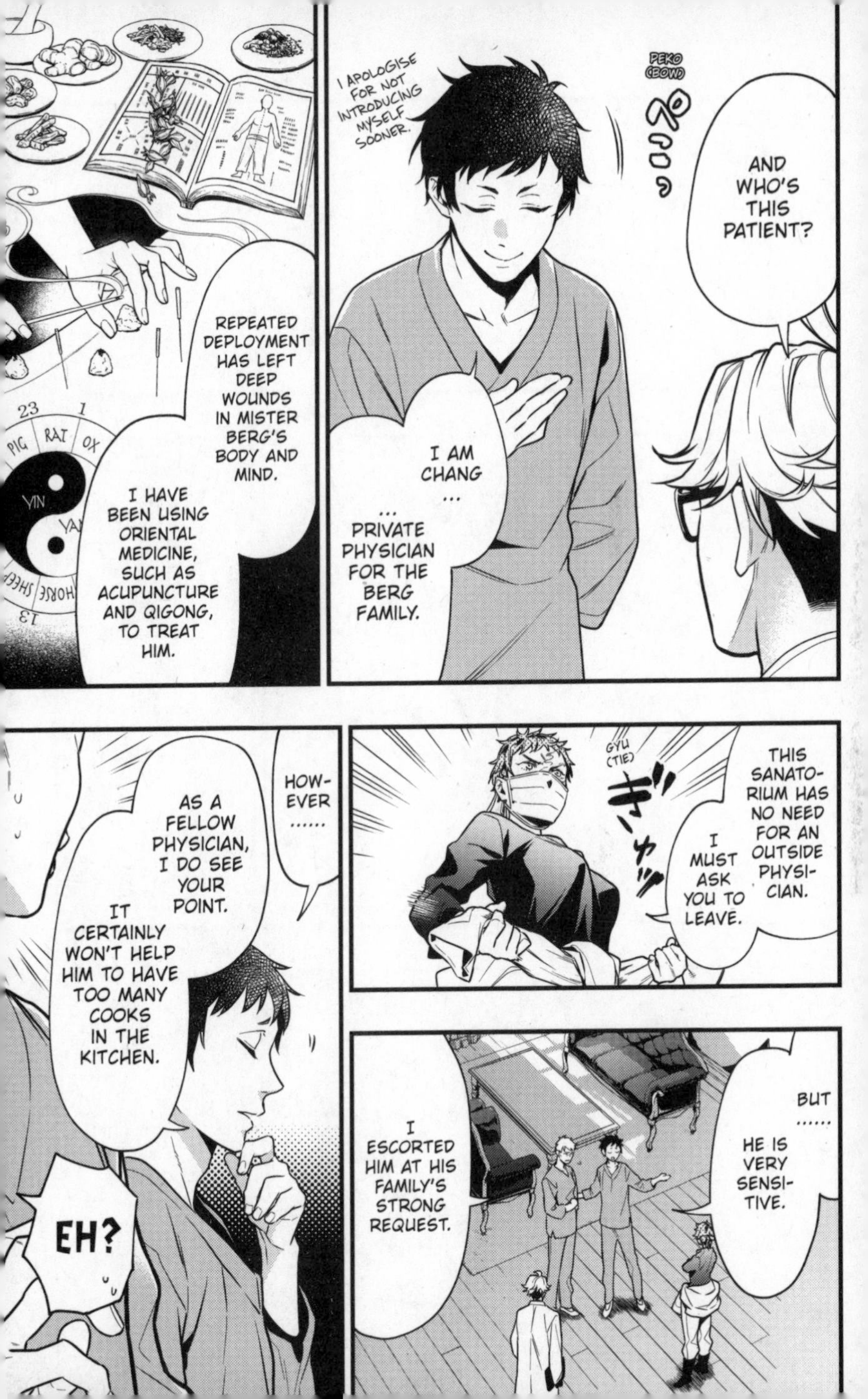
AND WHO'S THIS PATIENT?
PEKO (BOW)
I APOLOGISE FOR NOT INTRODUCING MYSELF SOONER.
I AM CHANG ...
... PRIVATE PHYSICIAN FOR THE BERG FAMILY.
REPEATED DEPLOYMENT HAS LEFT DEEP WOUNDS IN MISTER BERG'S BODY AND MIND.
I HAVE BEEN USING ORIENTAL MEDICINE, SUCH AS ACUPUNCTURE AND QIGONG, TO TREAT HIM.
23
1
PIG
RAT
OX
YIN
HORSE
SHEEP
13
THIS SANATORIUM HAS NO NEED FOR AN OUTSIDE PHYSICIAN.
GYU (TIE)
I MUST ASK YOU TO LEAVE.
BUT ......
HE IS VERY SENSITIVE.
I ESCORTED HIM AT HIS FAMILY'S STRONG REQUEST.
HOW-EVER ......
AS A FELLOW PHYSICIAN, I DO SEE YOUR POINT.
IT CERTAINLY WON'T HELP HIM TO HAVE TOO MANY COOKS IN THE KITCHEN.
EH?

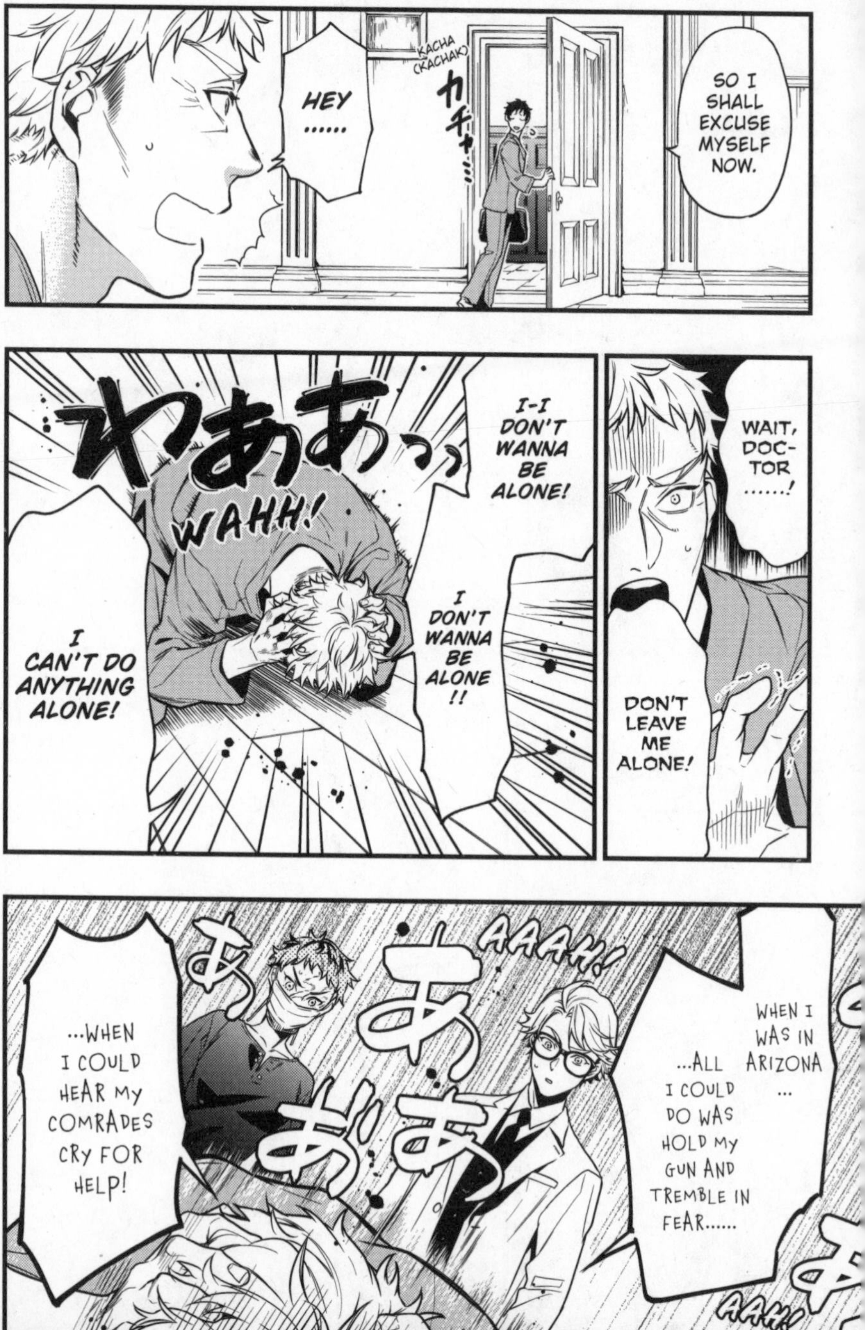
SO I SHALL EXCUSE MYSELF NOW.
KACHA (KACHAK)
カチャ
HEY ......
WAIT, DOCTOR......!
DON'T LEAVE ME ALONE!
I-I DON'T WANNA BE ALONE!
I DON'T WANNA BE ALONE !!
わあぁっっ
WAHH!
I CAN'T DO ANYTHING ALONE!
WHEN I WAS IN ARIZONA ...
...ALL I COULD DO WAS HOLD MY GUN AND TREMBLE IN FEAR......
AAAH!
ああああ
...WHEN I COULD HEAR MY COMRADES CRY FOR HELP!
AAAH!

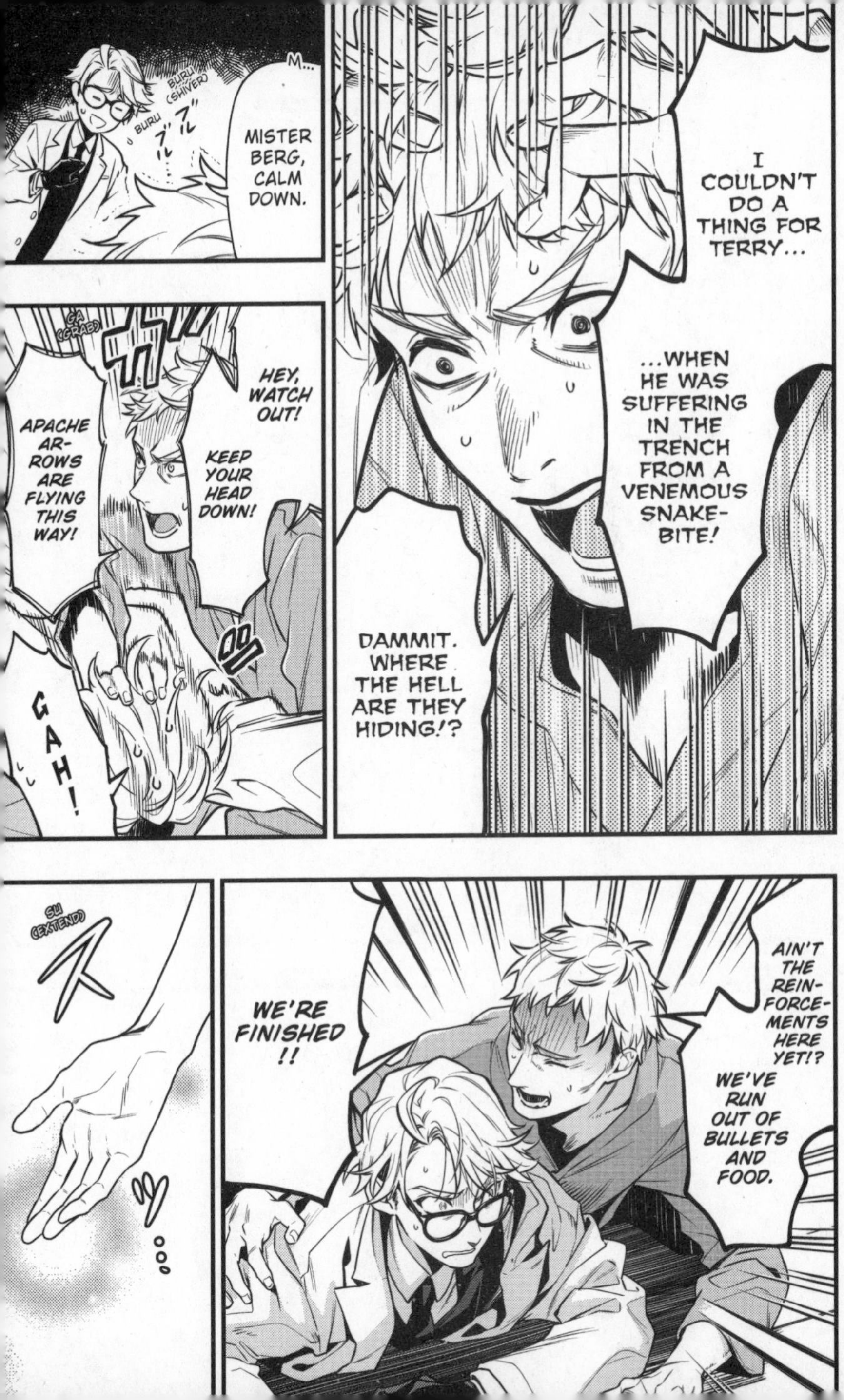
I COULDN'T DO A THING FOR TERRY...
...WHEN HE WAS SUFFERING IN THE TRENCH FROM A VENEMOUS SNAKE-BITE!
DAMMIT. WHERE THE HELL ARE THEY HIDING!?
M...
MISTER BERG, CALM DOWN.
BURU (SHIVER) BURU
HEY, WATCH OUT!
KEEP YOUR HEAD DOWN!
GA (GRAB)
APACHE AR-ROWS ARE FLYING THIS WAY!
GAH!
AIN'T THE REIN-FORCE-MENTS HERE YET!?
WE'VE RUN OUT OF BULLETS AND FOOD.
WE'RE FINISHED!!
SU (EXTEND)

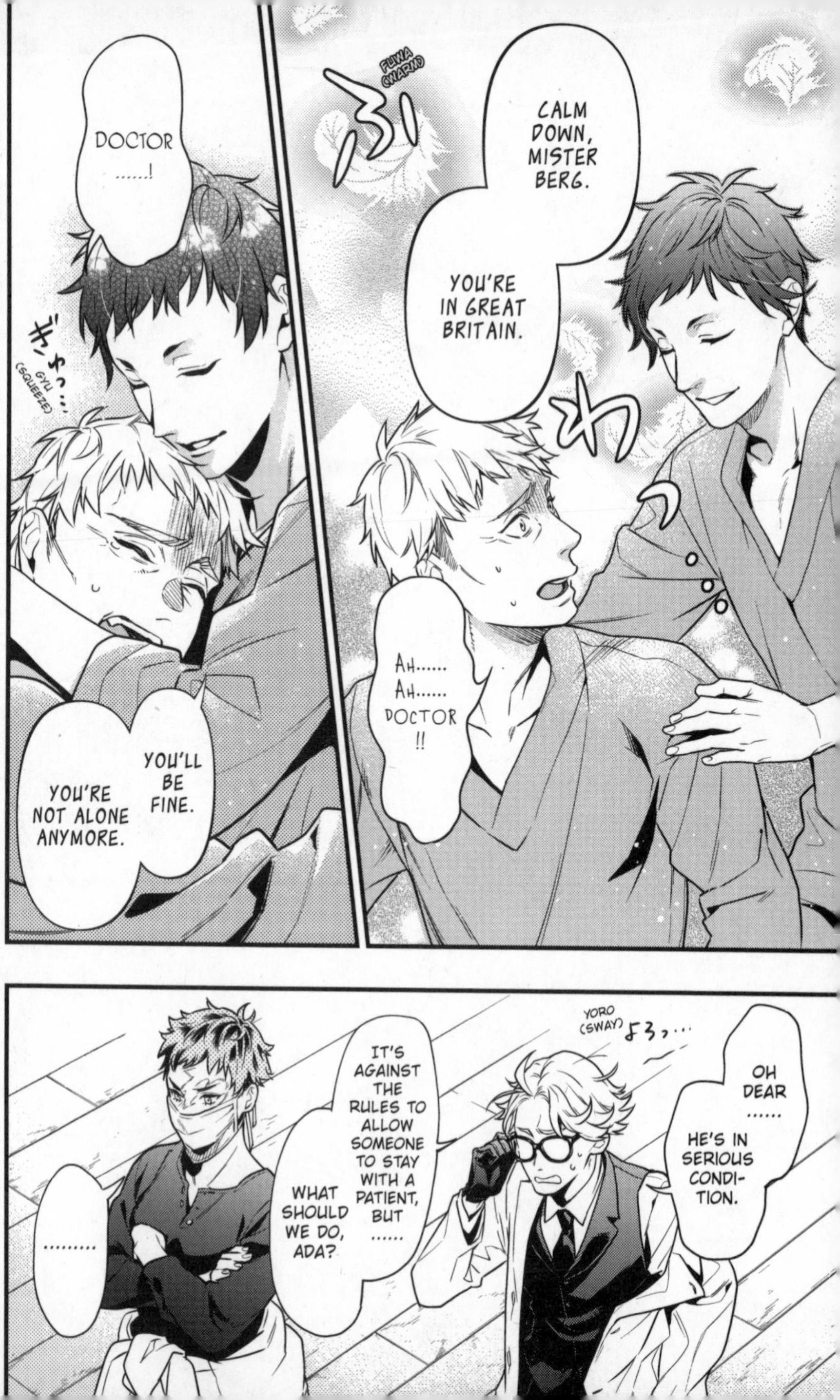
FUWA (WARM)
ふわ
CALM DOWN, MISTER BERG.
YOU'RE IN GREAT BRITAIN.
AH...... AH...... DOCTOR !!
DOCTOR ......!
ぎゅっ...
GYU (SQUEEZE)
YOU'LL BE FINE.
YOU'RE NOT ALONE ANYMORE.
YORO (SWAY) よろっ...
OH DEAR ......
HE'S IN SERIOUS CONDITION.
IT'S AGAINST THE RULES TO ALLOW SOMEONE TO STAY WITH A PATIENT, BUT ......
WHAT SHOULD WE DO, ADA?
....

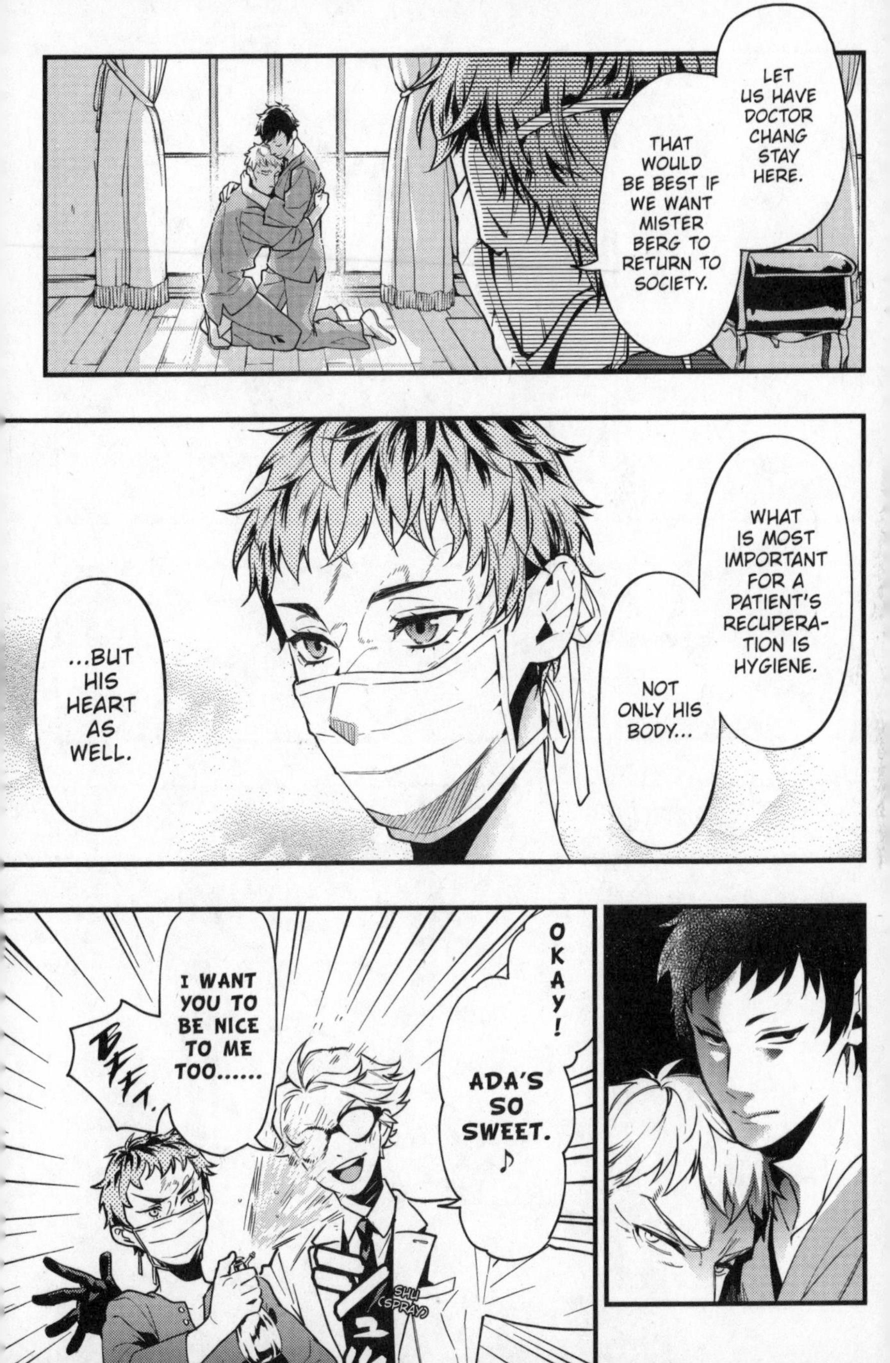
LET US HAVE DOCTOR CHANG STAY HERE.
THAT WOULD BE BEST IF WE WANT MISTER BERG TO RETURN TO SOCIETY.
WHAT IS MOST IMPORTANT FOR A PATIENT'S RECUPERATION IS HYGIENE.
NOT ONLY HIS BODY...
...BUT HIS HEART AS WELL.
OKAY!
ADA'S SO SWEET. ♪
I WANT YOU TO BE NICE TO ME TOO......
SHU (SPRAY)

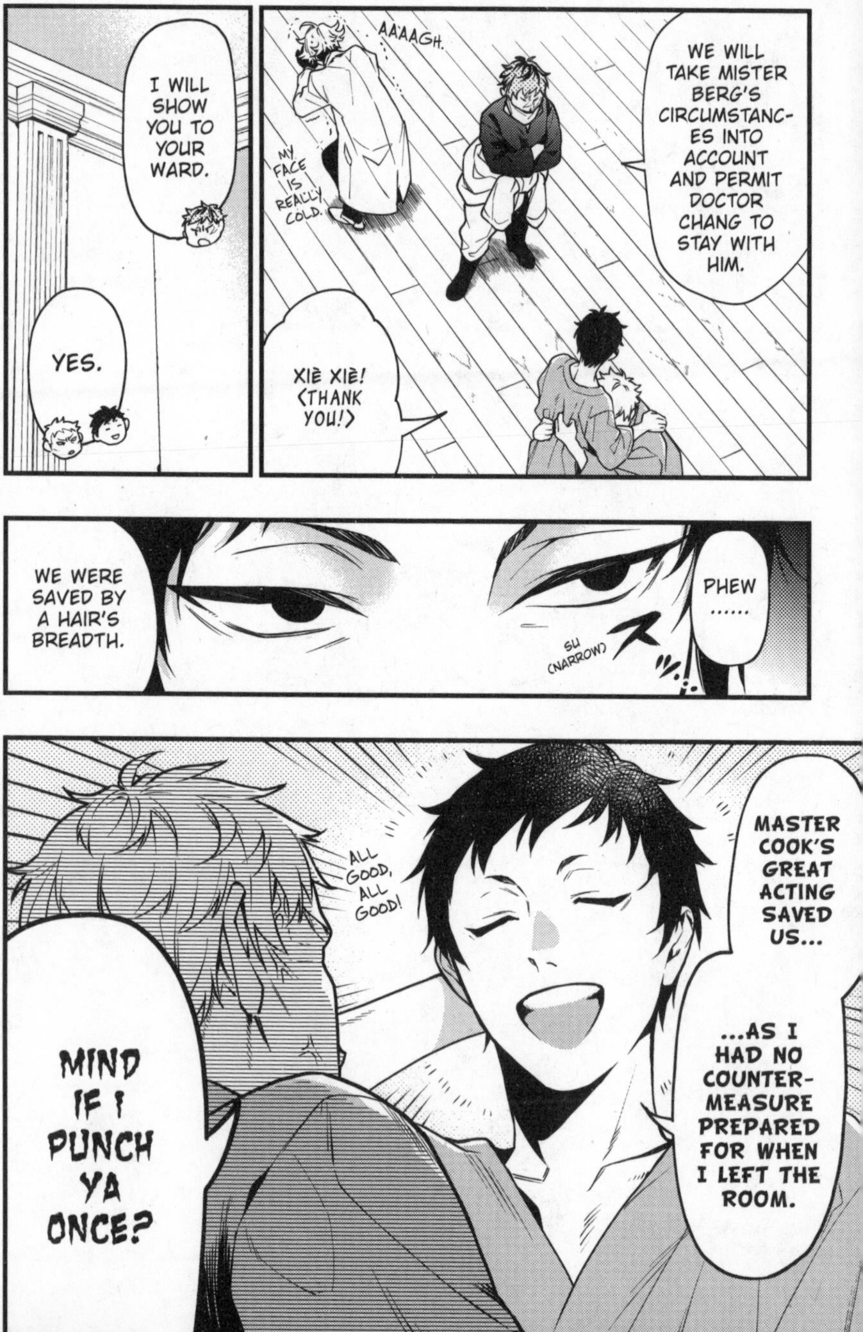
WE WILL TAKE MISTER BERG'S CIRCUMSTANCES INTO ACCOUNT AND PERMIT DOCTOR CHANG TO STAY WITH HIM.
AAAAGH.
MY FACE IS REALLY COLD.
XIÈ XIÈ! 〈THANK YOU!〉
I WILL SHOW YOU TO YOUR WARD.
YES.
PHEW ......
SU (NARROW)
WE WERE SAVED BY A HAIR'S BREADTH.
MASTER COOK'S GREAT ACTING SAVED US...
ALL GOOD, ALL GOOD!
...AS I HAD NO COUNTER-MEASURE PREPARED FOR WHEN I LEFT THE ROOM.
MIND IF I PUNCH YA ONCE?

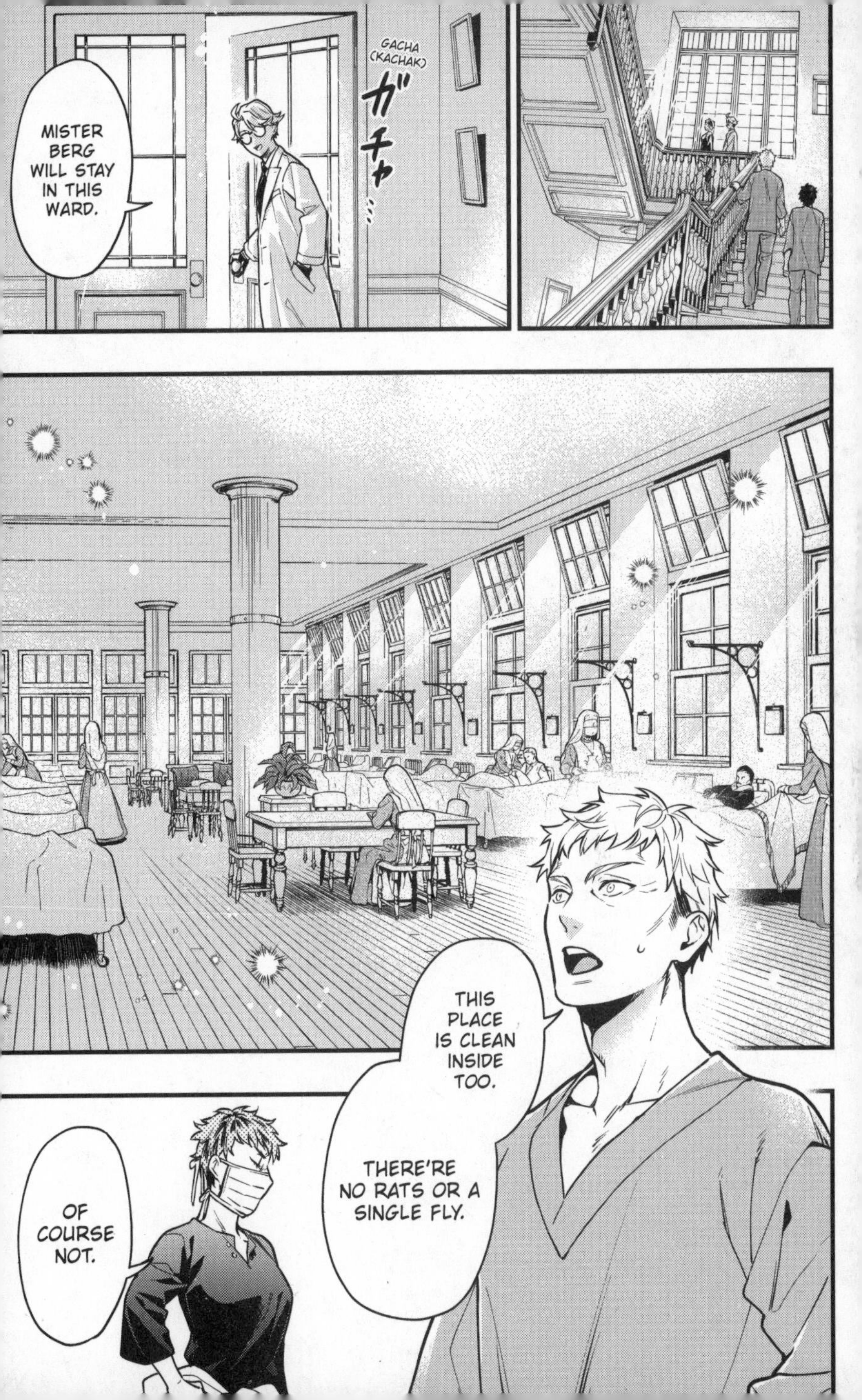
GACHA (KACHAK)
ガチャ…
MISTER BERG WILL STAY IN THIS WARD.
THIS PLACE IS CLEAN INSIDE TOO.
THERE'RE NO RATS OR A SINGLE FLY.
OF COURSE NOT.

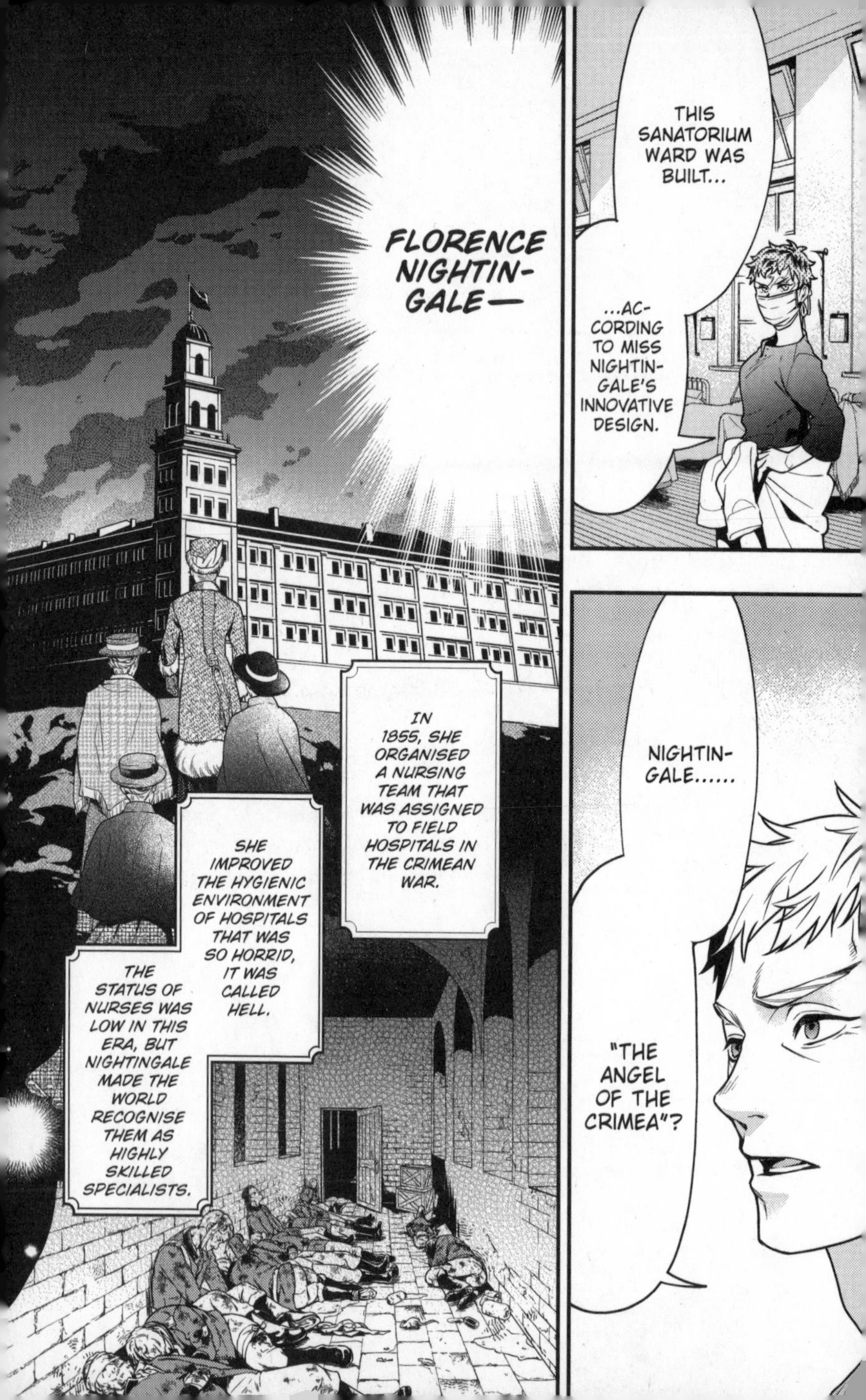
THIS SANATORIUM WARD WAS BUILT...
...ACCORDING TO MISS NIGHTIN-GALE'S INNOVATIVE DESIGN.
NIGHTIN-GALE......
"THE ANGEL OF THE CRIMEA"?
FLORENCE NIGHTIN-GALE—
IN 1855, SHE ORGANISED A NURSING TEAM THAT WAS ASSIGNED TO FIELD HOSPITALS IN THE CRIMEAN WAR.
SHE IMPROVED THE HYGIENIC ENVIRONMENT OF HOSPITALS THAT WAS SO HORRID, IT WAS CALLED HELL.
THE STATUS OF NURSES WAS LOW IN THIS ERA, BUT NIGHTINGALE MADE THE WORLD RECOGNISE THEM AS HIGHLY SKILLED SPECIALISTS.

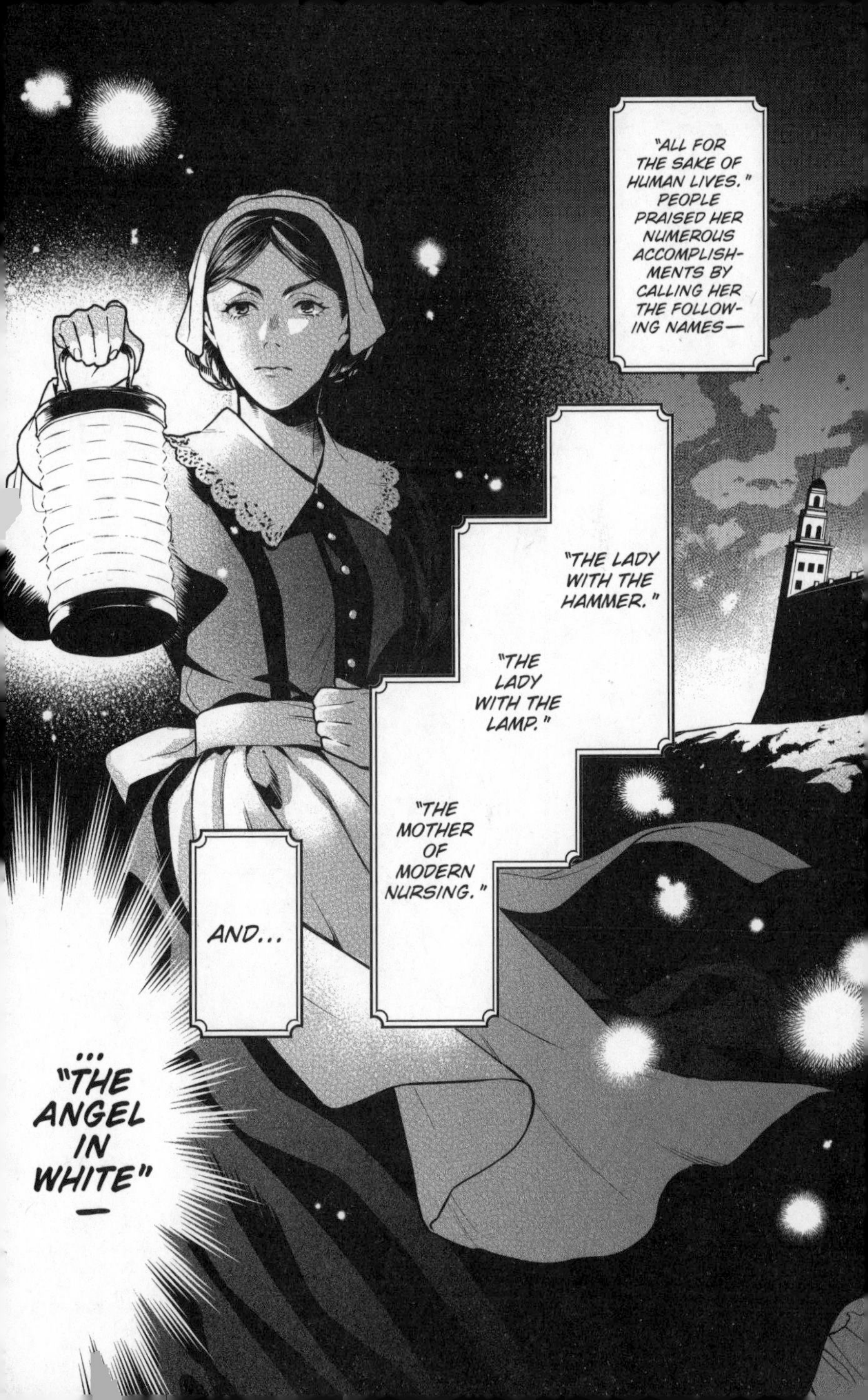
"ALL FOR THE SAKE OF HUMAN LIVES." PEOPLE PRAISED HER NUMEROUS ACCOMPLISHMENTS BY CALLING HER THE FOLLOWING NAMES—
"THE LADY WITH THE HAMMER."
"THE LADY WITH THE LAMP."
"THE MOTHER OF MODERN NURSING."
AND...
... "THE ANGEL IN WHITE" —

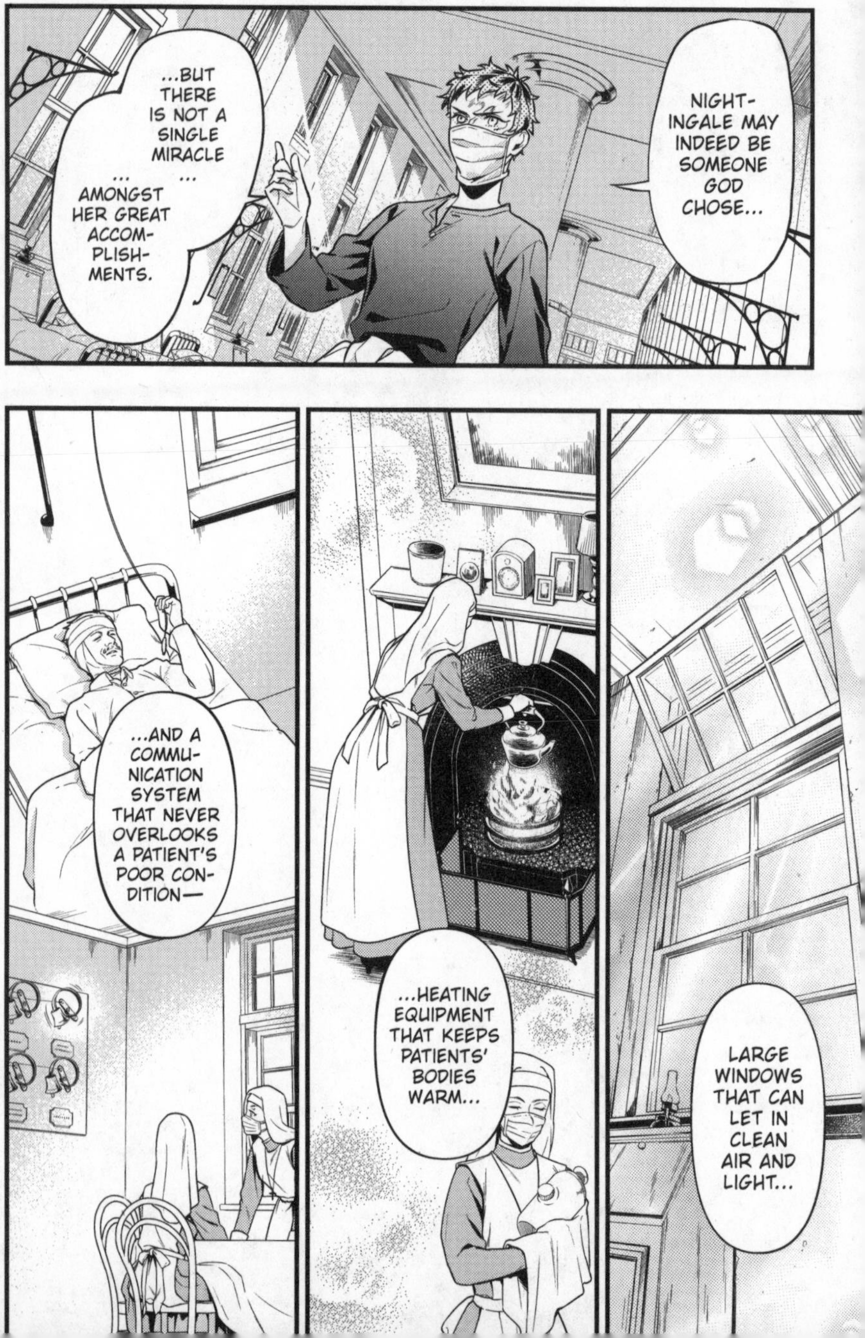
NIGHT-INGALE MAY INDEED BE SOMEONE GOD CHOSE...
...BUT THERE IS NOT A SINGLE MIRACLE... ...AMONGST HER GREAT ACCOM-PLISH-MENTS.
LARGE WINDOWS THAT CAN LET IN CLEAN AIR AND LIGHT...
...HEATING EQUIPMENT THAT KEEPS PATIENTS' BODIES WARM...
...AND A COMMU-NICATION SYSTEM THAT NEVER OVERLOOKS A PATIENT'S POOR CON-DITION—

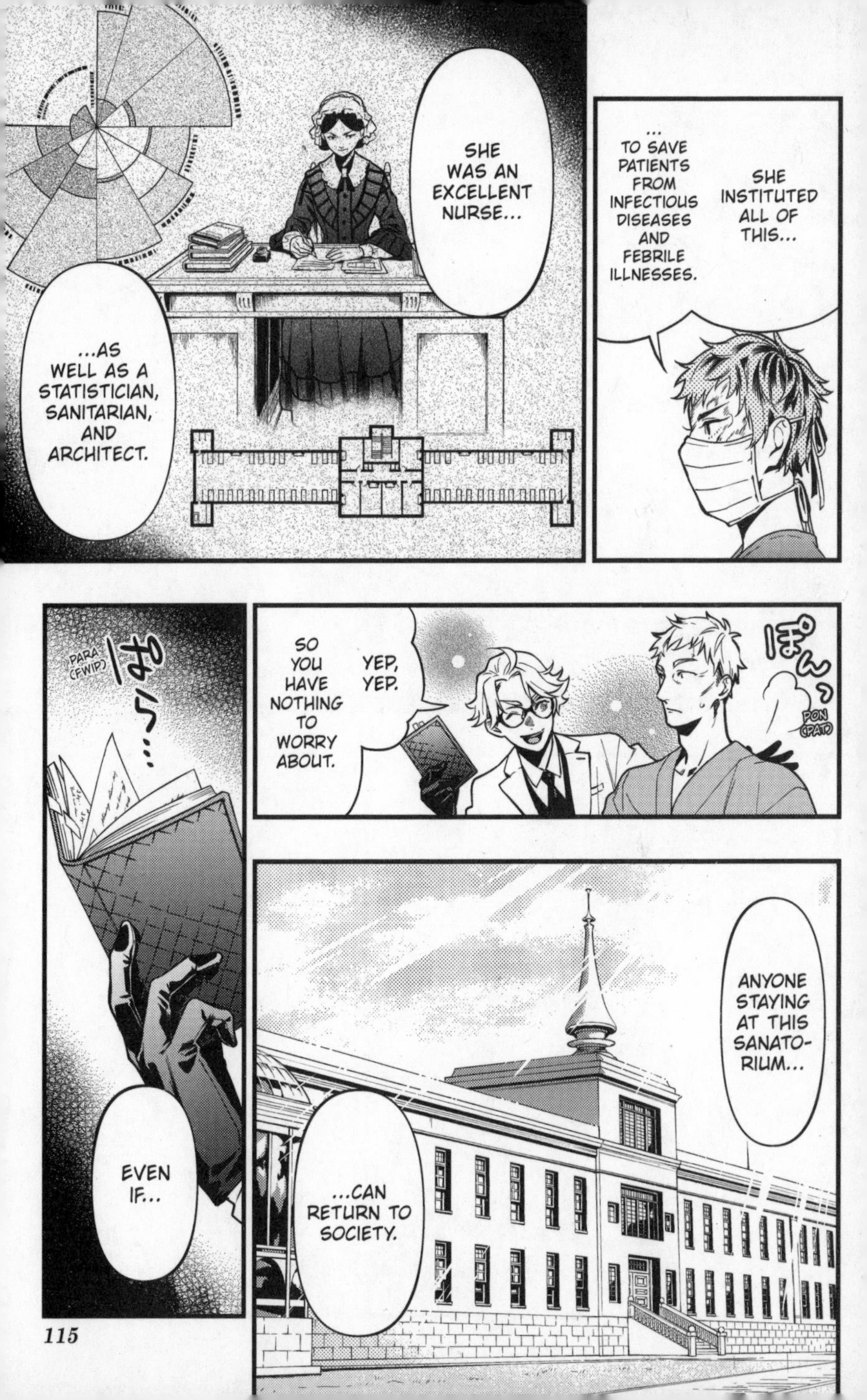
SHE INSTITUTED ALL OF THIS...
... TO SAVE PATIENTS FROM INFECTIOUS DISEASES AND FEBRILE ILLNESSES.
SHE WAS AN EXCELLENT NURSE...
...AS WELL AS A STATISTICIAN, SANITARIAN, AND ARCHITECT.
ぽんっ
PON (PAT)
YEP, YEP.
SO YOU HAVE NOTHING TO WORRY ABOUT.
ANYONE STAYING AT THIS SANATO-RIUM...
...CAN RETURN TO SOCIETY.
ぱら…
PARA (FWIP)
EVEN IF...

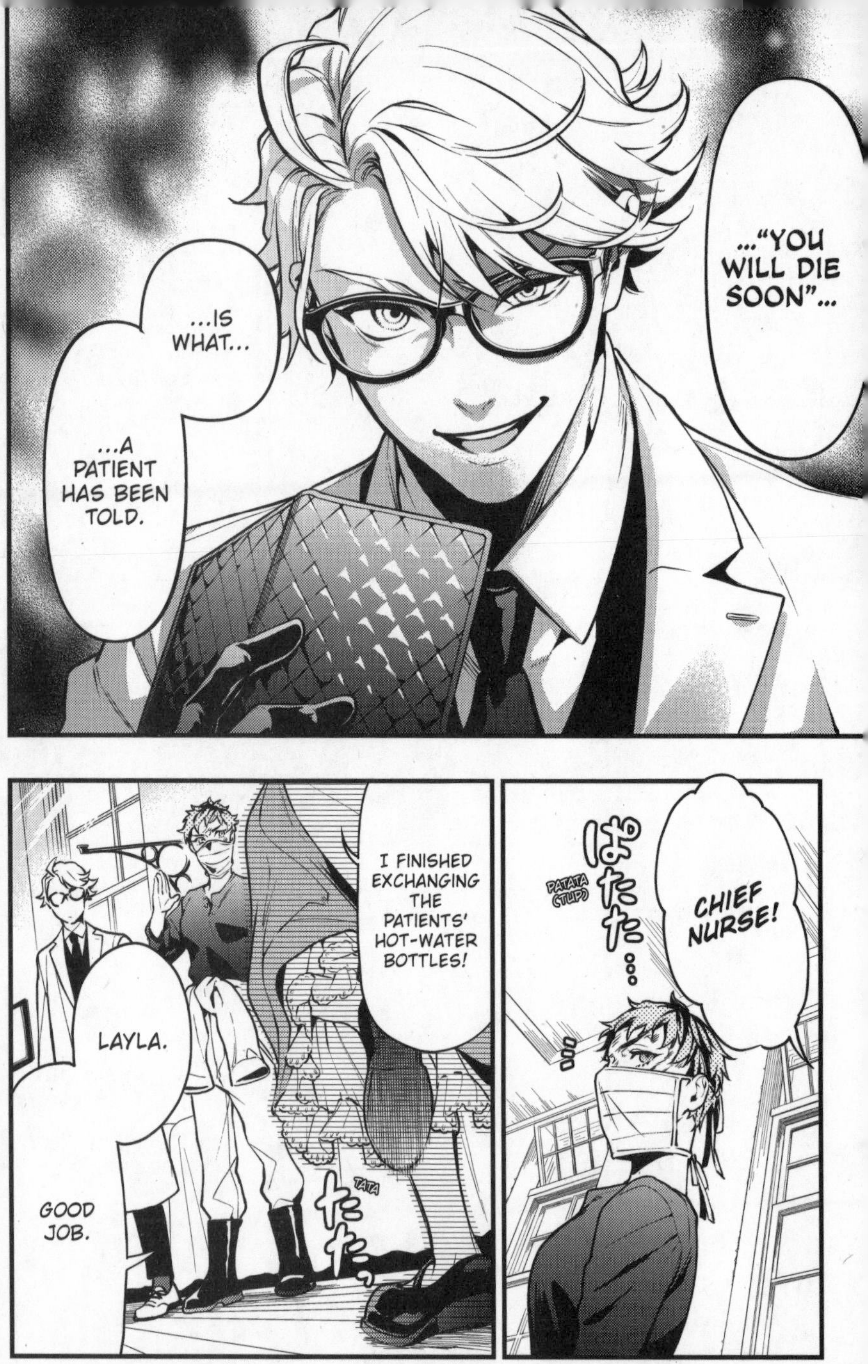
..."YOU WILL DIE SOON"...
...IS WHAT...
...A PATIENT HAS BEEN TOLD.
CHIEF NURSE!
ぱたた…
PATATA (TUP)
...
I FINISHED EXCHANGING THE PATIENTS' HOT-WATER BOTTLES!
TATA
たたっ
LAYLA.
GOOD JOB.

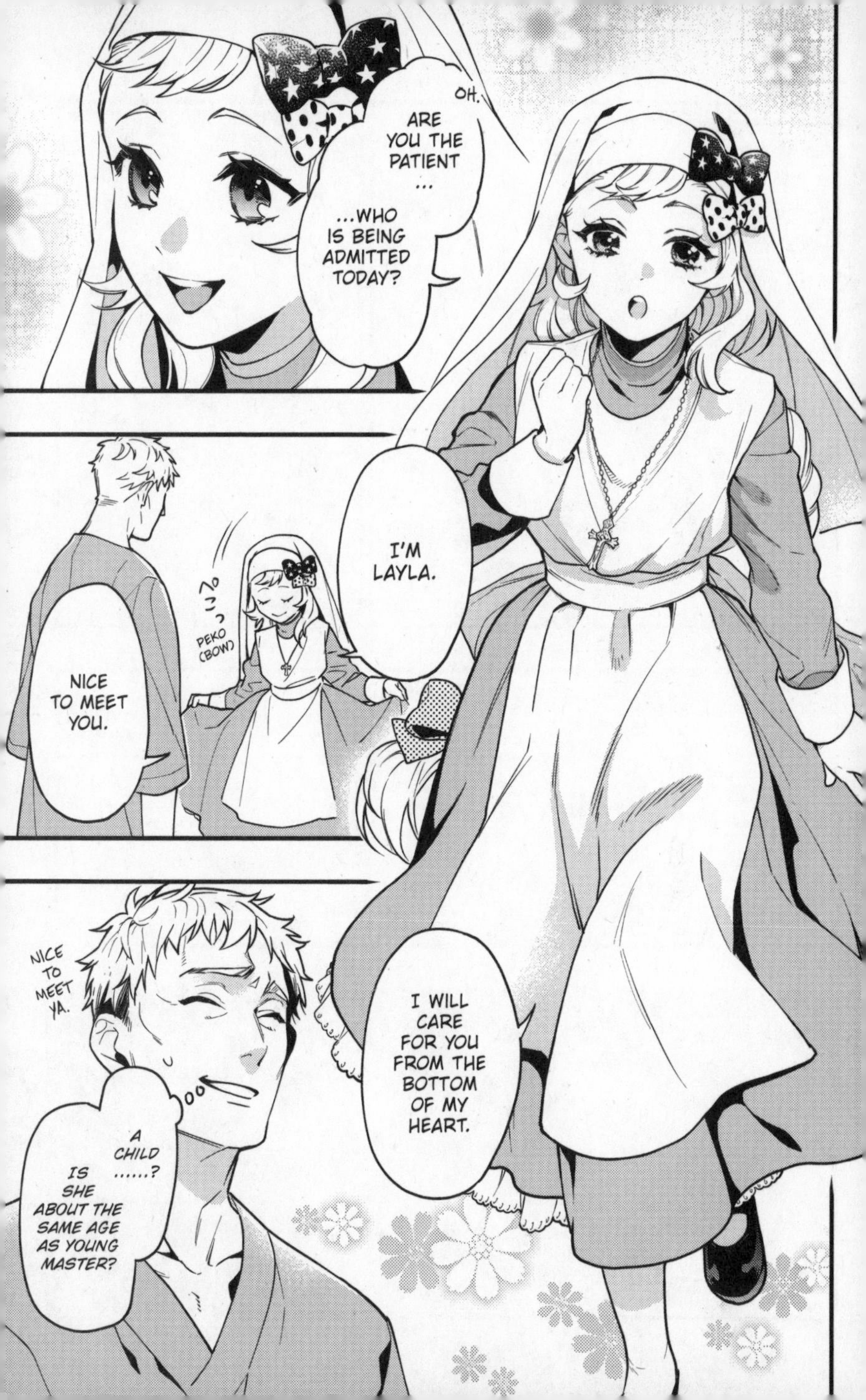
OH.
ARE YOU THE PATIENT ...
...WHO IS BEING ADMITTED TODAY?
I'M LAYLA.
NICE TO MEET YOU.
PEKO (BOW)
I WILL CARE FOR YOU FROM THE BOTTOM OF MY HEART.
NICE TO MEET YA.
A CHILD ......?
IS SHE ABOUT THE SAME AGE AS YOUNG MASTER?

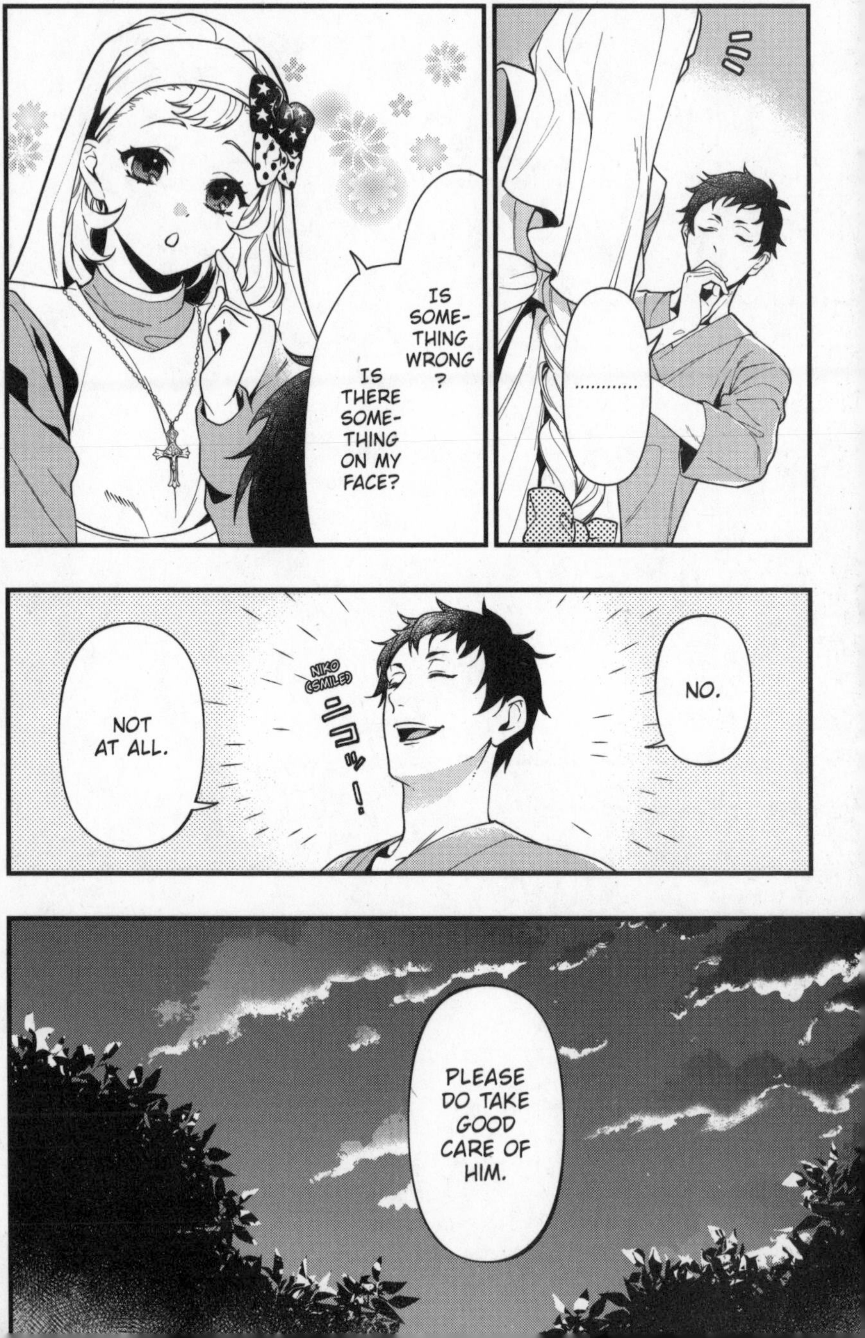
....
IS SOMETHING WRONG?
IS THERE SOMETHING ON MY FACE?
NO.
NIKO (SMILED)
ニコッ!
NOT AT ALL.
PLEASE DO TAKE GOOD CARE OF HIM.

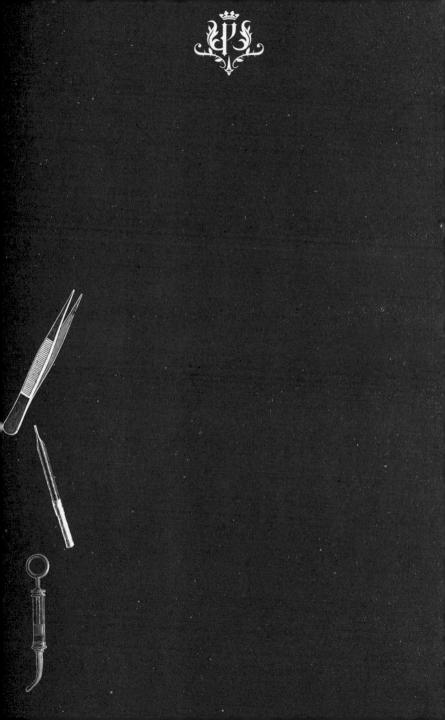

Black Butler

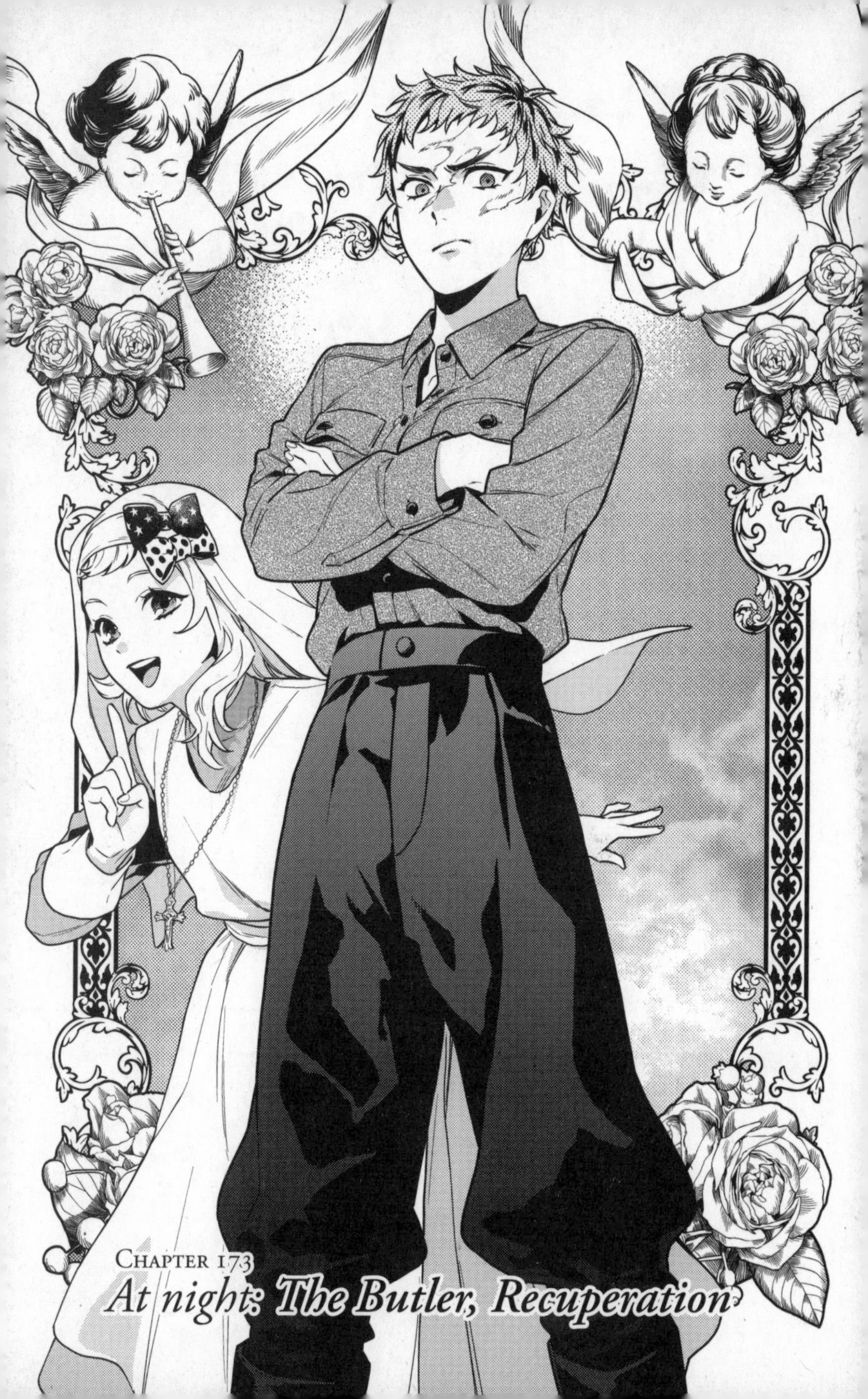
CHAPTER 173
At night: The Butler, Recuperation

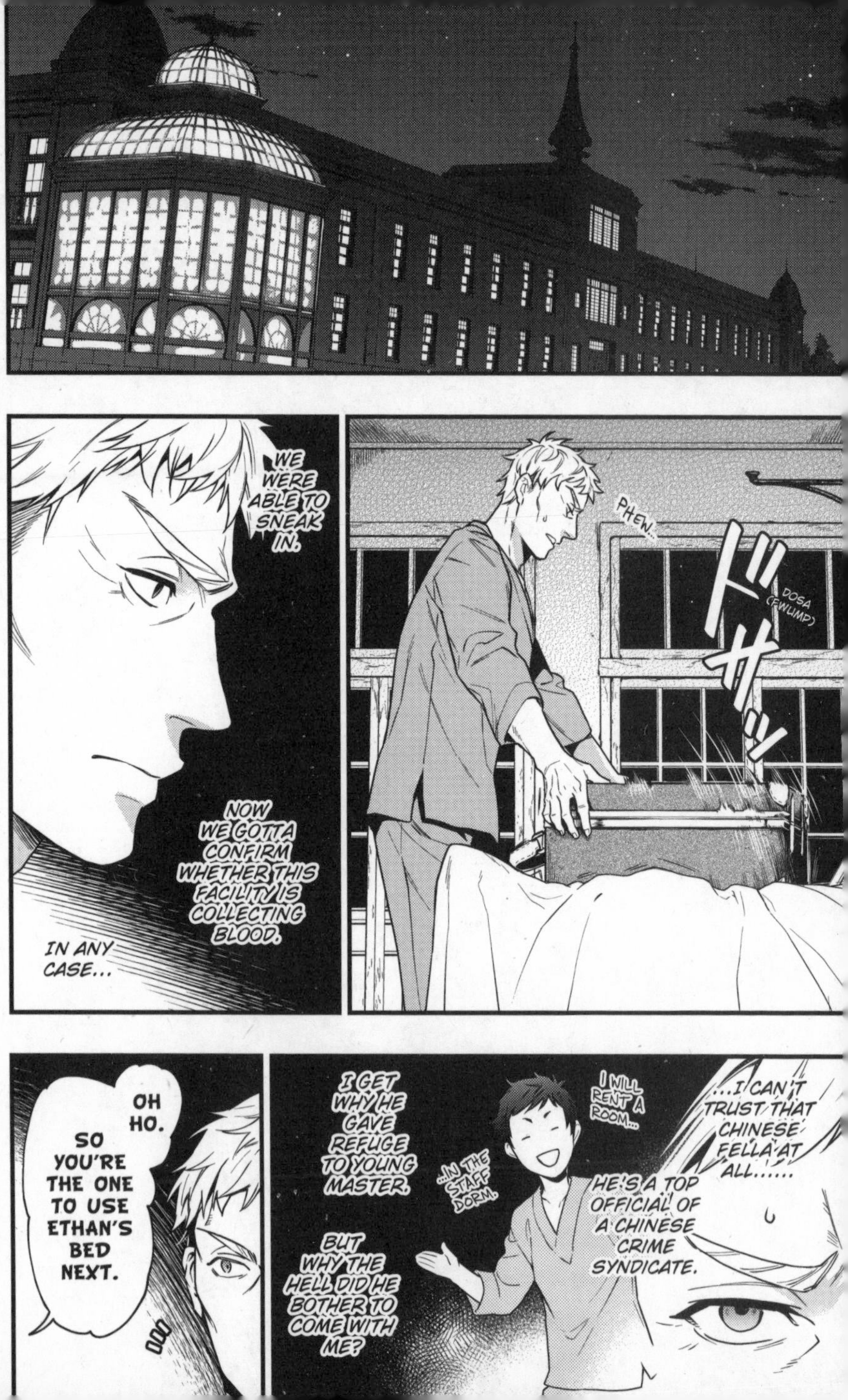
PHEW...
ドサッ
DOSA (FWUMP)
WE WERE ABLE TO SNEAK IN.
NOW WE GOTTA CONFIRM WHETHER THIS FACILITY IS COLLECTING BLOOD.
IN ANY CASE...
...I CAN'T TRUST THAT CHINESE FELLA AT ALL......
HE'S A TOP OFFICIAL OF A CHINESE CRIME SYNDICATE.
I WILL RENT A ROOM...
...IN THE STAFF DORM.
I GET WHY HE GAVE REFUGE TO YOUNG MASTER.
BUT WHY THE HELL DID HE BOTHER TO COME WITH ME?
OH HO.
SO YOU'RE THE ONE TO USE ETHAN'S BED NEXT.

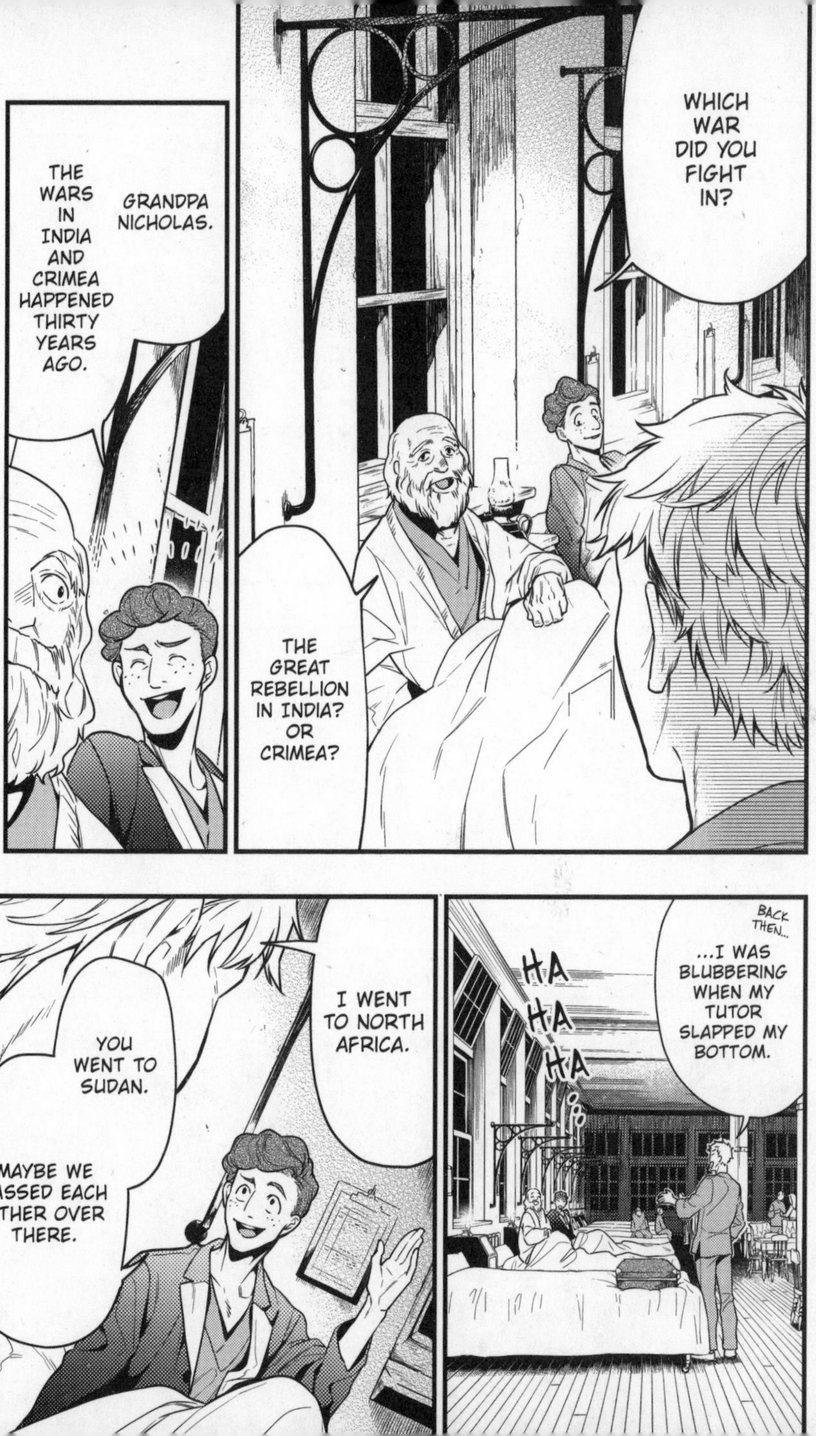
WHICH WAR DID YOU FIGHT IN?
THE GREAT REBELLION IN INDIA? OR CRIMEA?
GRANDPA NICHOLAS.
THE WARS IN INDIA AND CRIMEA HAPPENED THIRTY YEARS AGO.
BACK THEN...
...I WAS BLUBBERING WHEN MY TUTOR SLAPPED MY BOTTOM.
HA HA HA
I WENT TO NORTH AFRICA.
YOU WENT TO SUDAN.
MAYBE WE PASSED EACH OTHER OVER THERE.

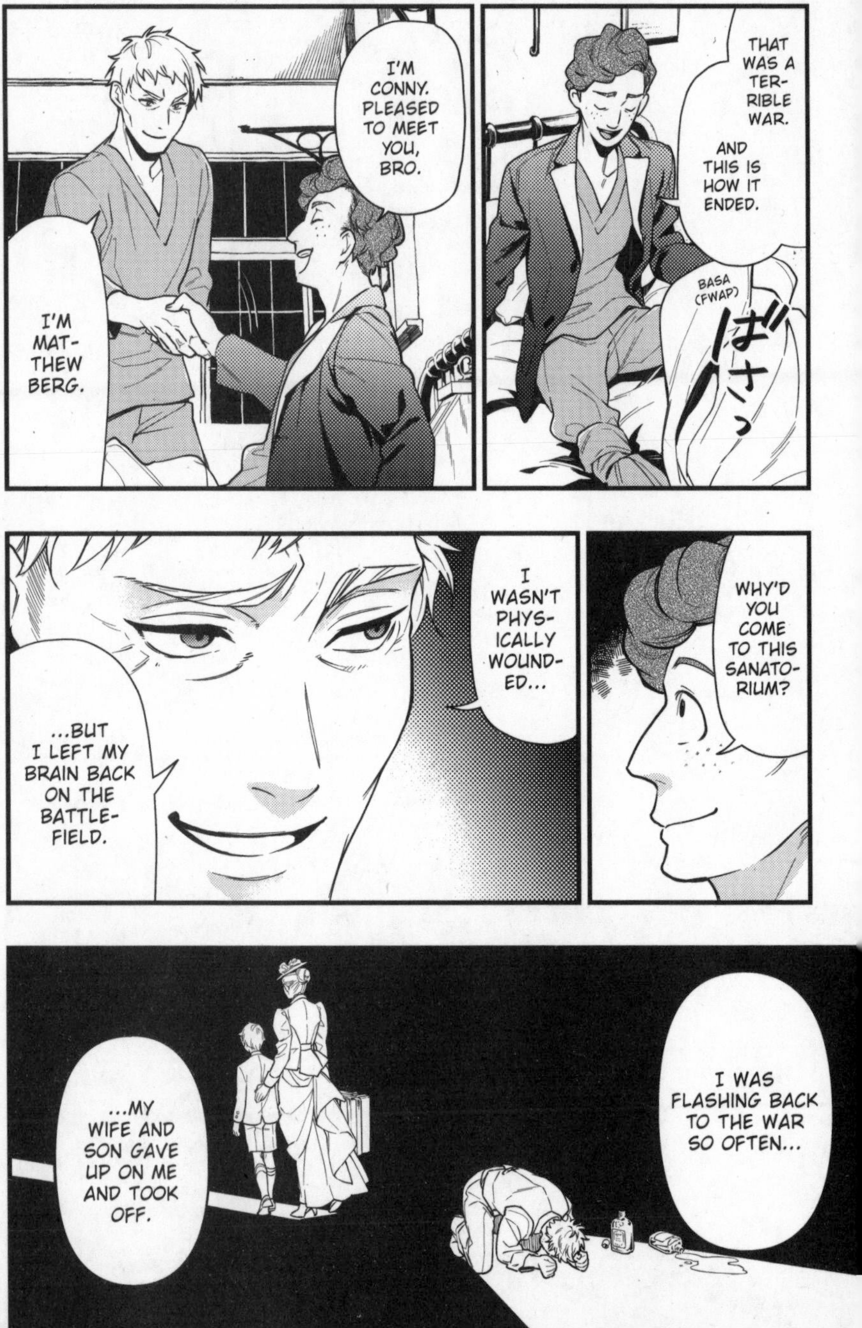

THAT WAS A TERRIBLE WAR.
AND THIS IS HOW IT ENDED.
BASA (FWAP)
ばさっ
I'M CONNY. PLEASED TO MEET YOU, BRO.
I'M MATTHEW BERG.
WHY'D YOU COME TO THIS SANATORIUM?
I WASN'T PHYSICALLY WOUNDED...
...BUT I LEFT MY BRAIN BACK ON THE BATTLEFIELD.
I WAS FLASHING BACK TO THE WAR SO OFTEN...
...MY WIFE AND SON GAVE UP ON ME AND TOOK OFF.

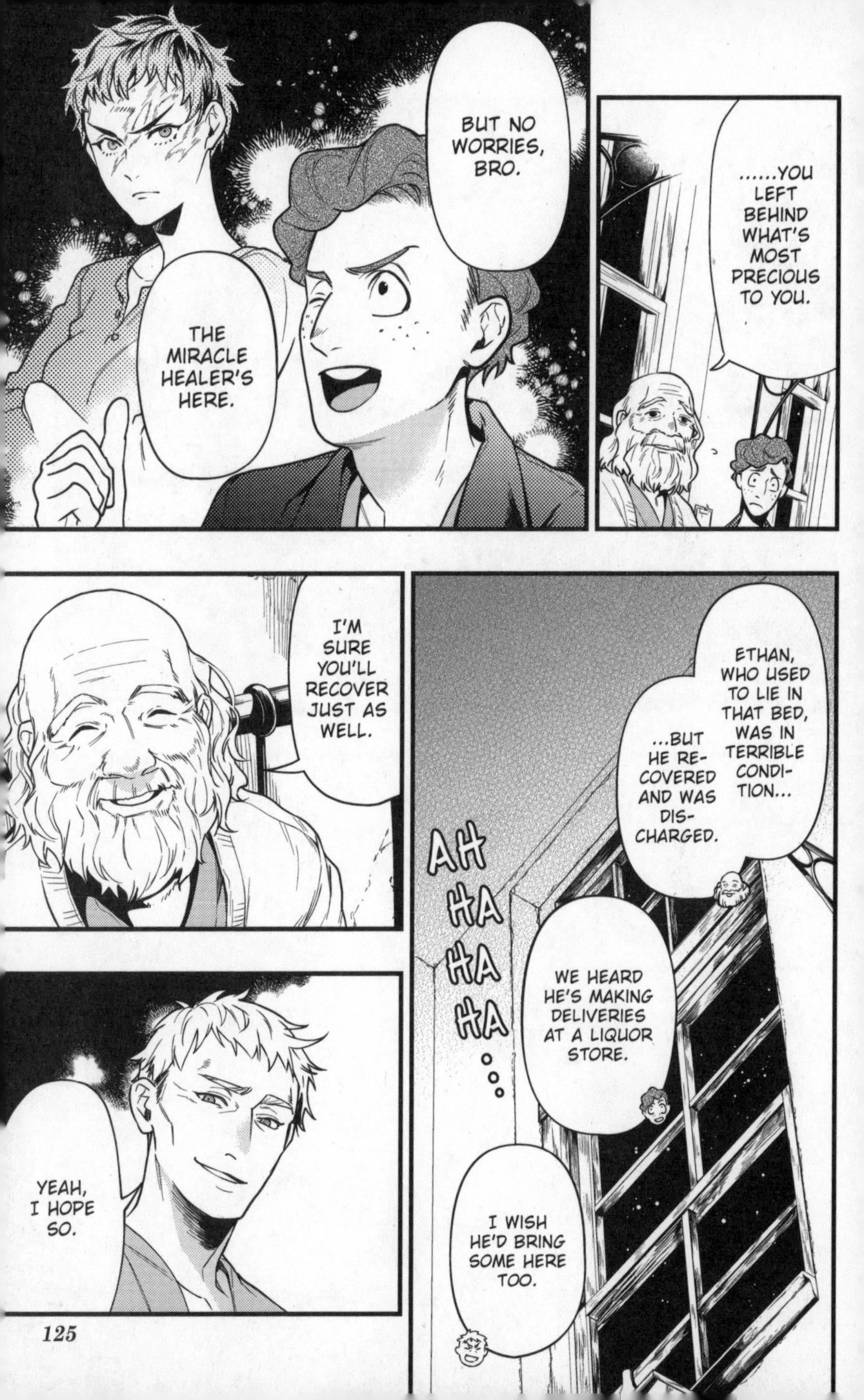
......YOU LEFT BEHIND WHAT'S MOST PRECIOUS TO YOU.
BUT NO WORRIES, BRO.
THE MIRACLE HEALER'S HERE.
ETHAN, WHO USED TO LIE IN THAT BED, WAS IN TERRIBLE CONDITION...
...BUT HE RECOVERED AND WAS DISCHARGED.
WE HEARD HE'S MAKING DELIVERIES AT A LIQUOR STORE.
AH HA HA HA...
I WISH HE'D BRING SOME HERE TOO.
I'M SURE YOU'LL RECOVER JUST AS WELL.
YEAH, I HOPE SO.

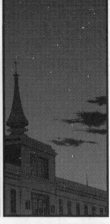

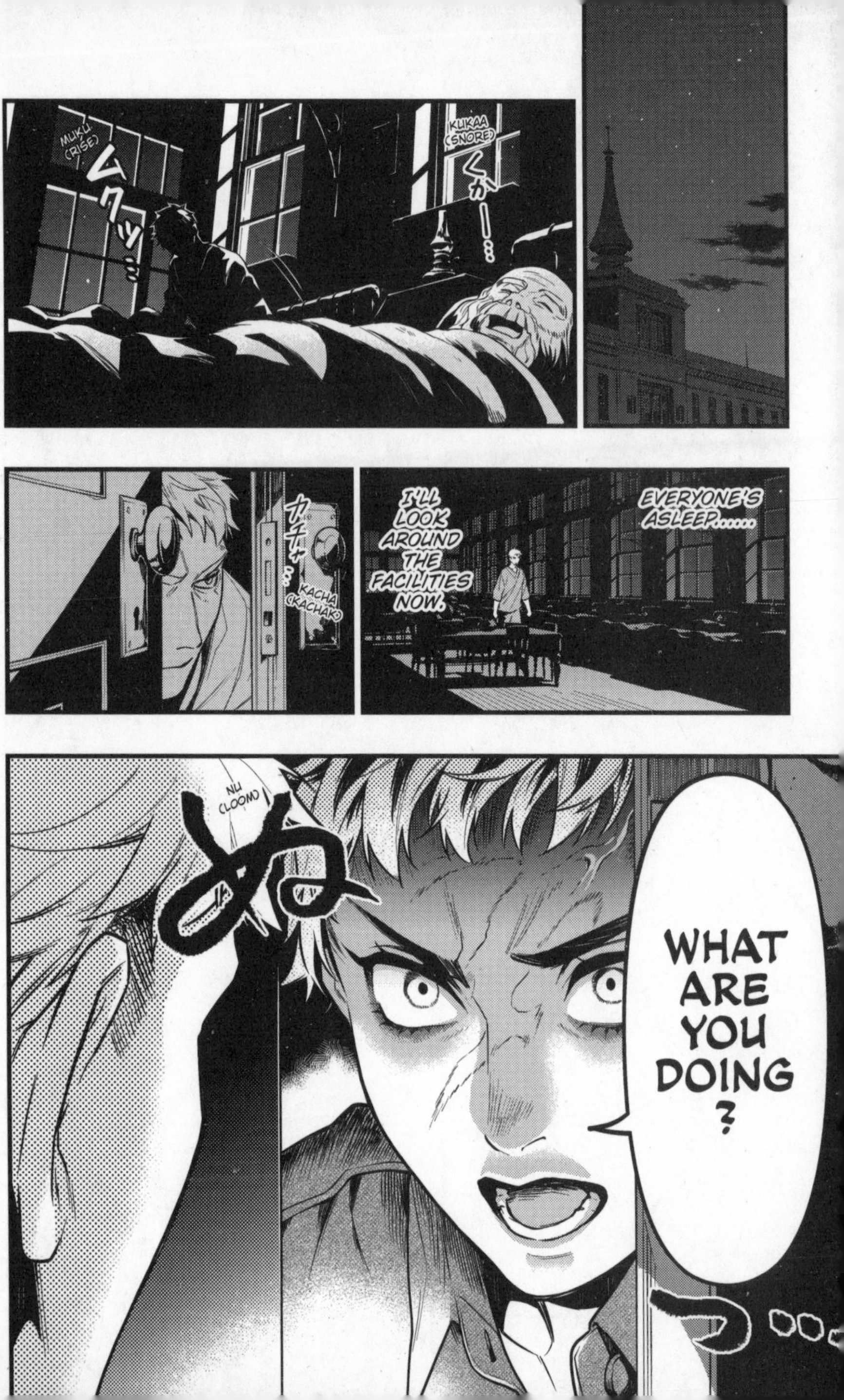
KUKAA (SNORE)
くかー…
MUKU (RISE)
ムクッ…
EVERYONE'S ASLEEP......
I'LL LOOK AROUND THE FACILITIES NOW.
カチャ…
KACHA (KACHAK)
WHAT ARE YOU DOING?
NU (LOOM)
ぬっ

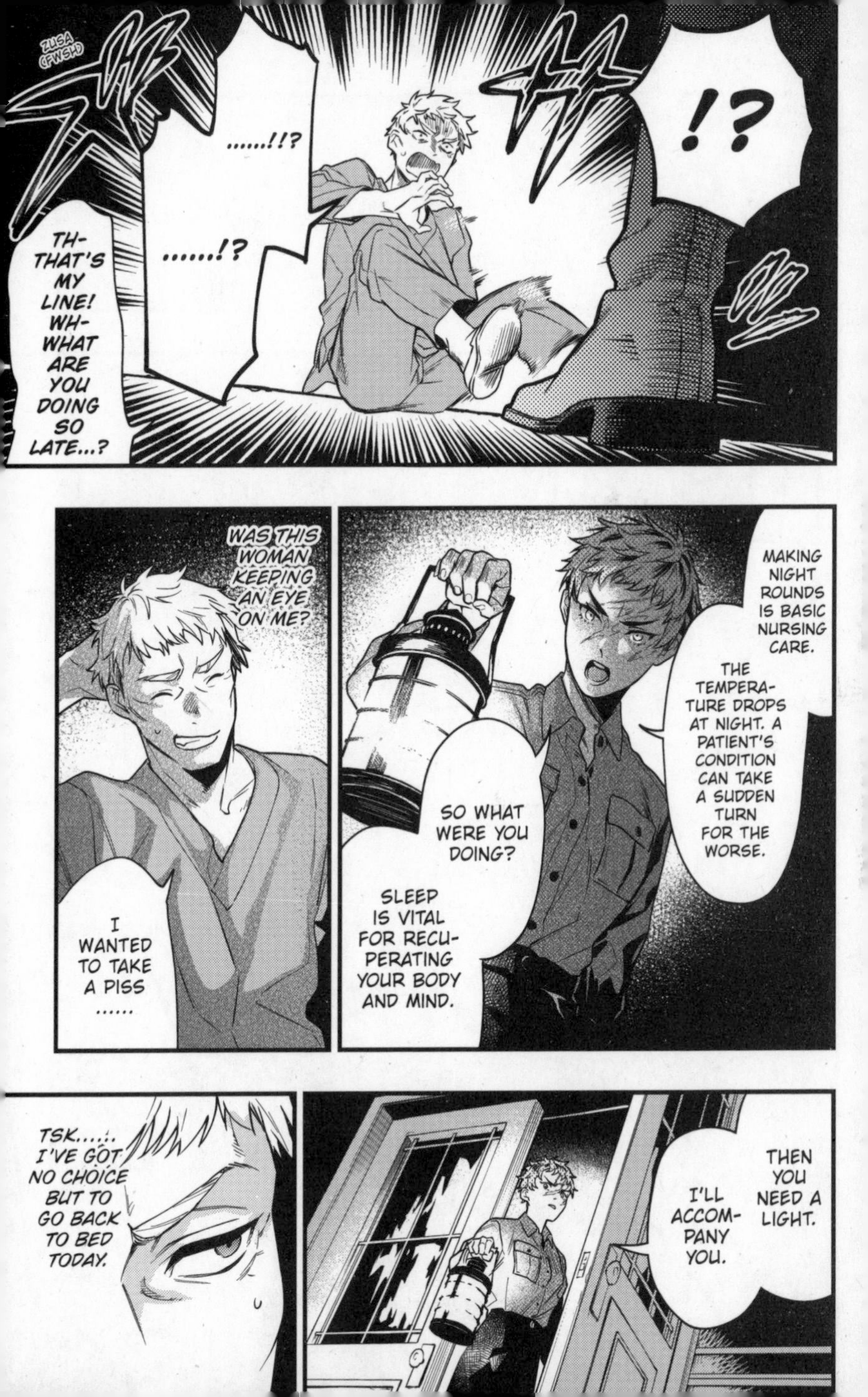
!?
......!!?
ZUSA (FWSH)
......!?
TH-THAT'S MY LINE! WH-WHAT ARE YOU DOING SO LATE...?
MAKING NIGHT ROUNDS IS BASIC NURSING CARE.
THE TEMPERATURE DROPS AT NIGHT. A PATIENT'S CONDITION CAN TAKE A SUDDEN TURN FOR THE WORSE.
SO WHAT WERE YOU DOING?
SLEEP IS VITAL FOR RECUPERATING YOUR BODY AND MIND.
WAS THIS WOMAN KEEPING AN EYE ON ME?
I WANTED TO TAKE A PISS ......
THEN YOU NEED A LIGHT.
I'LL ACCOMPANY YOU.
TSK...... I'VE GOT NO CHOICE BUT TO GO BACK TO BED TODAY.

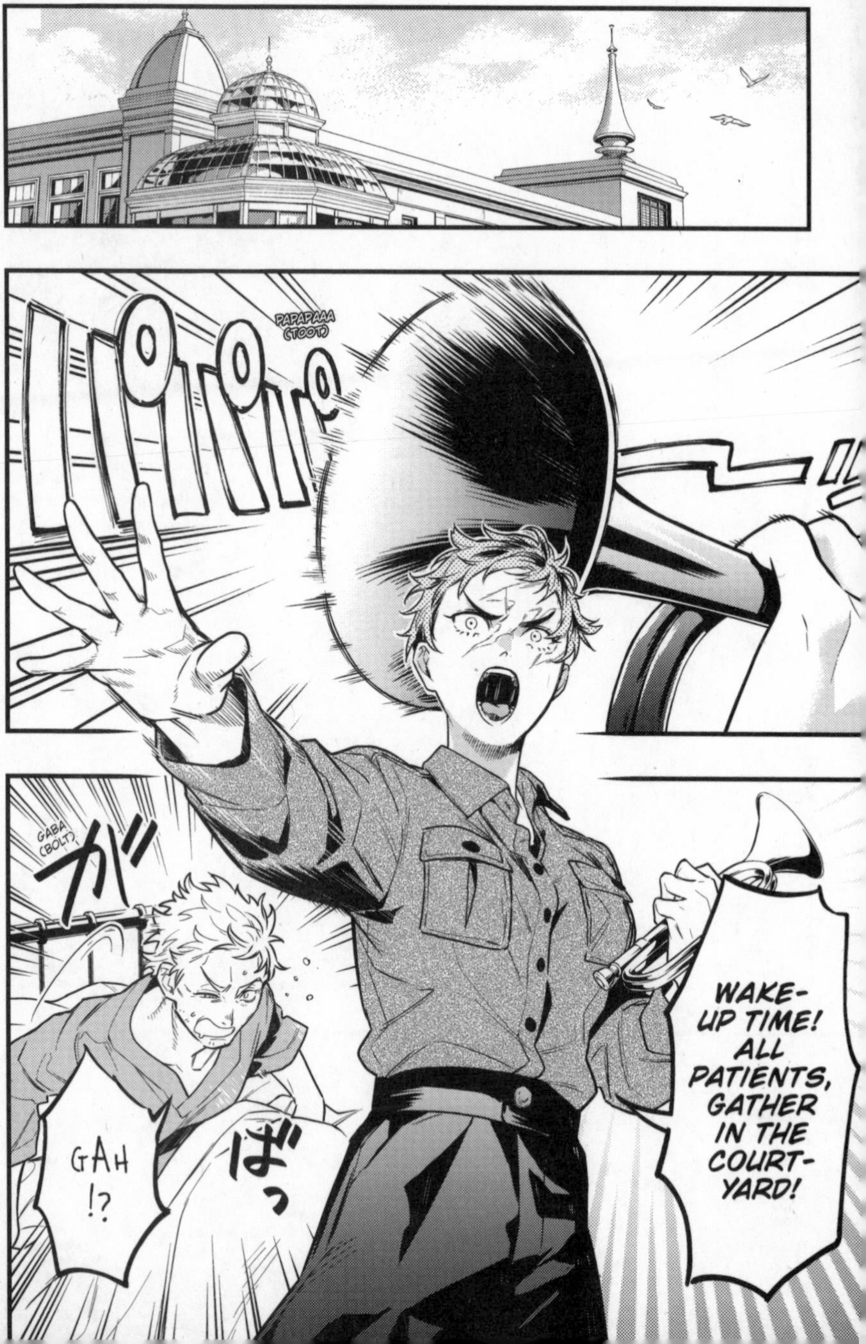
PAPAPAAA (TOOT)
WAKE-UP TIME! ALL PATIENTS, GATHER IN THE COURTYARD!
GABA (BOLT)
GAH!?

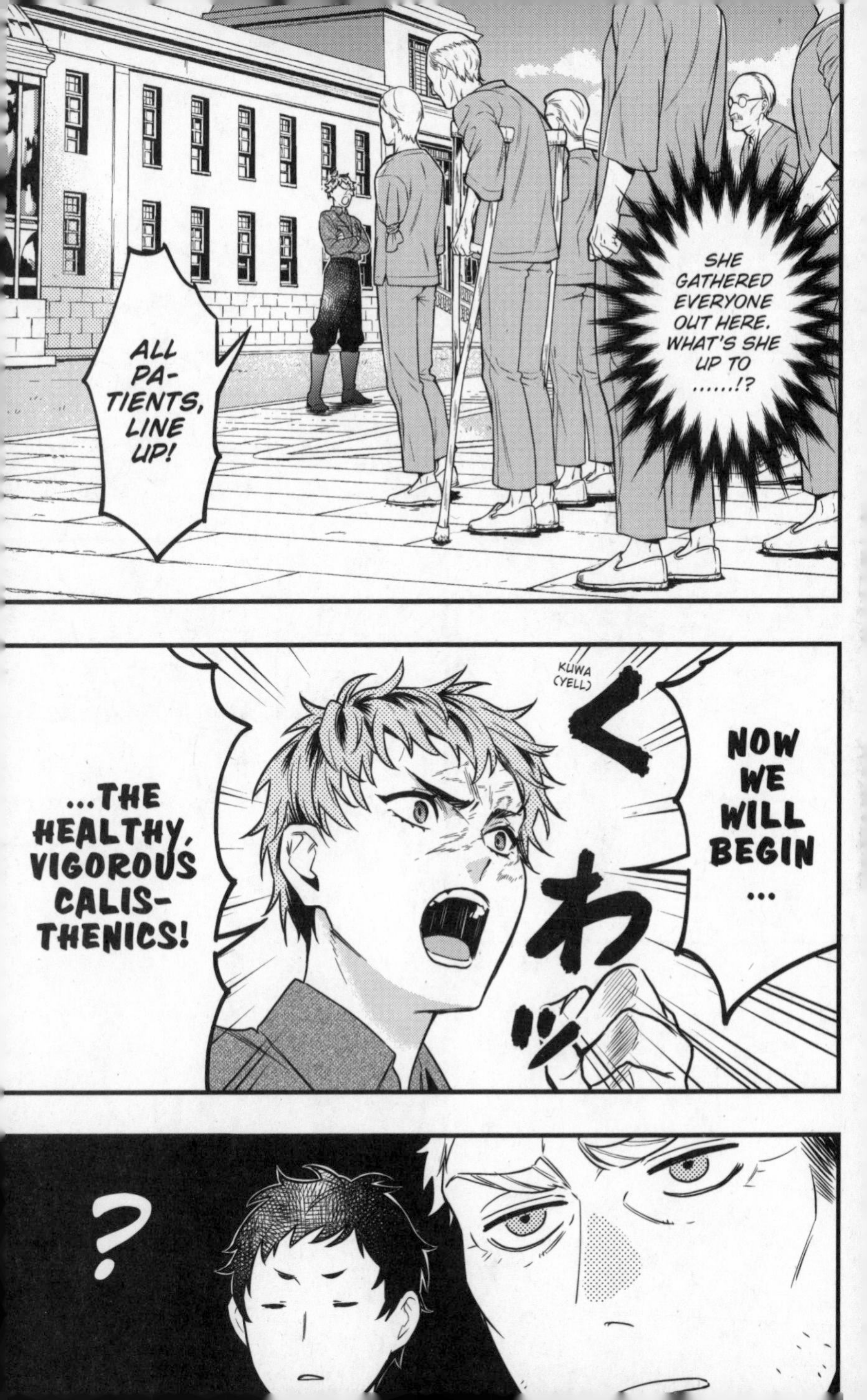
SHE GATHERED EVERYONE OUT HERE. WHAT'S SHE UP TO ......!?
ALL PATIENTS, LINE UP!
KUWA (YELL)
くわッ
NOW WE WILL BEGIN ...
...THE HEALTHY, VIGOROUS CALISTHENICS!
?

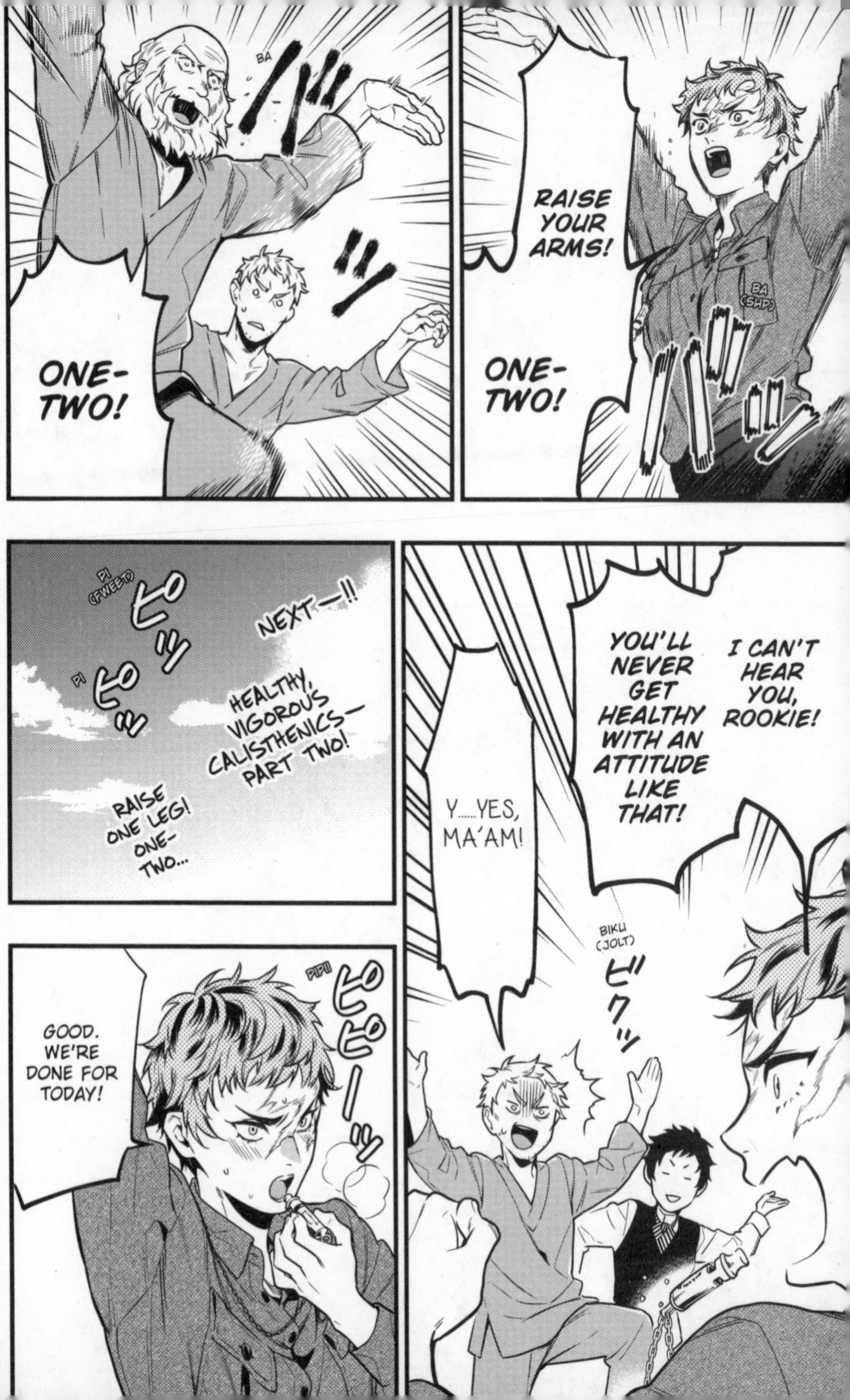
RAISE YOUR ARMS!
ONE-TWO!
BA (SHP)
BA
ONE-TWO!
I CAN'T HEAR YOU, ROOKIE!
YOU'LL NEVER GET HEALTHY WITH AN ATTITUDE LIKE THAT!
Y......YES, MA'AM!
BIKU (JOLT)
ビクッ
PI (FWEET)
ピッ
PI
ピッ
NEXT—!!
HEALTHY, VIGOROUS CALISTHENICS—PART TWO!
RAISE ONE LEG! ONE-TWO...
GOOD. WE'RE DONE FOR TODAY!
PIPII
ピピーーッ

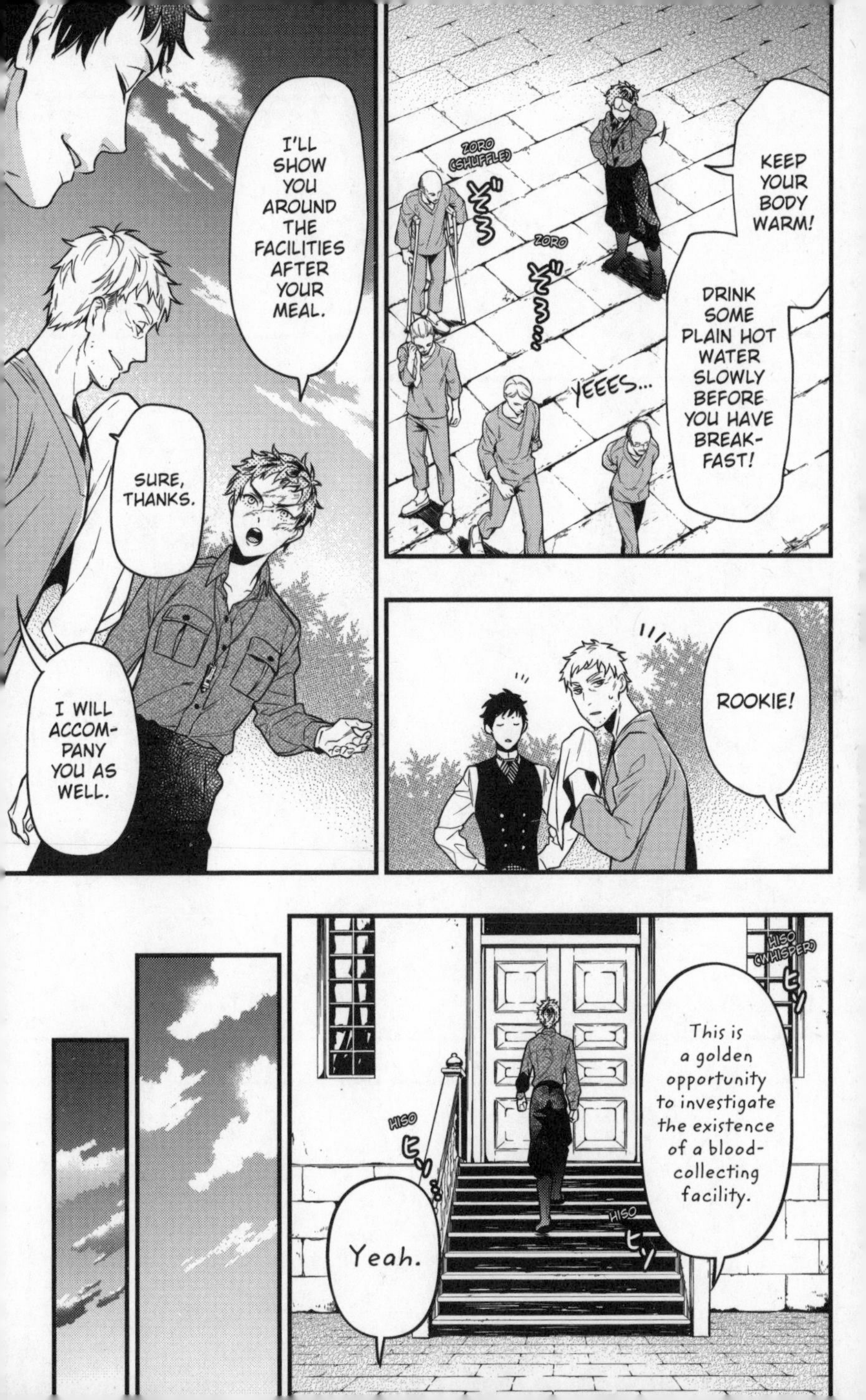
KEEP YOUR BODY WARM!
DRINK SOME PLAIN HOT WATER SLOWLY BEFORE YOU HAVE BREAKFAST!
ZORO
YEEES...
ZORO (SHUFFLE)
ROOKIE!
I'LL SHOW YOU AROUND THE FACILITIES AFTER YOUR MEAL.
SURE, THANKS.
I WILL ACCOMPANY YOU AS WELL.
HISO (WHISPER)
This is a golden opportunity to investigate the existence of a blood-collecting facility.
HISO
HISO
Yeah.

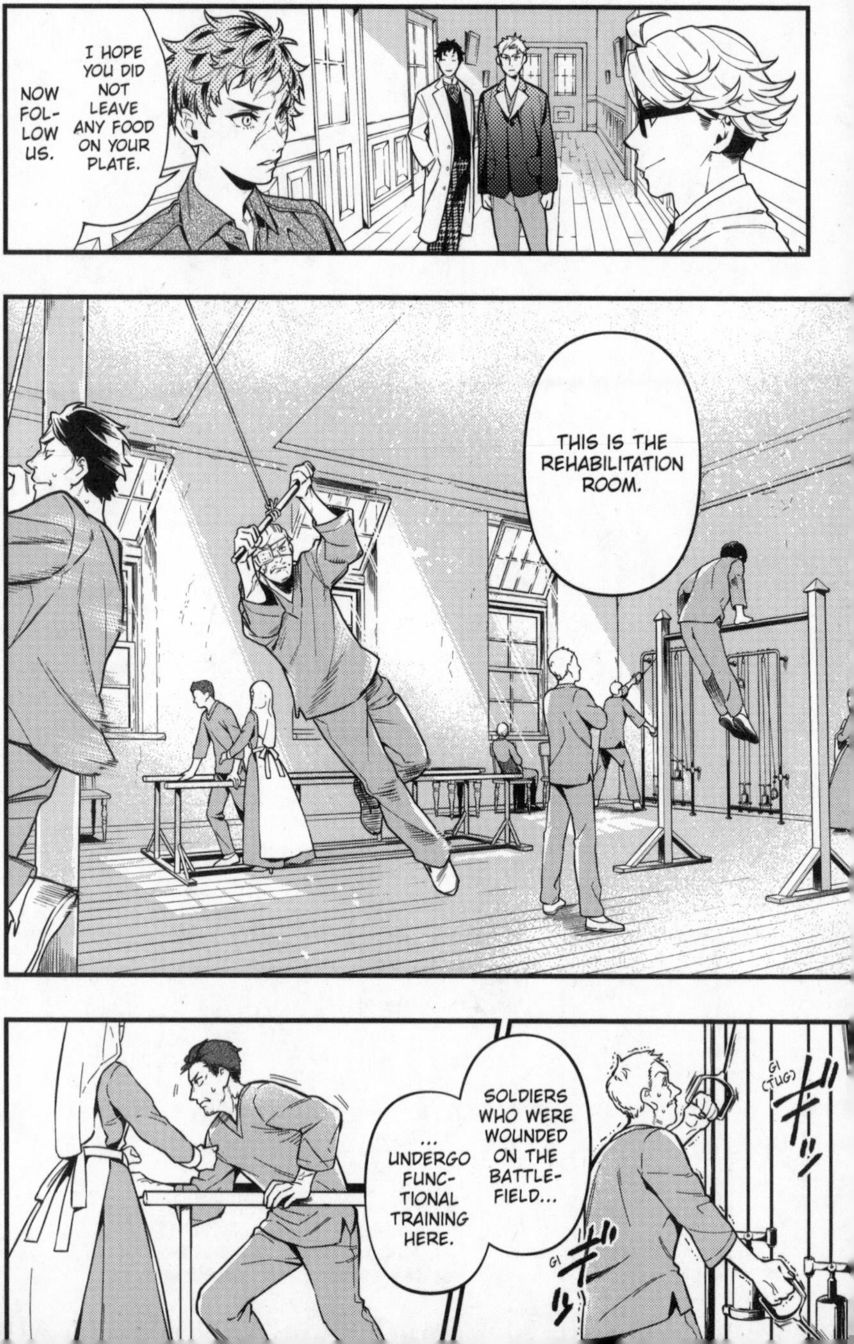
I HOPE YOU DID NOT LEAVE ANY FOOD ON YOUR PLATE.
NOW FOL-LOW US.
THIS IS THE REHABILITATION ROOM.
GI (TUG)
SOLDIERS WHO WERE WOUNDED ON THE BATTLE-FIELD...
...UNDERGO FUNC-TIONAL TRAINING HERE.
GI

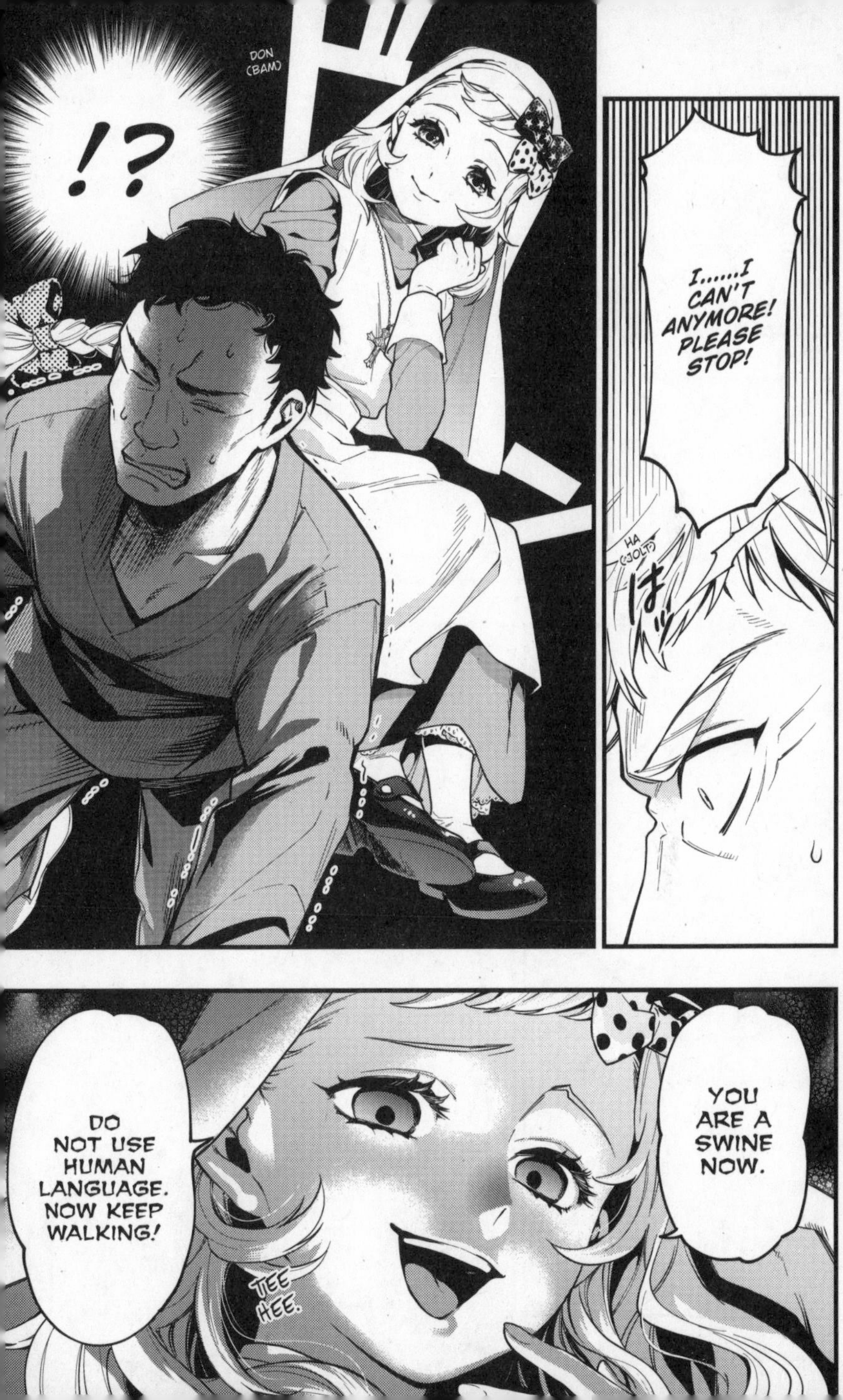
I......I CAN'T ANYMORE! PLEASE STOP!
HA (JOLT)
はッ
DON (BAM)
ド
!?
YOU ARE A SWINE NOW.
DO NOT USE HUMAN LANGUAGE. NOW KEEP WALKING!
TEE HEE.

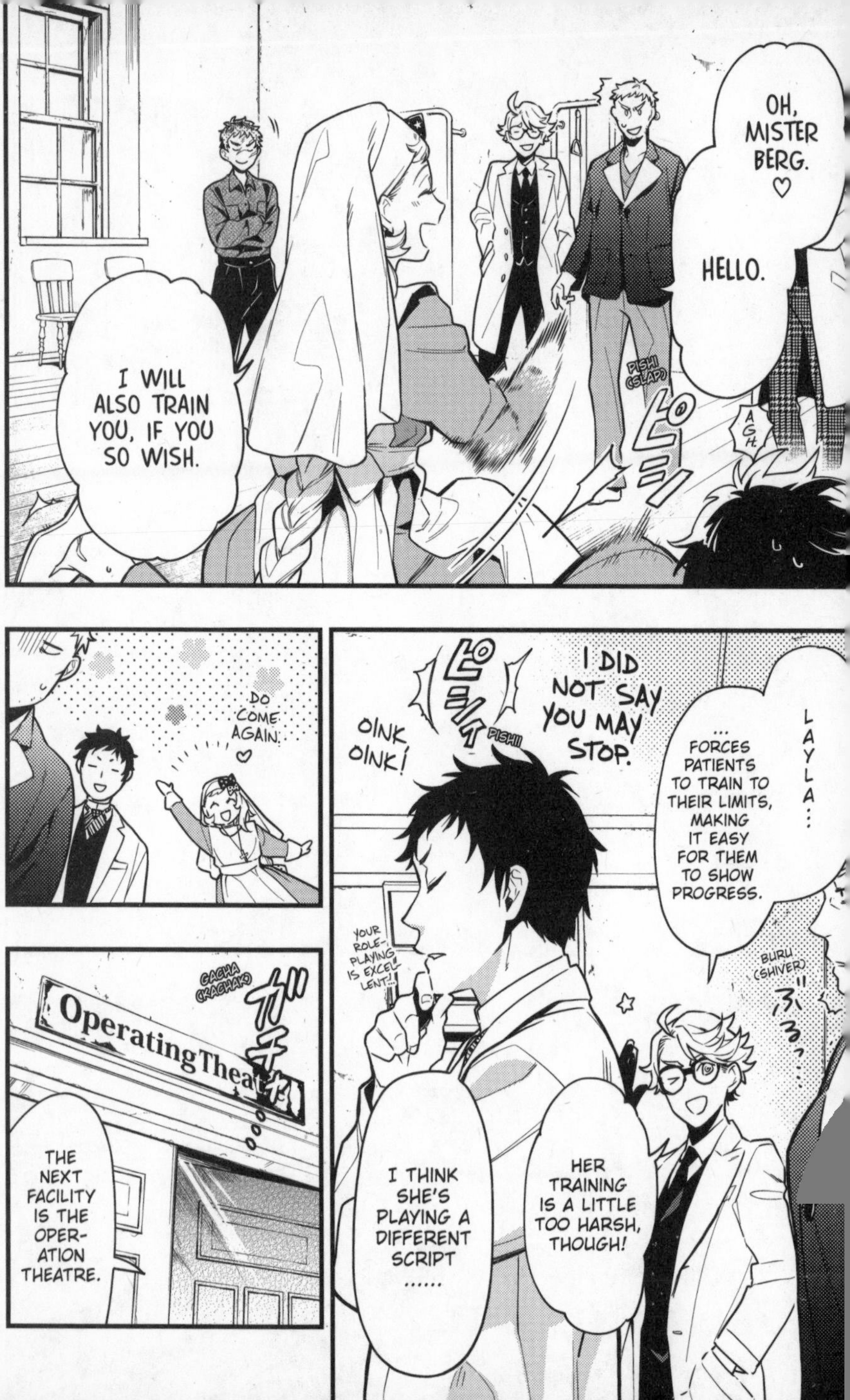
OH, MISTER BERG. ♡
HELLO.
PISHI (SLAP)
AGH.
I WILL ALSO TRAIN YOU, IF YOU SO WISH.
LAYLA...
... FORCES PATIENTS TO TRAIN TO THEIR LIMITS, MAKING IT EASY FOR THEM TO SHOW PROGRESS.
I DID NOT SAY YOU MAY STOP.
PISHI!
OINK OINK!
BURU (SHIVER)
YOUR ROLE-PLAYING IS EXCELLENT!...
HER TRAINING IS A LITTLE TOO HARSH, THOUGH!
I THINK SHE'S PLAYING A DIFFERENT SCRIPT ......
DO COME AGAIN. ♡
GACHA (KACHAK)
Operating Thea
THE NEXT FACILITY IS THE OPERATION THEATRE.

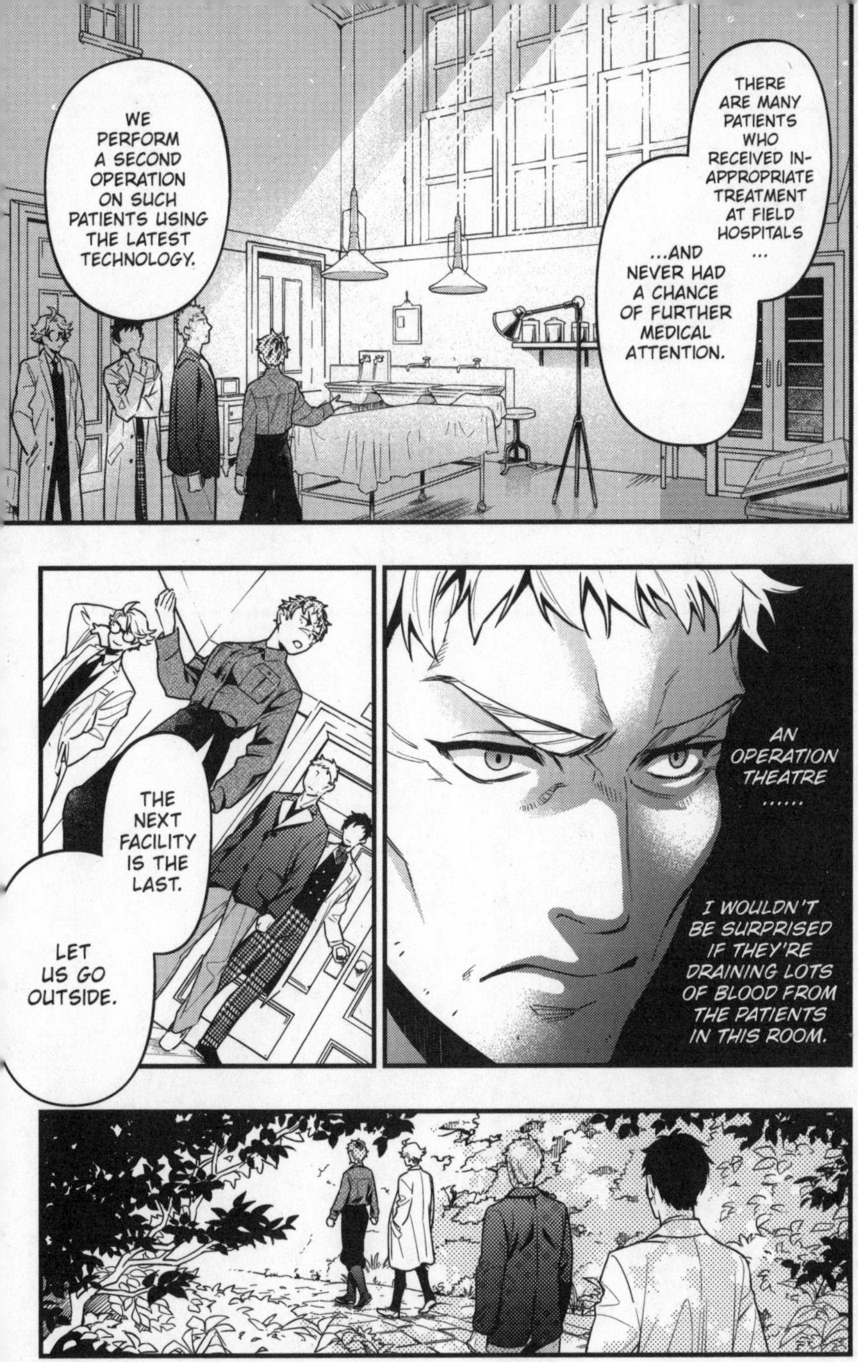
THERE ARE MANY PATIENTS WHO RECEIVED IN-APPROPRIATE TREATMENT AT FIELD HOSPITALS ...
...AND NEVER HAD A CHANCE OF FURTHER MEDICAL ATTENTION.
WE PERFORM A SECOND OPERATION ON SUCH PATIENTS USING THE LATEST TECHNOLOGY.
AN OPERATION THEATRE ......
I WOULDN'T BE SURPRISED IF THEY'RE DRAINING LOTS OF BLOOD FROM THE PATIENTS IN THIS ROOM.
THE NEXT FACILITY IS THE LAST.
LET US GO OUTSIDE.

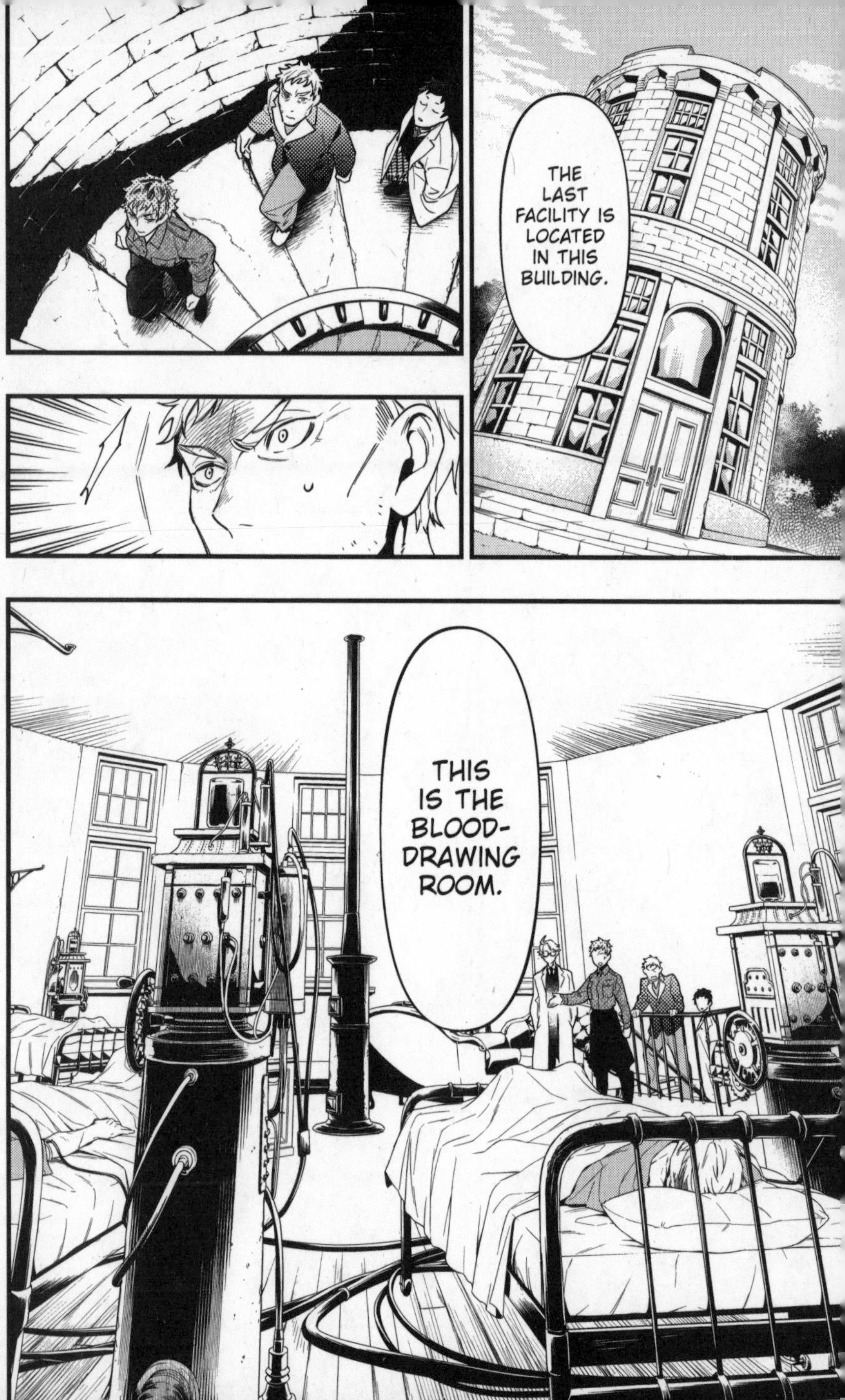
THE LAST FACILITY IS LOCATED IN THIS BUILDING.
THIS IS THE BLOOD-DRAWING ROOM.

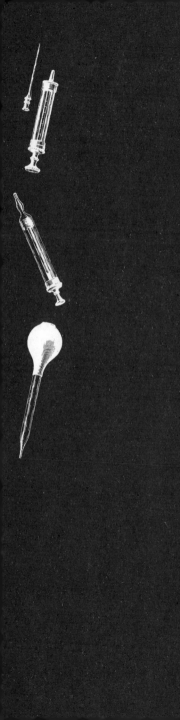

Black Butler

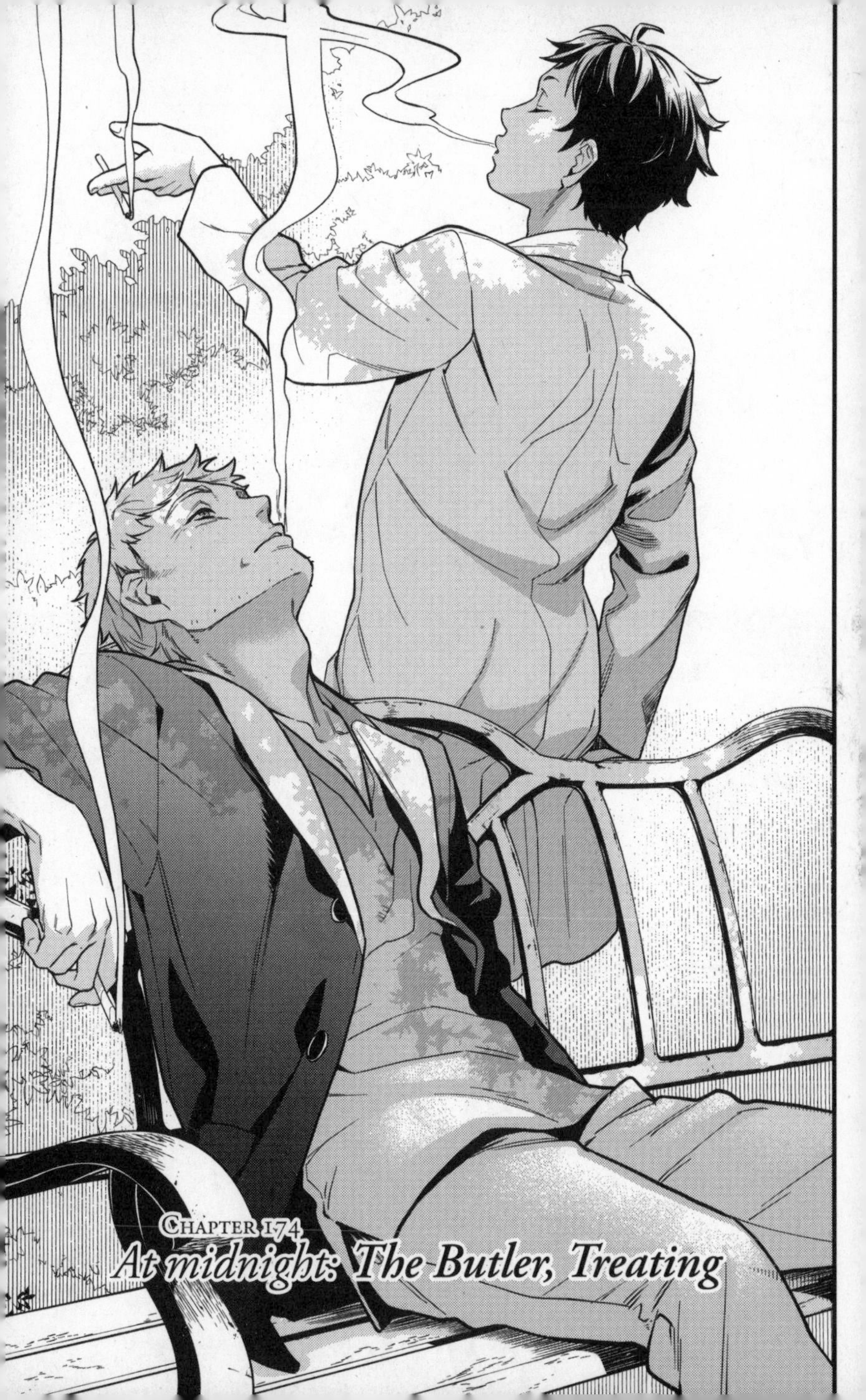
Chapter 174
At midnight: The Butler, Treating

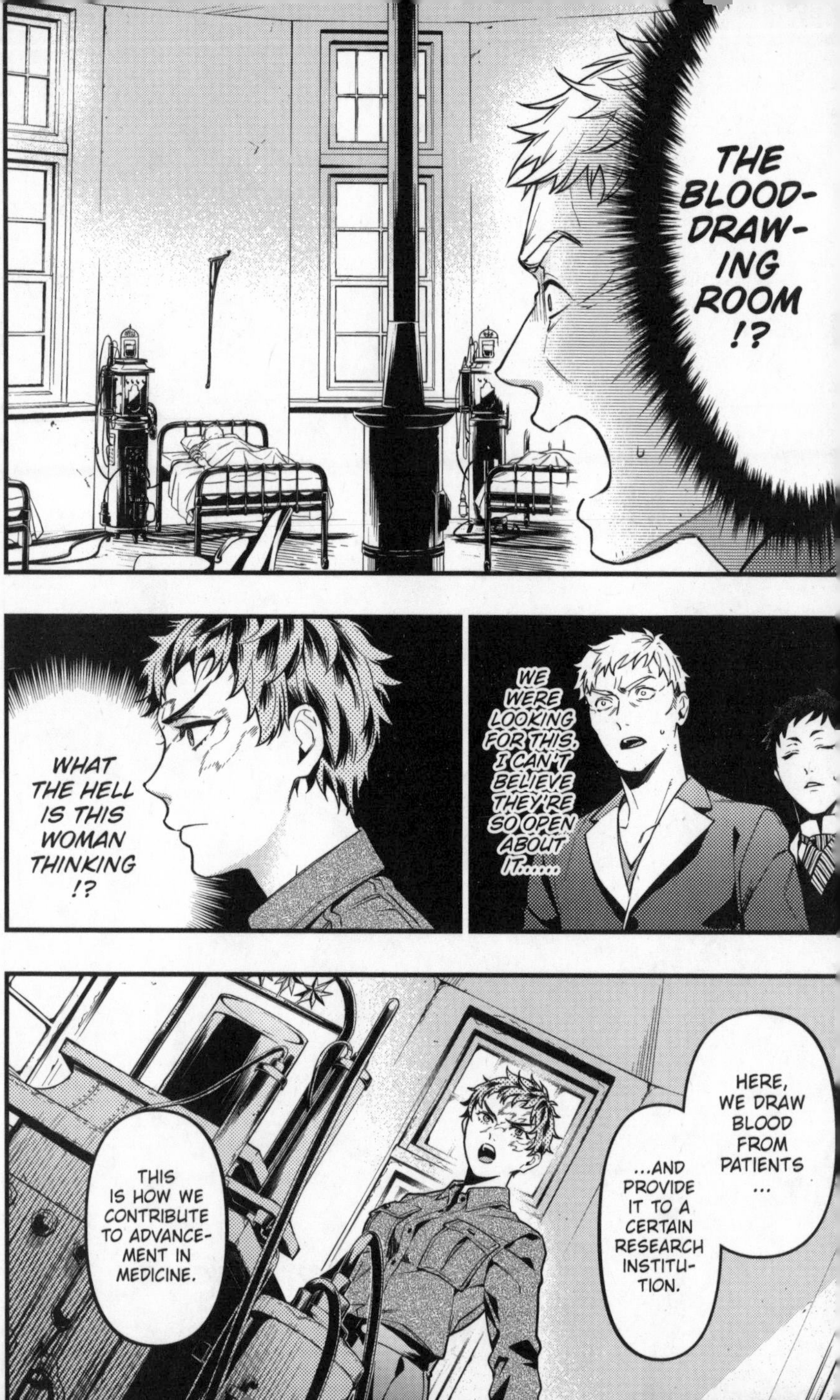
THE BLOOD-DRAW-ING ROOM!?
WE WERE LOOKING FOR THIS. I CAN'T BELIEVE THEY'RE SO OPEN ABOUT IT......
WHAT THE HELL IS THIS WOMAN THINKING!?
HERE, WE DRAW BLOOD FROM PATIENTS...
...AND PROVIDE IT TO A CERTAIN RESEARCH INSTITUTION.
THIS IS HOW WE CONTRIBUTE TO ADVANCEMENT IN MEDICINE.

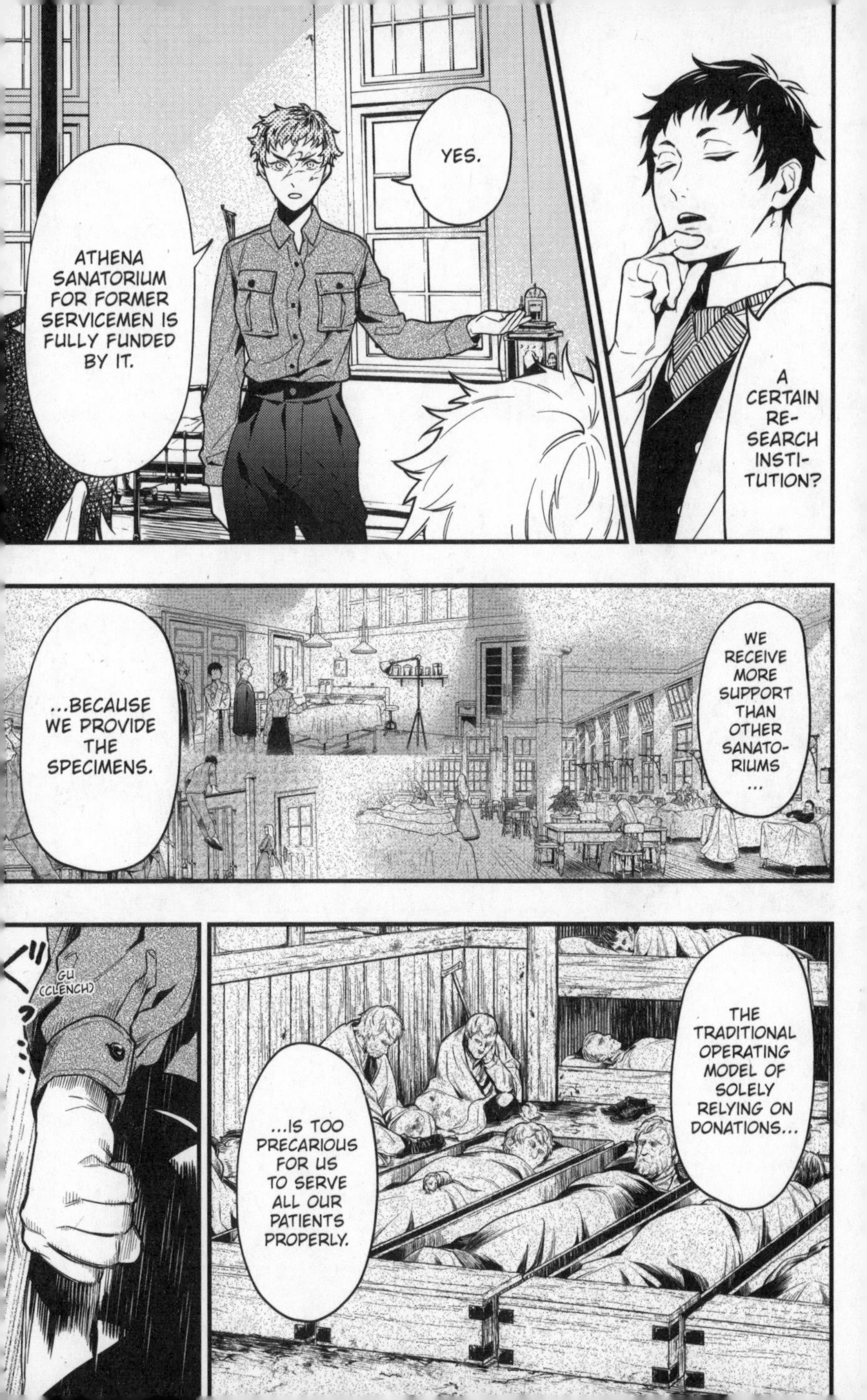
A CERTAIN RE-SEARCH INSTI-TUTION?
YES.
ATHENA SANATORIUM FOR FORMER SERVICEMEN IS FULLY FUNDED BY IT.
WE RECEIVE MORE SUPPORT THAN OTHER SANATO-RIUMS...
...BECAUSE WE PROVIDE THE SPECIMENS.
THE TRADITIONAL OPERATING MODEL OF SOLELY RELYING ON DONATIONS...
...IS TOO PRECARIOUS FOR US TO SERVE ALL OUR PATIENTS PROPERLY.
GU (CLENCH)

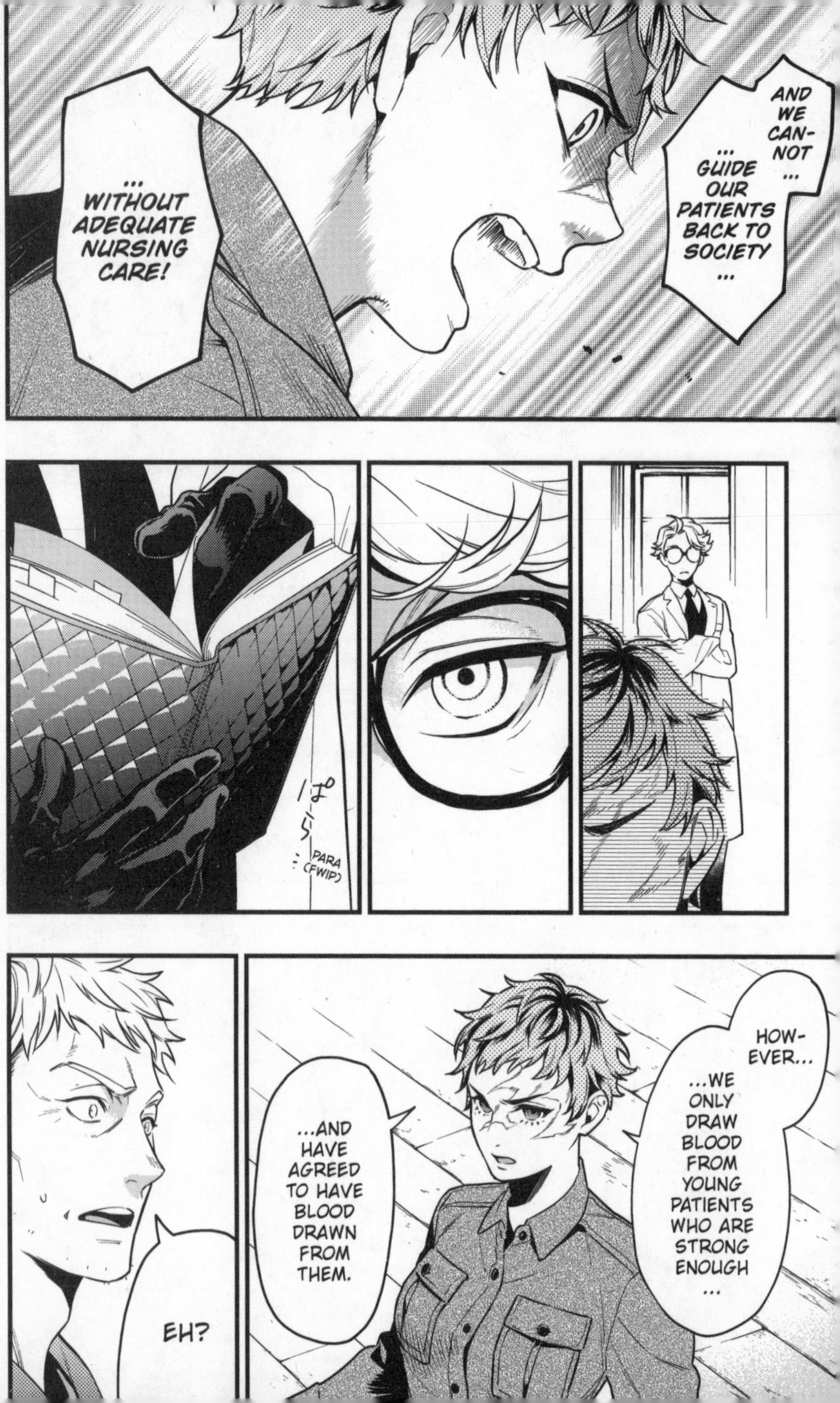
AND WE CAN-NOT ...
... GUIDE OUR PATIENTS BACK TO SOCIETY ...
... WITHOUT ADEQUATE NURSING CARE!
ぱら
PARA (FWIP)
HOW-EVER...
...WE ONLY DRAW BLOOD FROM YOUNG PATIENTS WHO ARE STRONG ENOUGH ...
...AND HAVE AGREED TO HAVE BLOOD DRAWN FROM THEM.
EH?

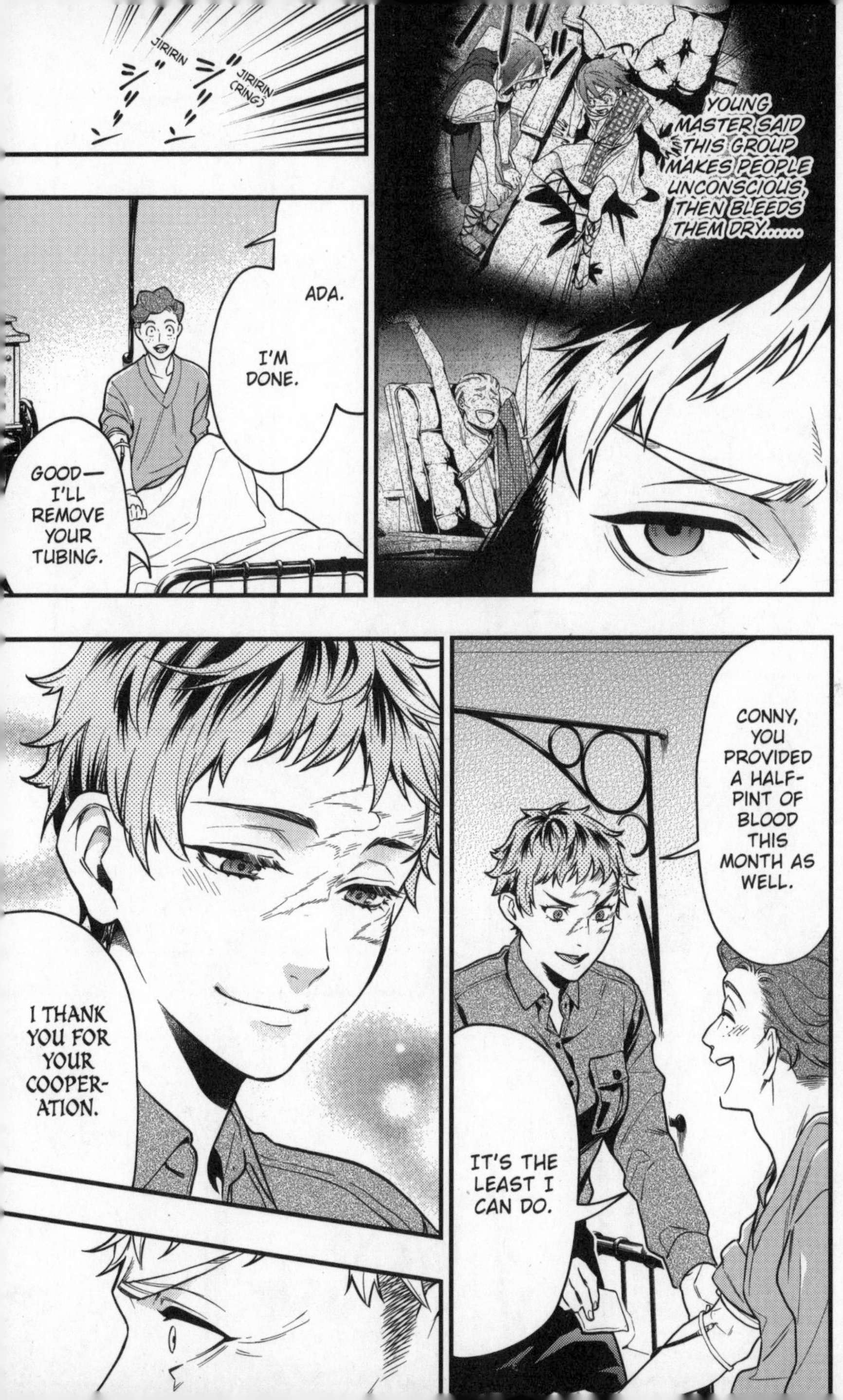
YOUNG MASTER SAID THIS GROUP MAKES PEOPLE UNCONSCIOUS, THEN BLEEDS THEM DRY......
JIRIRIN
JIRIRIN (RING)
ADA.
I'M DONE.
GOOD— I'LL REMOVE YOUR TUBING.
CONNY, YOU PROVIDED A HALF-PINT OF BLOOD THIS MONTH AS WELL.
IT'S THE LEAST I CAN DO.
I THANK YOU FOR YOUR COOPERATION.

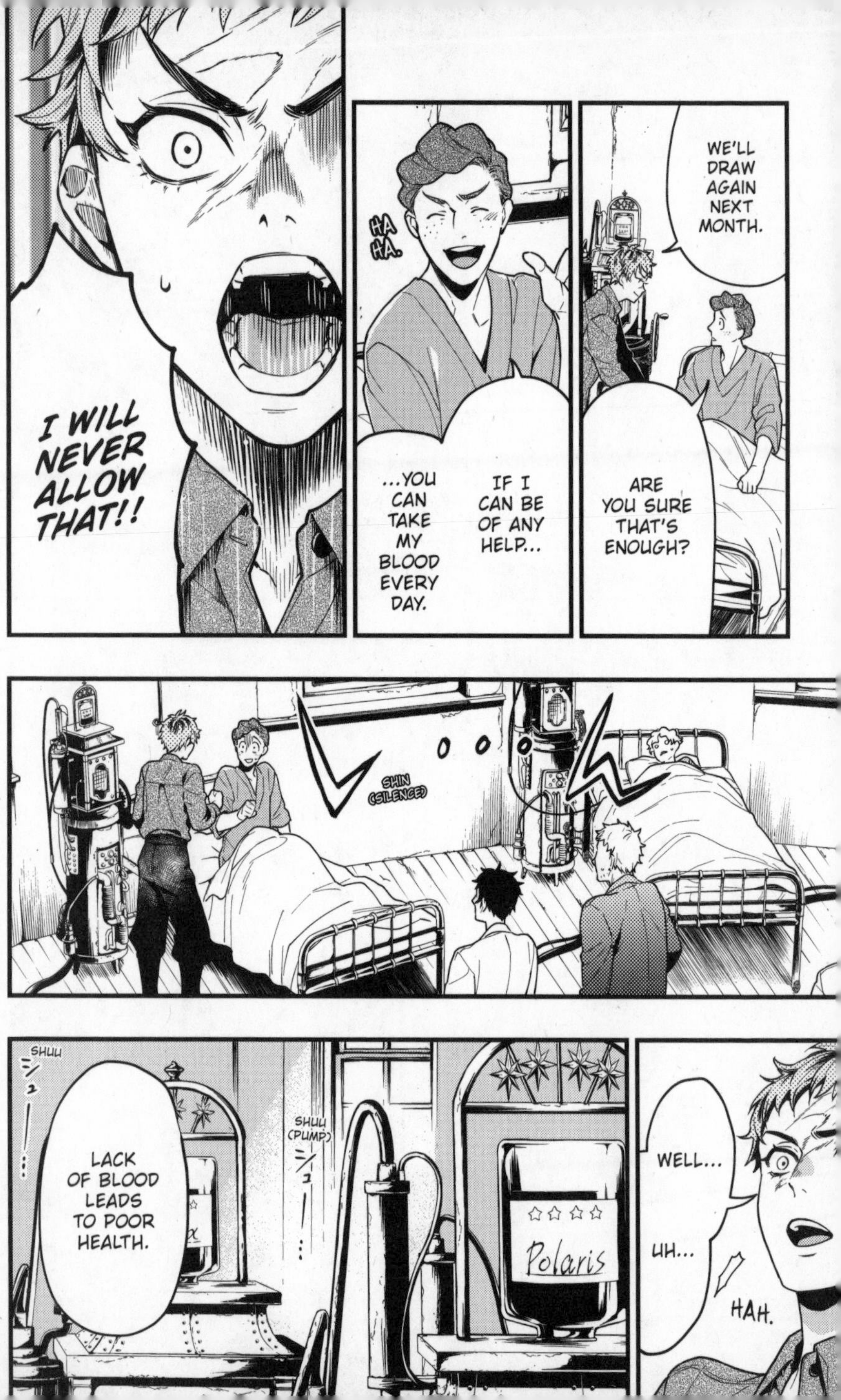
WE'LL DRAW AGAIN NEXT MONTH.
ARE YOU SURE THAT'S ENOUGH?
HA HA.
IF I CAN BE OF ANY HELP...
...YOU CAN TAKE MY BLOOD EVERY DAY.
I WILL NEVER ALLOW THAT!!
SHIN (SILENCED)
WELL...
UH...
HAH.
SHUU (PUMP)
Polaris
SHUU
LACK OF BLOOD LEADS TO POOR HEALTH.

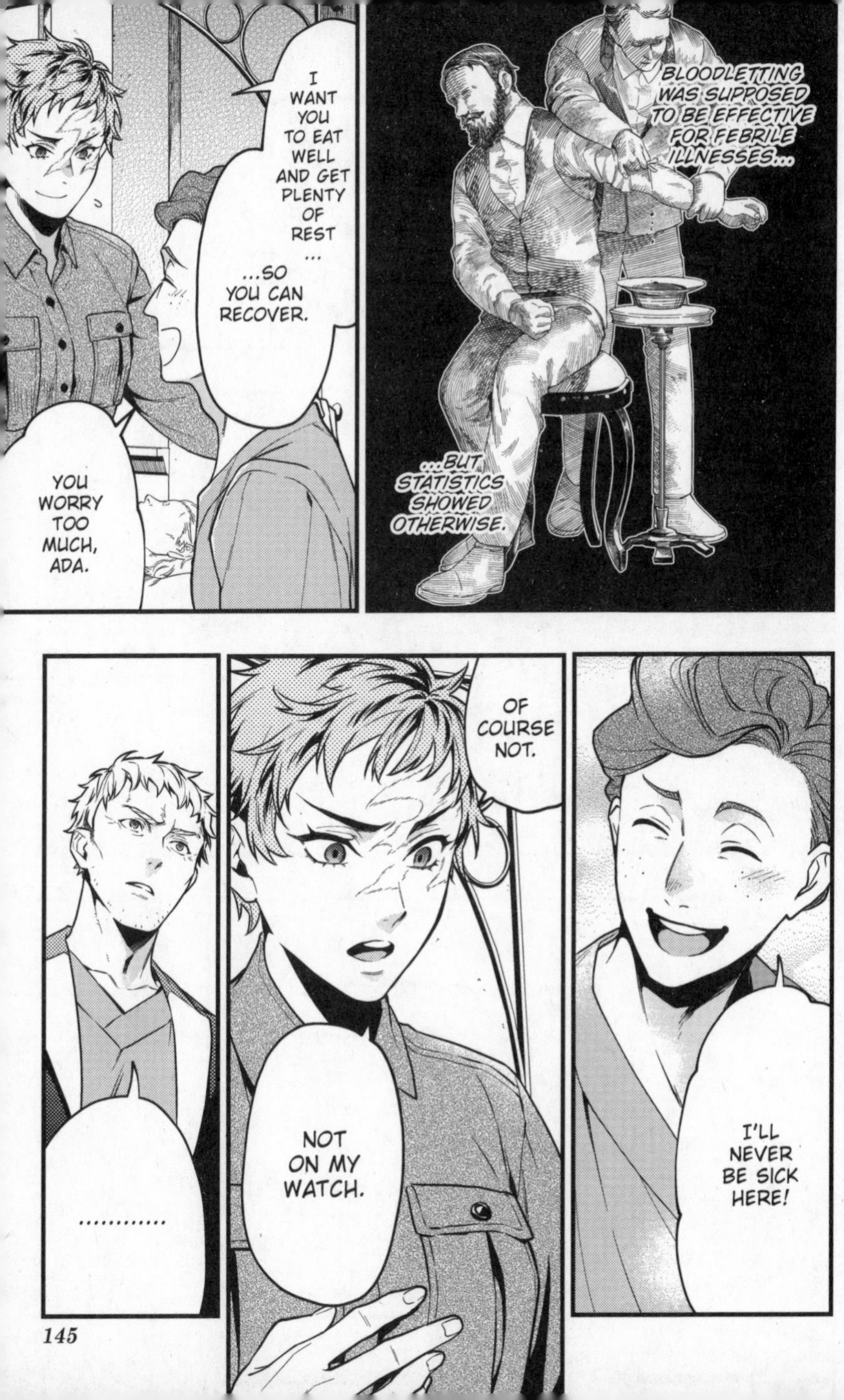
BLOODLETTING WAS SUPPOSED TO BE EFFECTIVE FOR FEBRILE ILLNESSES...
...BUT STATISTICS SHOWED OTHERWISE.
I WANT YOU TO EAT WELL AND GET PLENTY OF REST ...
...SO YOU CAN RECOVER.
YOU WORRY TOO MUCH, ADA.
I'LL NEVER BE SICK HERE!
OF COURSE NOT.
NOT ON MY WATCH.
....

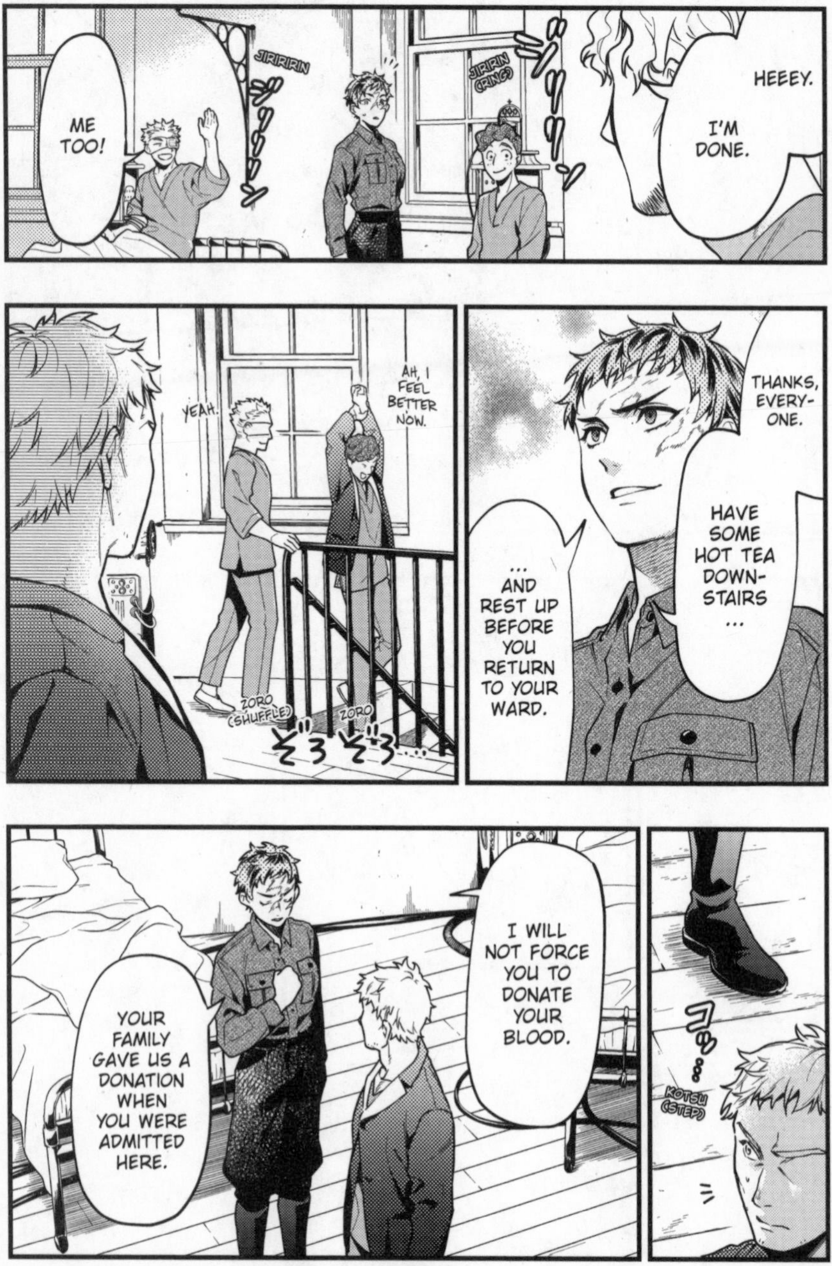
HEEEY.
I'M DONE.
JIRIRIN (RING)
JIRIRIRIN
ME TOO!
THANKS, EVERY-ONE.
HAVE SOME HOT TEA DOWN-STAIRS ...
... AND REST UP BEFORE YOU RETURN TO YOUR WARD.
AH, I FEEL BETTER NOW.
YEAH.
ZORO (SHUFFLE)
ZORO
KOTSU (STEP)
I WILL NOT FORCE YOU TO DONATE YOUR BLOOD.
YOUR FAMILY GAVE US A DONATION WHEN YOU WERE ADMITTED HERE.

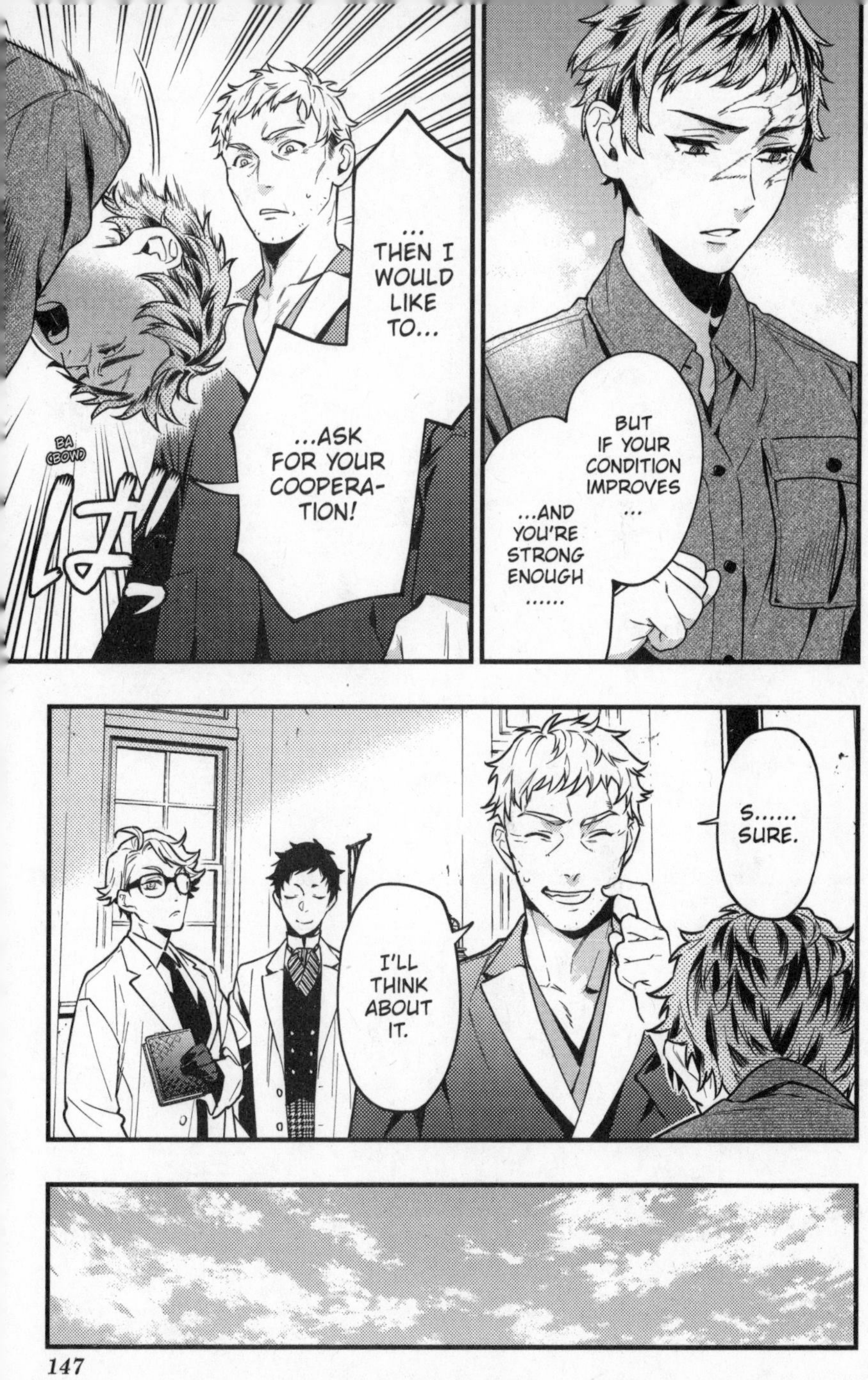
BUT IF YOUR CONDITION IMPROVES ...
...AND YOU'RE STRONG ENOUGH ......
... THEN I WOULD LIKE TO...
...ASK FOR YOUR COOPERATION!
BA (BOW)
ばっ
S...... SURE.
I'LL THINK ABOUT IT.

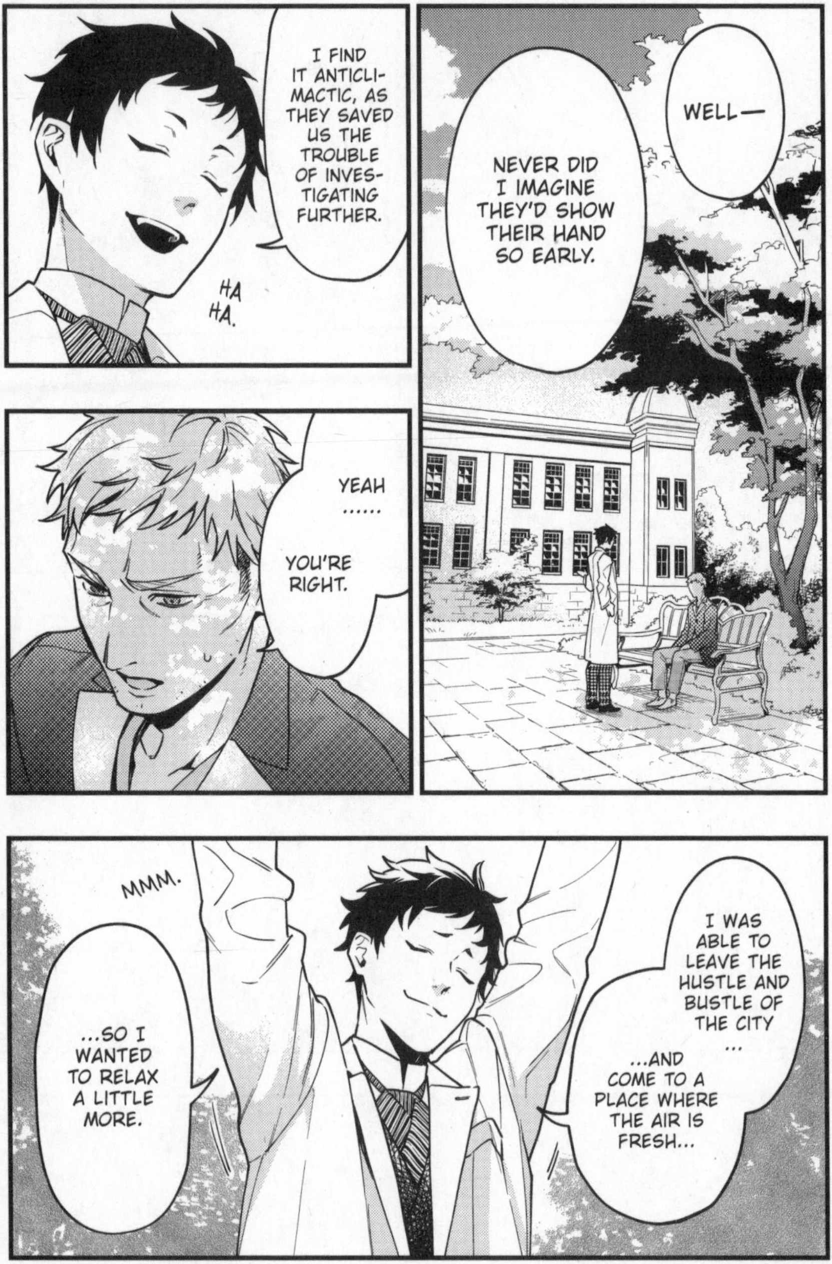
WELL—
NEVER DID I IMAGINE THEY'D SHOW THEIR HAND SO EARLY.
I FIND IT ANTICLI-MACTIC, AS THEY SAVED US THE TROUBLE OF INVES-TIGATING FURTHER.
HA HA.
YEAH ......
YOU'RE RIGHT.
I WAS ABLE TO LEAVE THE HUSTLE AND BUSTLE OF THE CITY ...
...AND COME TO A PLACE WHERE THE AIR IS FRESH...
MMM.
...SO I WANTED TO RELAX A LITTLE MORE.

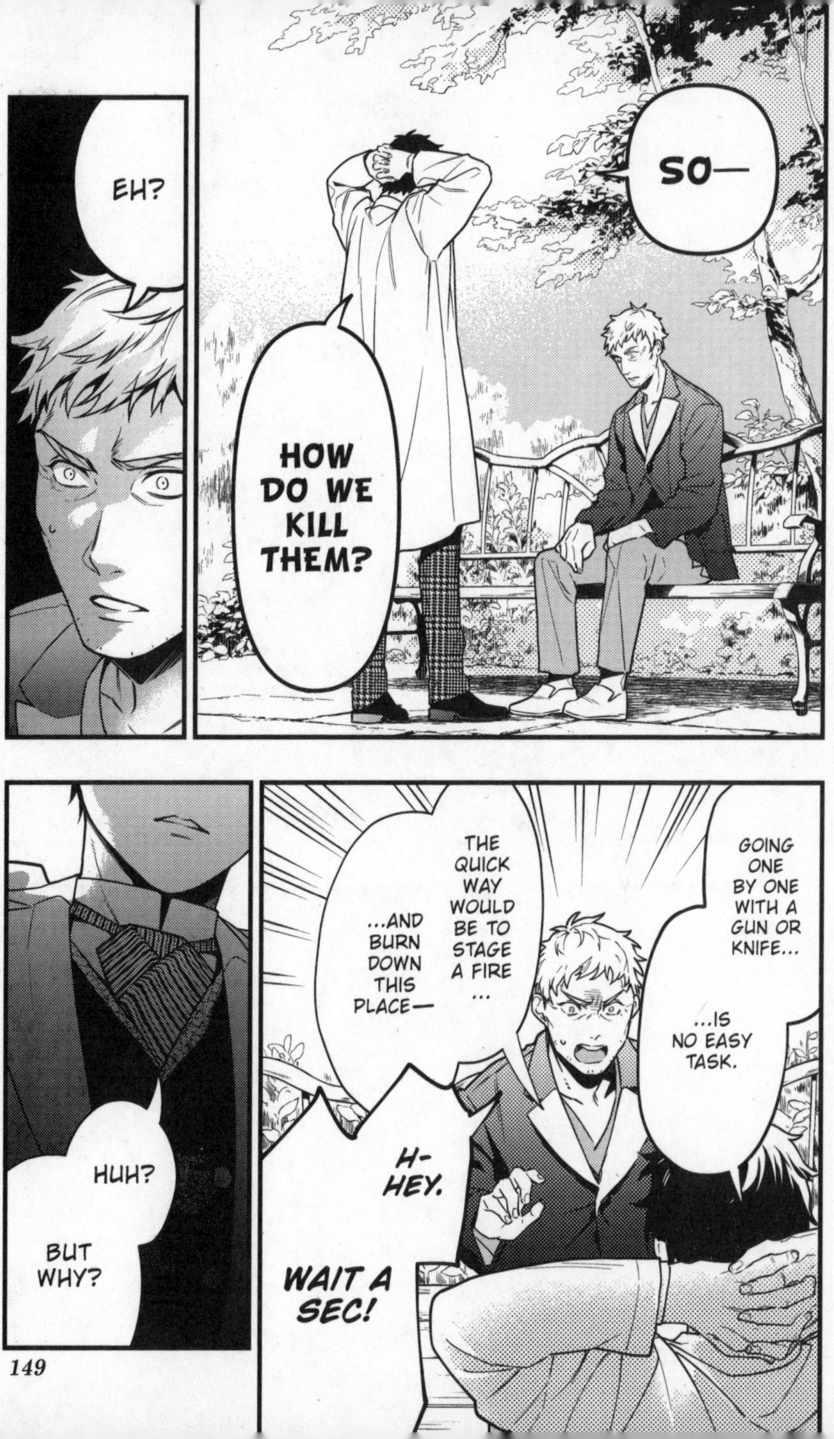
SO—
HOW DO WE KILL THEM?
EH?
GOING ONE BY ONE WITH A GUN OR KNIFE...
...IS NO EASY TASK.
THE QUICK WAY WOULD BE TO STAGE A FIRE...
...AND BURN DOWN THIS PLACE—
H-HEY.
WAIT A SEC!
HUH?
BUT WHY?

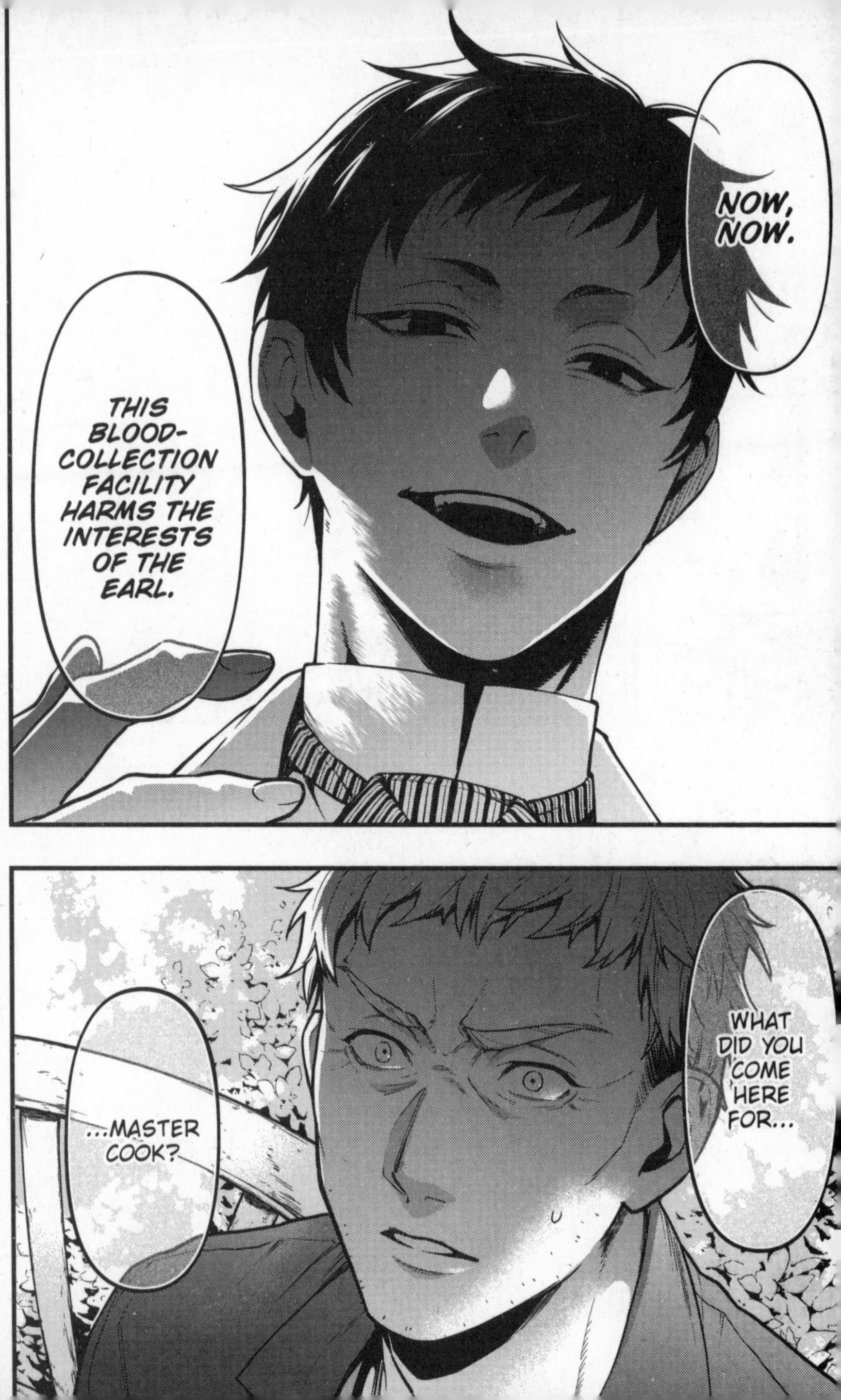
NOW, NOW.
THIS BLOOD-COLLECTION FACILITY HARMS THE INTERESTS OF THE EARL.
WHAT DID YOU COME HERE FOR...
...MASTER COOK?

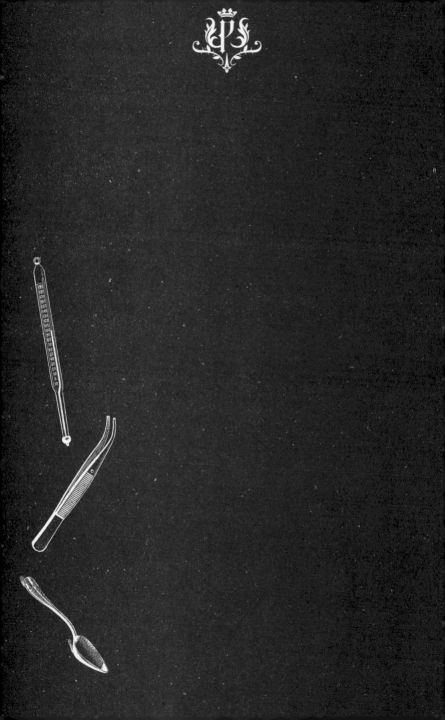

Black Butler

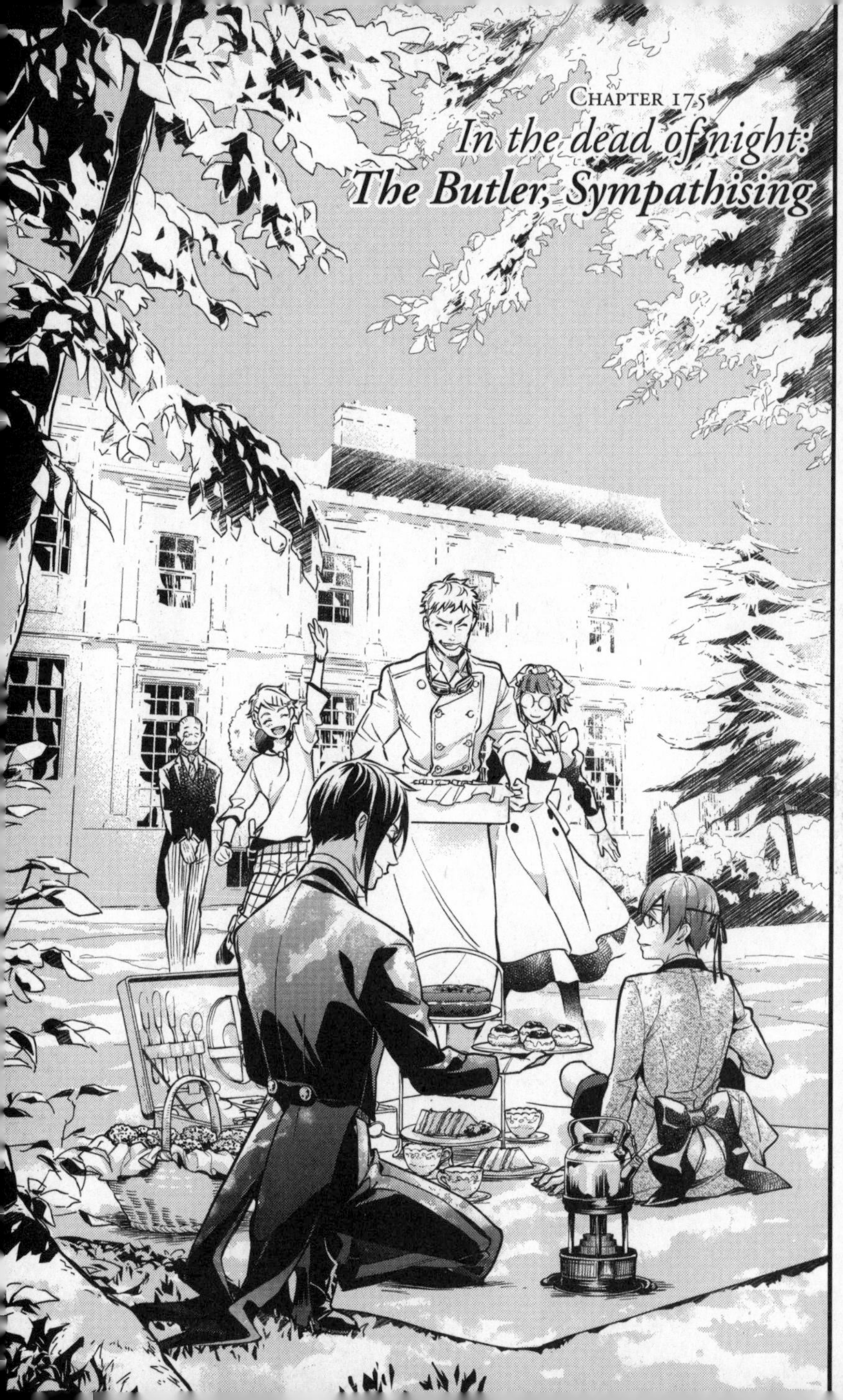
Chapter 175
In the dead of night:
The Butler, Sympathising

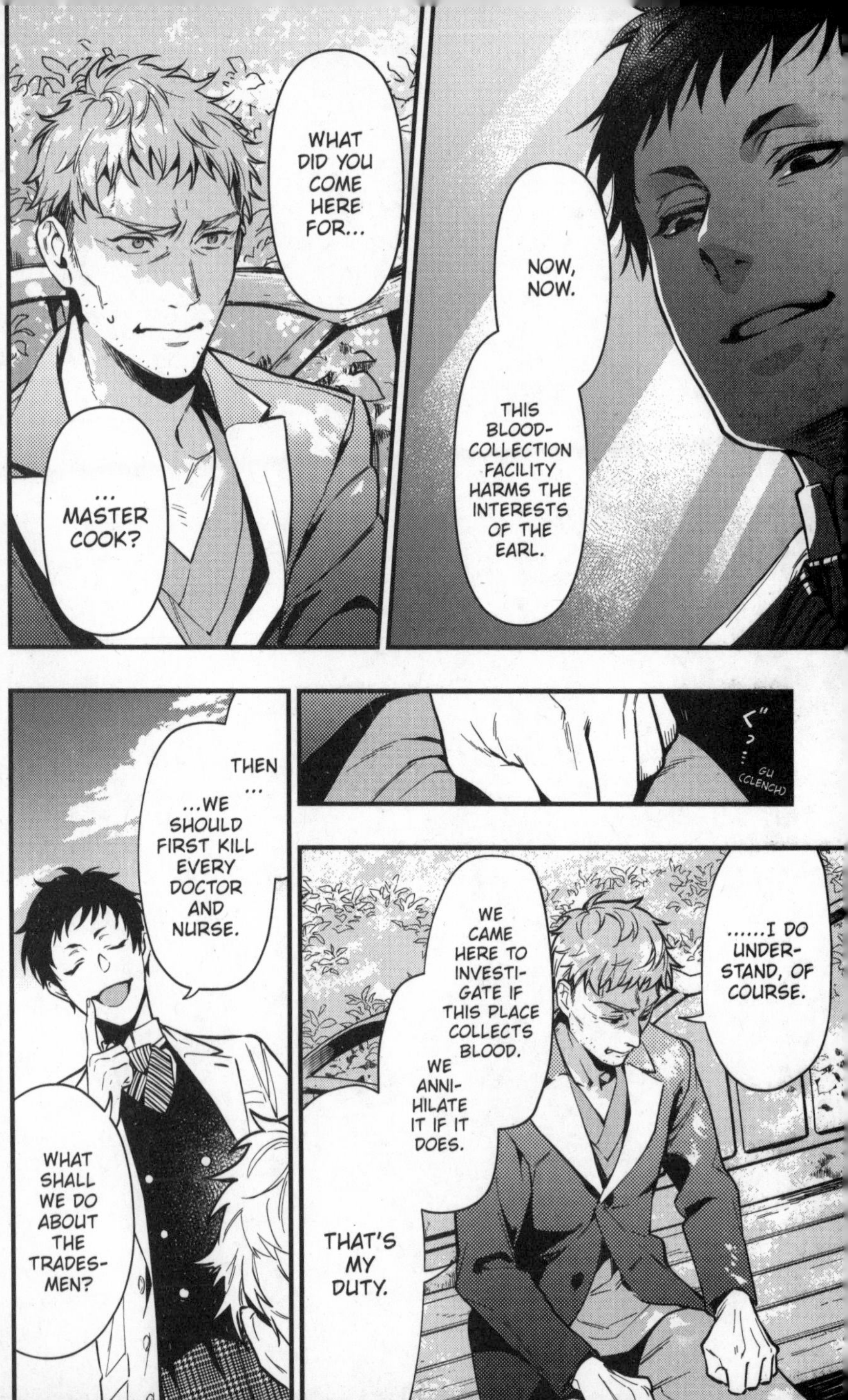
NOW, NOW.
THIS BLOOD-COLLECTION FACILITY HARMS THE INTERESTS OF THE EARL.
WHAT DID YOU COME HERE FOR...
... MASTER COOK?
ぐっ…
GU (CLENCH)
......I DO UNDERSTAND, OF COURSE.
WE CAME HERE TO INVESTIGATE IF THIS PLACE COLLECTS BLOOD.
WE ANNIHILATE IT IF IT DOES.
THAT'S MY DUTY.
THEN ...
...WE SHOULD FIRST KILL EVERY DOCTOR AND NURSE.
WHAT SHALL WE DO ABOUT THE TRADESMEN?

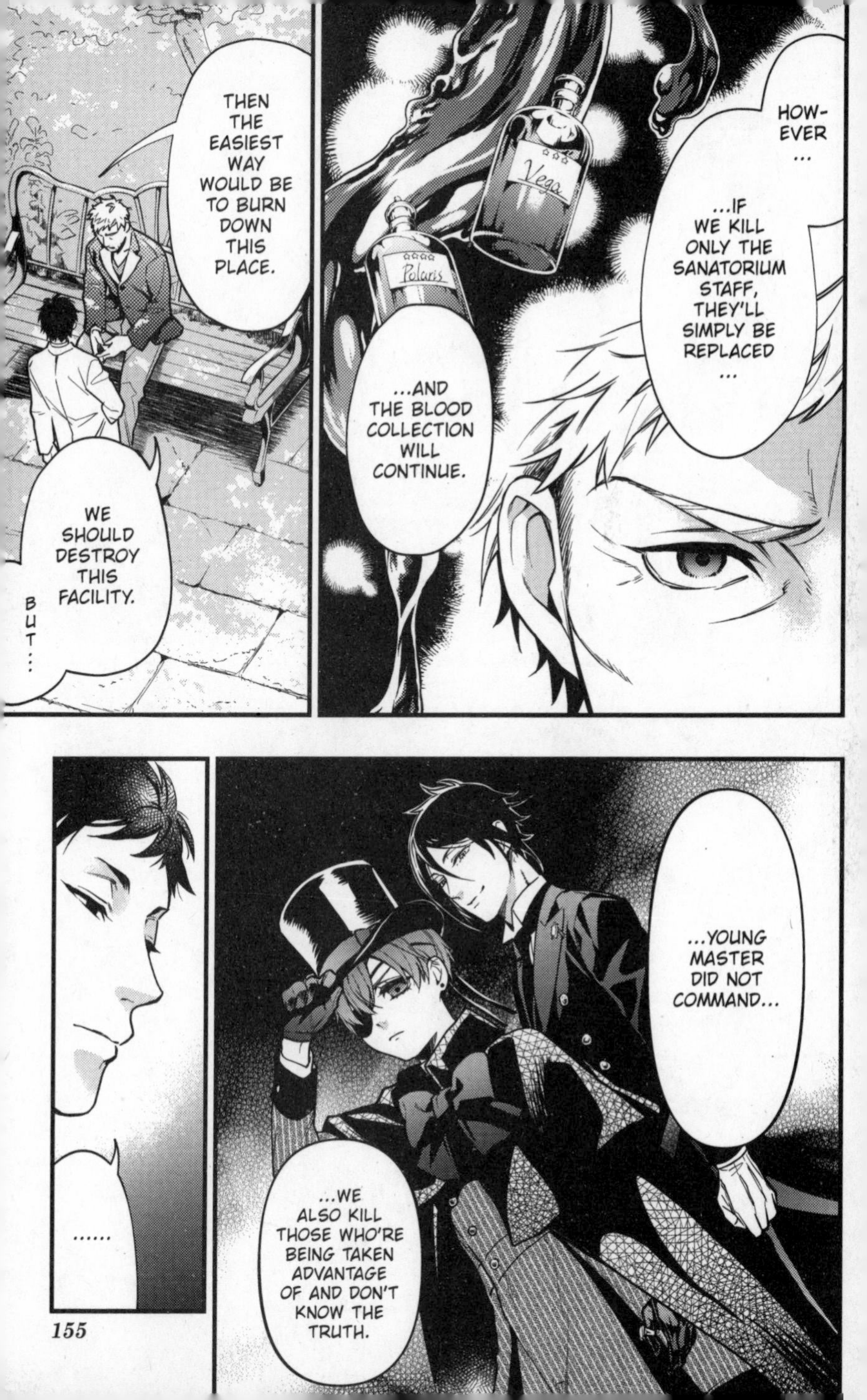
HOW-EVER...
...IF WE KILL ONLY THE SANATORIUM STAFF, THEY'LL SIMPLY BE REPLACED...
...AND THE BLOOD COLLECTION WILL CONTINUE.
Vega
Polaris
THEN THE EASIEST WAY WOULD BE TO BURN DOWN THIS PLACE.
WE SHOULD DESTROY THIS FACILITY.
BUT...
...YOUNG MASTER DID NOT COMMAND...
...WE ALSO KILL THOSE WHO'RE BEING TAKEN ADVANTAGE OF AND DON'T KNOW THE TRUTH.
......

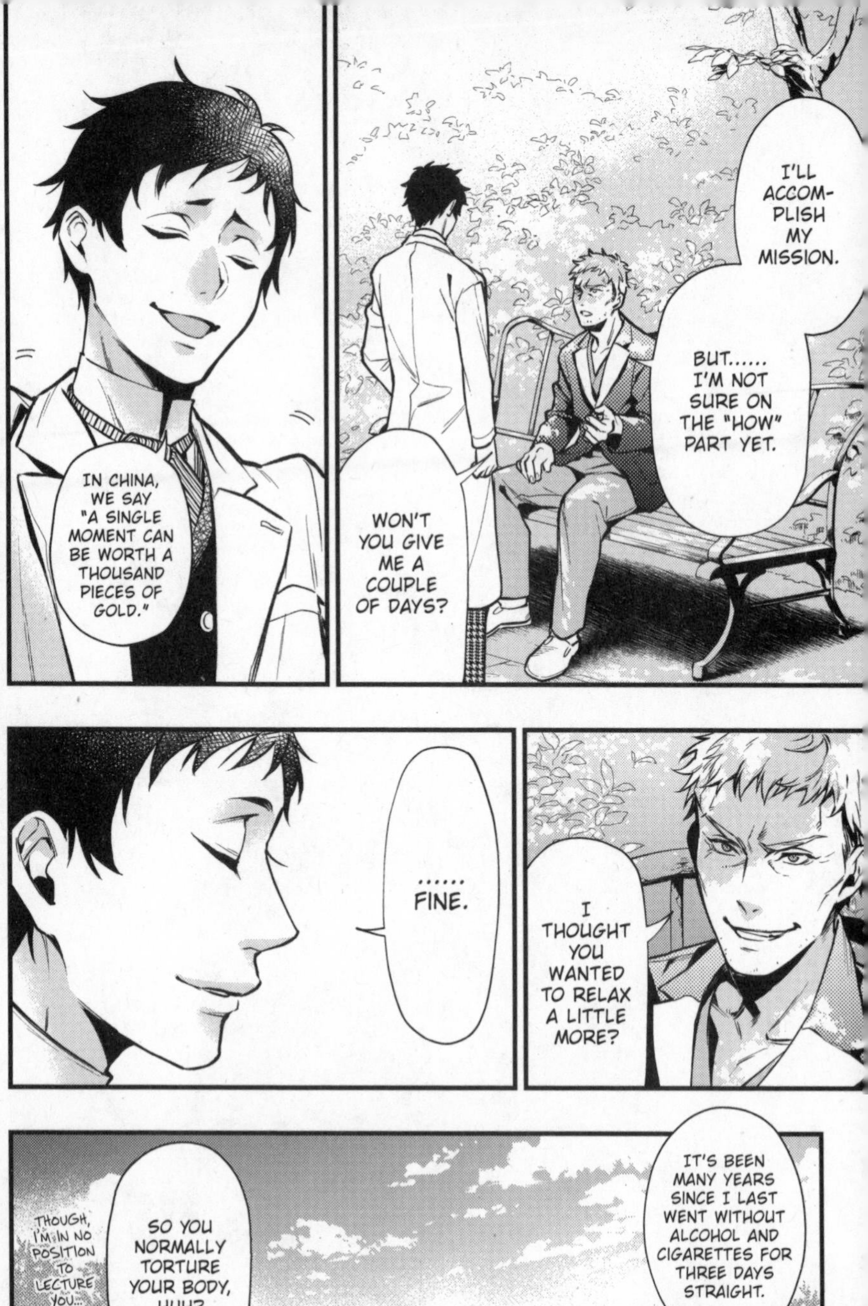
I'LL ACCOMPLISH MY MISSION.
BUT...... I'M NOT SURE ON THE "HOW" PART YET.
WON'T YOU GIVE ME A COUPLE OF DAYS?
IN CHINA, WE SAY "A SINGLE MOMENT CAN BE WORTH A THOUSAND PIECES OF GOLD."
I THOUGHT YOU WANTED TO RELAX A LITTLE MORE?
......FINE.
IT'S BEEN MANY YEARS SINCE I LAST WENT WITHOUT ALCOHOL AND CIGARETTES FOR THREE DAYS STRAIGHT.
SO YOU NORMALLY TORTURE YOUR BODY, HUH?
THOUGH, I'M IN NO POSITION TO LECTURE YOU...

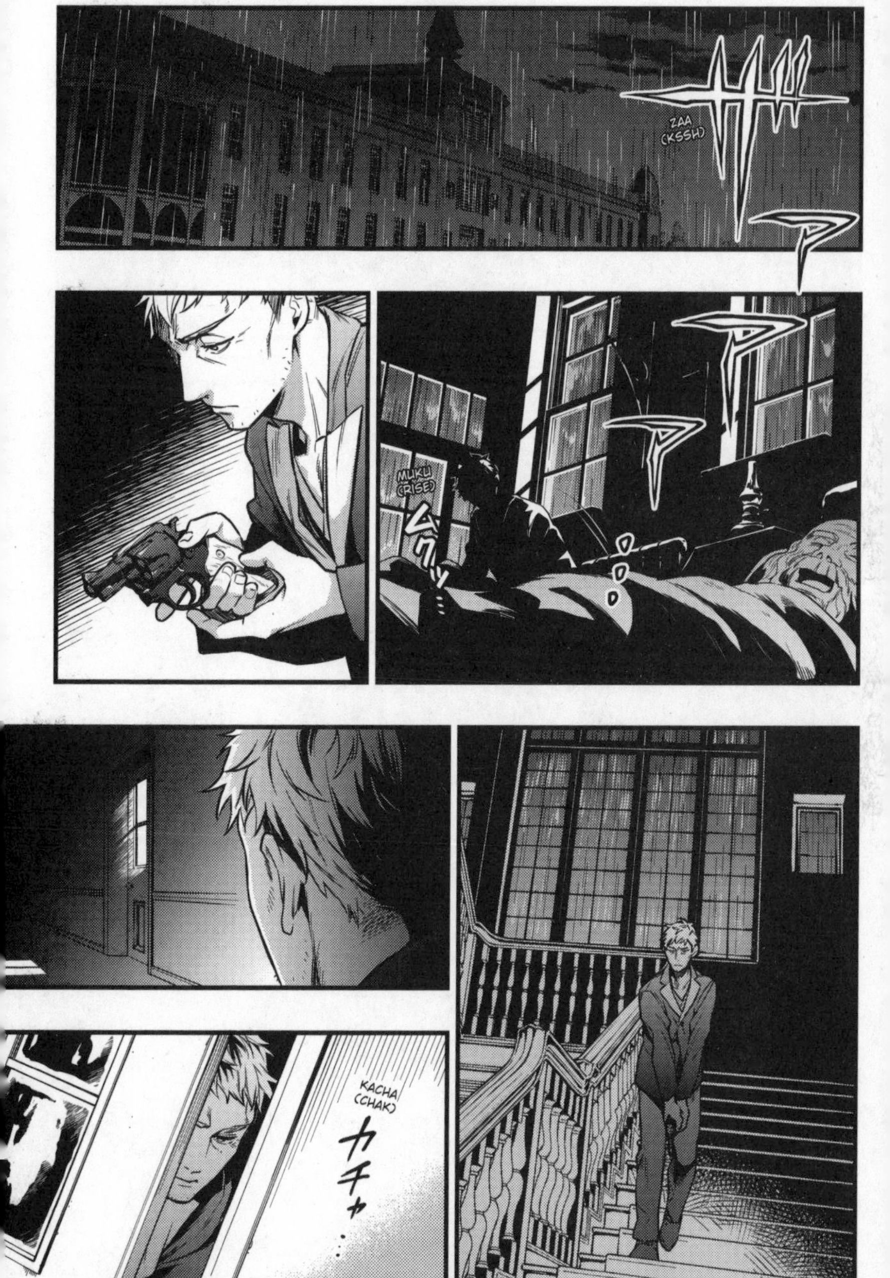
ZAA (KSSH)
ザァァア
MUKU (RISE)
ムクッ
KACHA (CHAK)
カチャ…

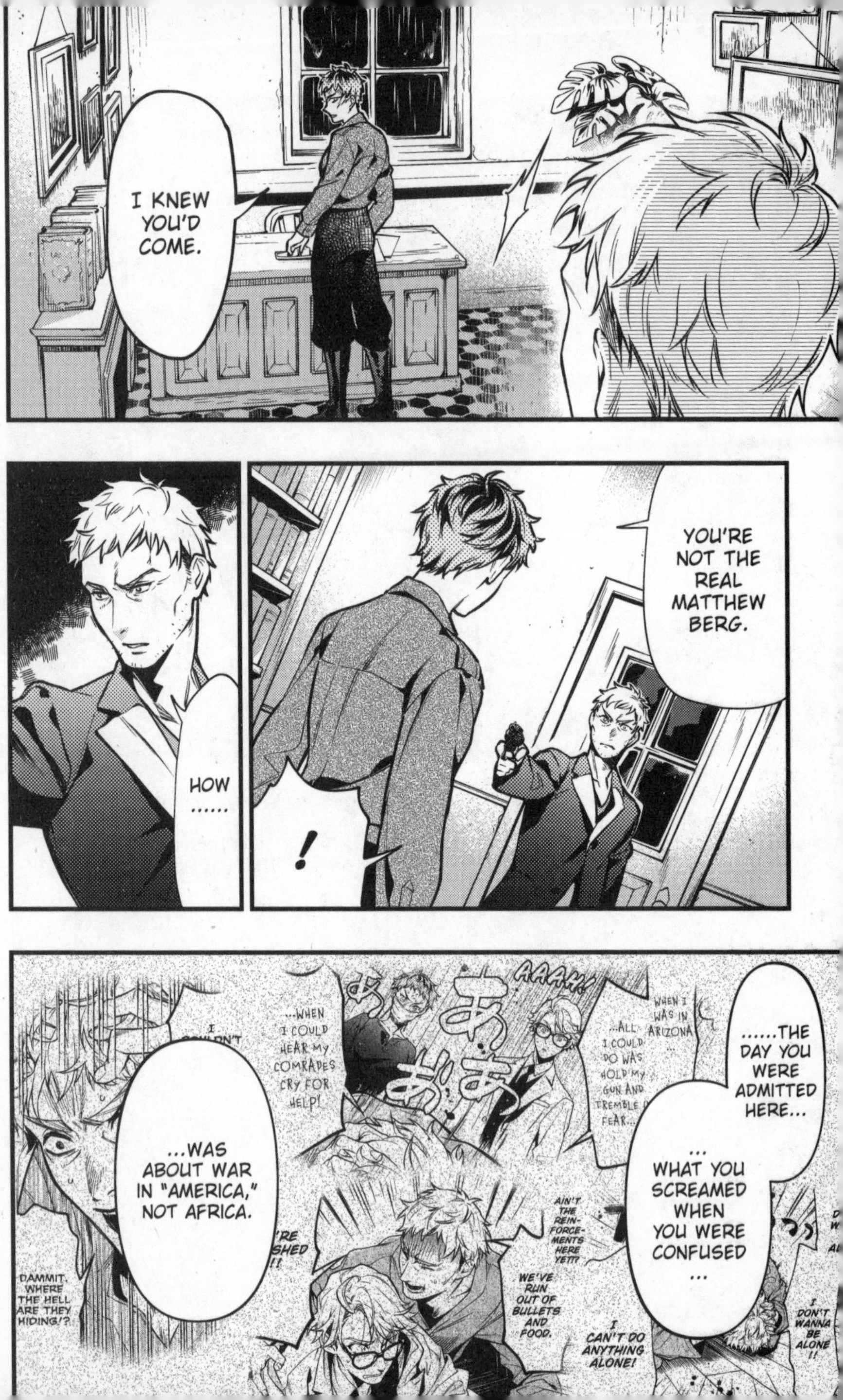
I KNEW YOU'D COME.
YOU'RE NOT THE REAL MATTHEW BERG.
!
HOW ......
......THE DAY YOU WERE ADMITTED HERE...
... WHAT YOU SCREAMED WHEN YOU WERE CONFUSED ...
WHEN I WAS IN ARIZONA ...
...ALL I COULD DO WAS HOLD MY GUN AND TREMBLE
AAAAH!
...WHEN I COULD HEAR MY COMRADES CRY FOR HELP!
...WAS ABOUT WAR IN "AMERICA," NOT AFRICA.
I DON'T WANNA BE ALONE!!
I CAN'T DO ANYTHING ALONE!
AIN'T THE REINFORCEMENTS HERE YET!?
WE'VE RUN OUT OF BULLETS AND FOOD.
DAMMIT, WHERE THE HELL ARE THEY HIDING!?

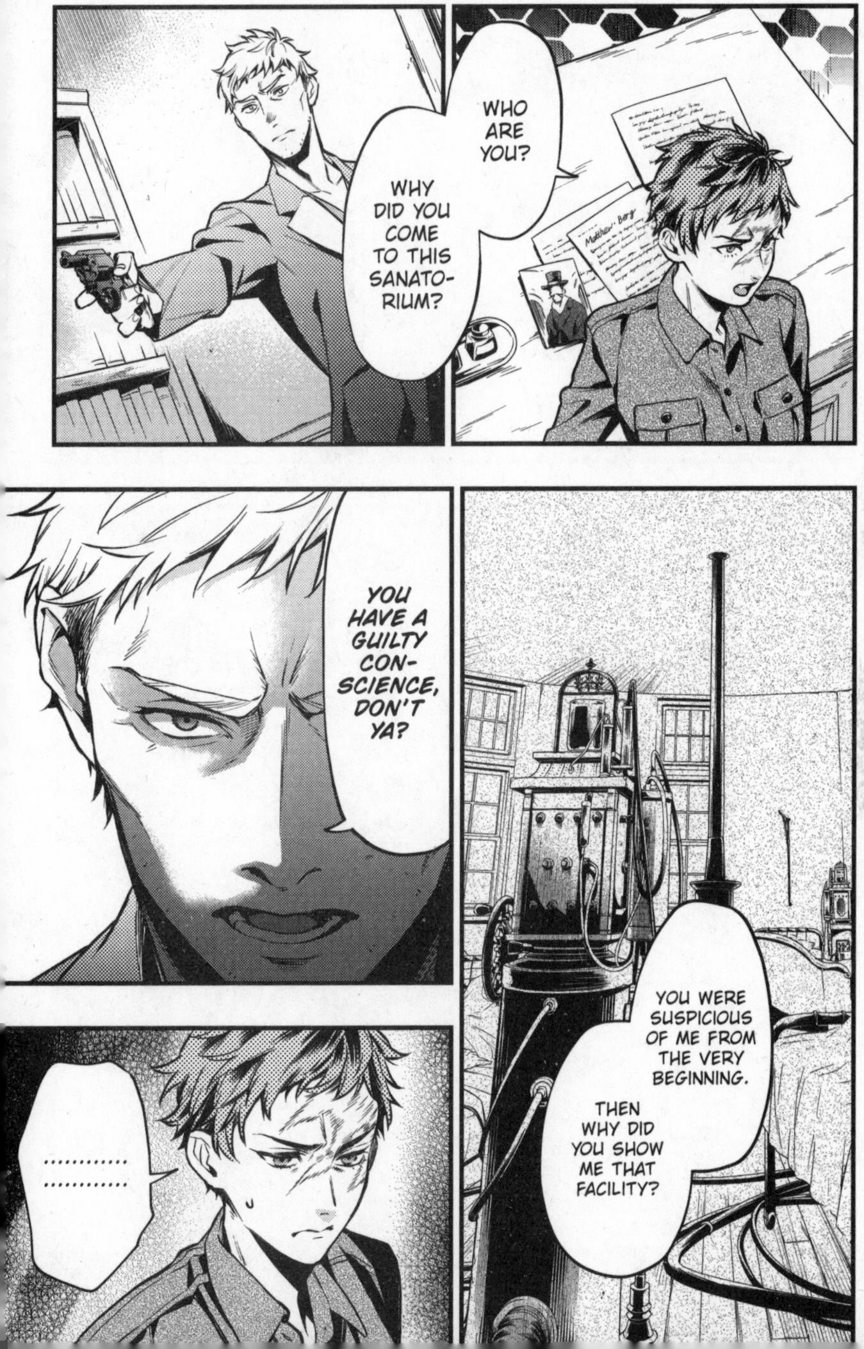
WHO ARE YOU?
WHY DID YOU COME TO THIS SANATORIUM?
YOU WERE SUSPICIOUS OF ME FROM THE VERY BEGINNING.
THEN WHY DID YOU SHOW ME THAT FACILITY?
YOU HAVE A GUILTY CONSCIENCE, DON'T YA?
....
....

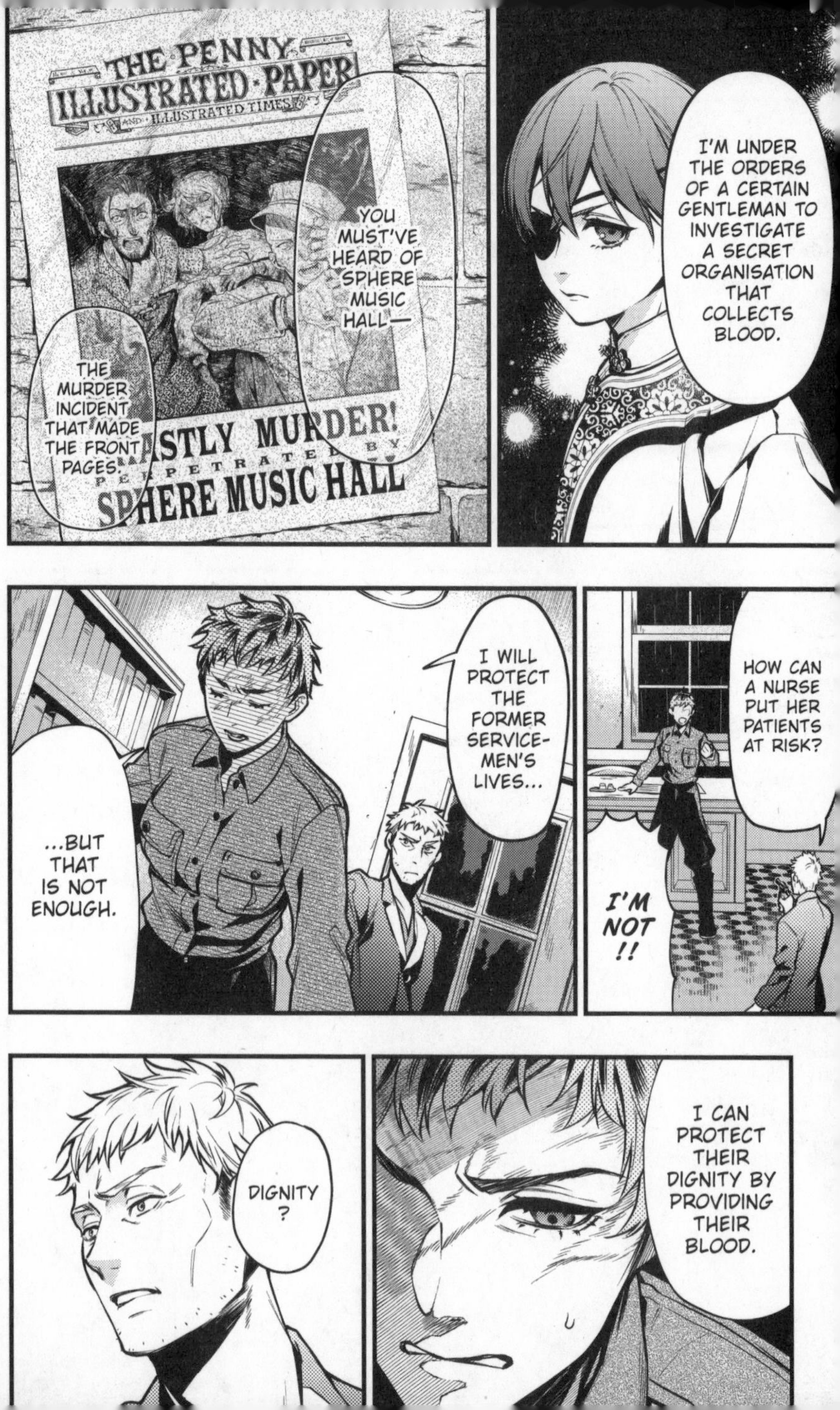
I'M UNDER THE ORDERS OF A CERTAIN GENTLEMAN TO INVESTIGATE A SECRET ORGANISATION THAT COLLECTS BLOOD.
THE PENNY ILLUSTRATED PAPER
AND ILLUSTRATED TIMES
ASTLY MURDER!
SPHERE MUSIC HALL
YOU MUST'VE HEARD OF SPHERE MUSIC HALL—
THE MURDER INCIDENT THAT MADE THE FRONT PAGES.
HOW CAN A NURSE PUT HER PATIENTS AT RISK?
I'M NOT !!
I WILL PROTECT THE FORMER SERVICE-MEN'S LIVES...
...BUT THAT IS NOT ENOUGH.
I CAN PROTECT THEIR DIGNITY BY PROVIDING THEIR BLOOD.
DIGNITY?

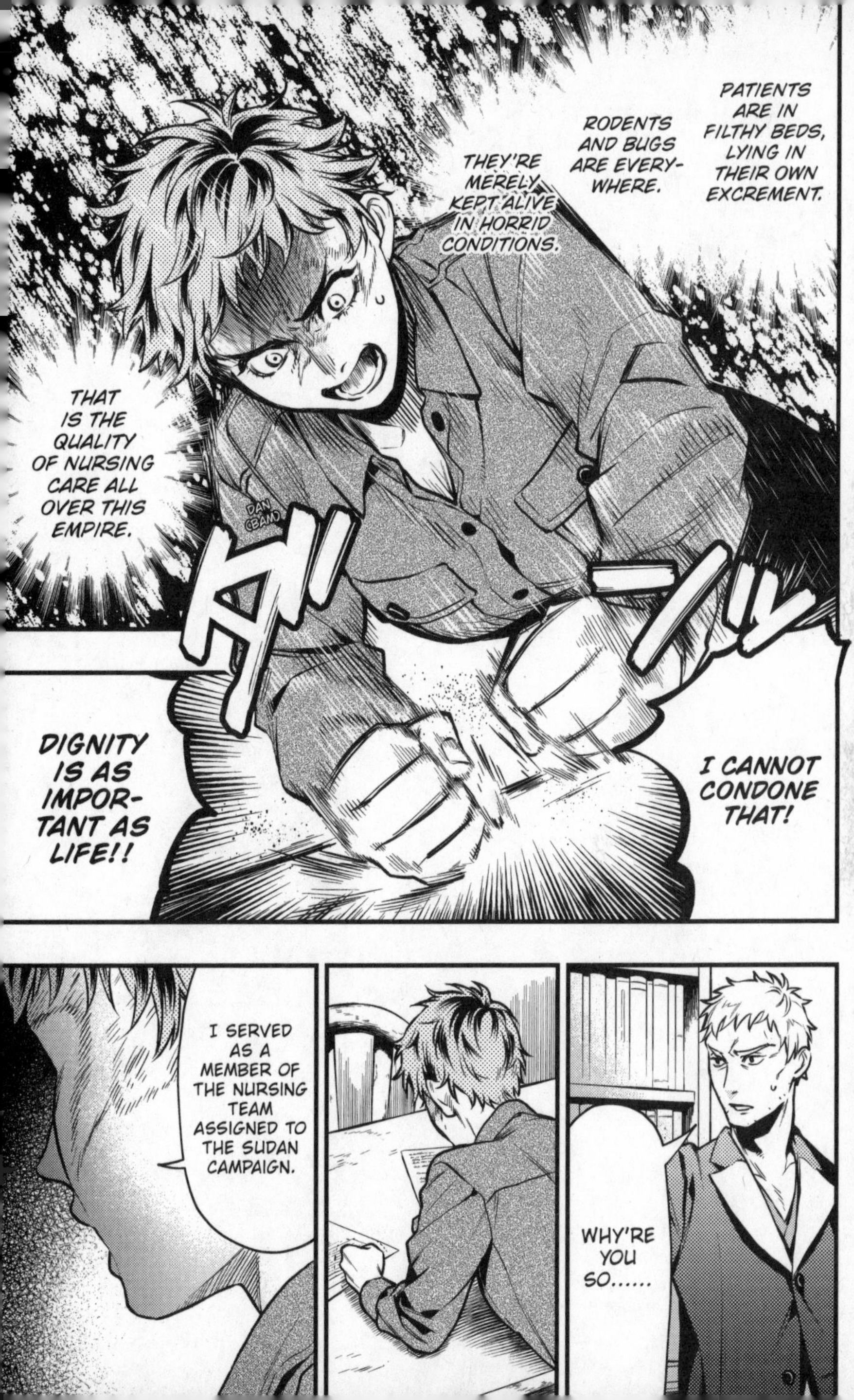
PATIENTS ARE IN FILTHY BEDS, LYING IN THEIR OWN EXCREMENT.
RODENTS AND BUGS ARE EVERY-WHERE.
THEY'RE MERELY KEPT ALIVE IN HORRID CONDITIONS.
THAT IS THE QUALITY OF NURSING CARE ALL OVER THIS EMPIRE.
DAN (BAM)
I CANNOT CONDONE THAT!
DIGNITY IS AS IMPOR-TANT AS LIFE!!
WHY'RE YOU SO......
I SERVED AS A MEMBER OF THE NURSING TEAM ASSIGNED TO THE SUDAN CAMPAIGN.

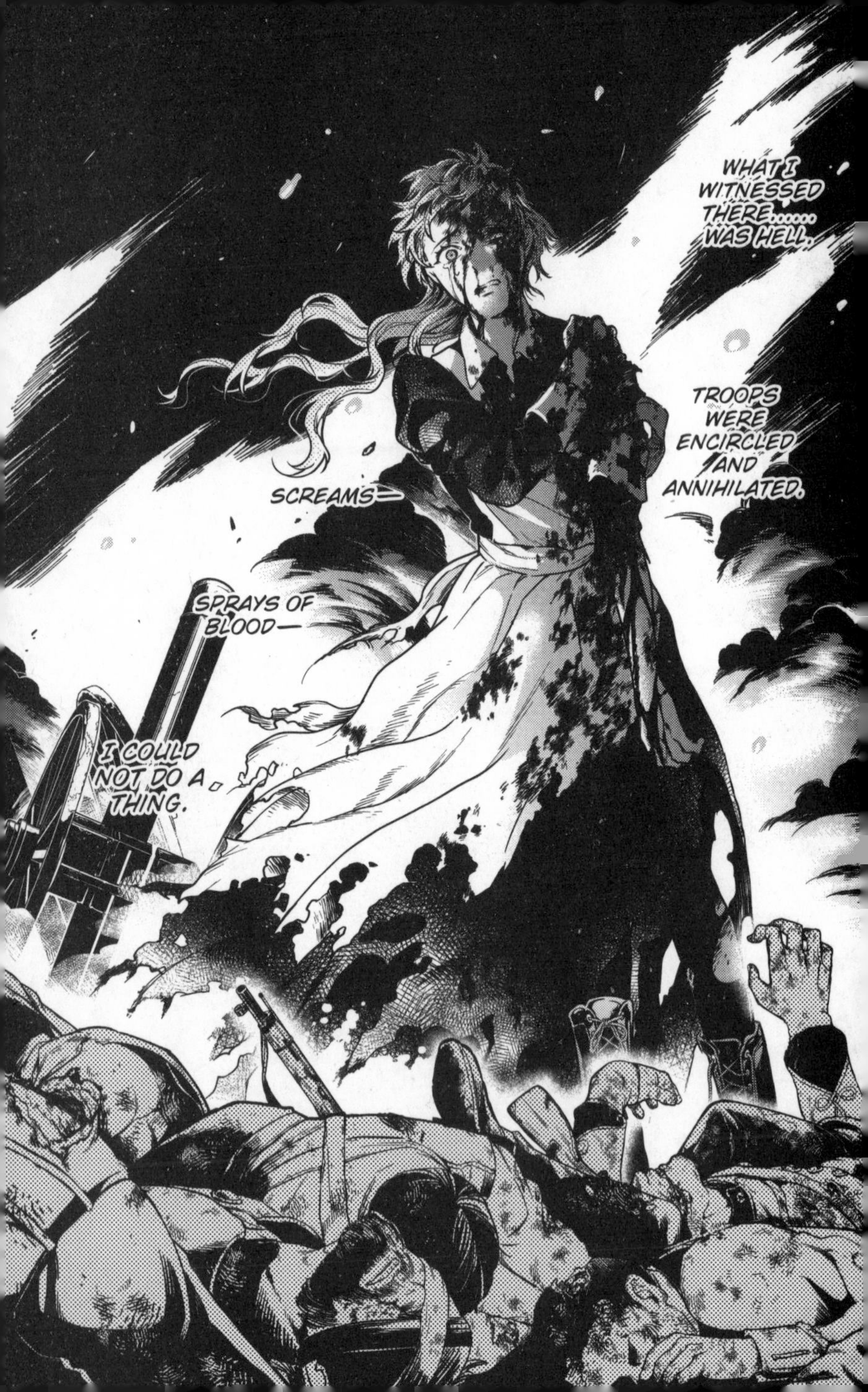
WHAT I WITNESSED THERE...... WAS HELL.
TROOPS WERE ENCIRCLED AND ANNIHILATED.
SCREAMS—
SPRAYS OF BLOOD—
I COULD NOT DO A THING.

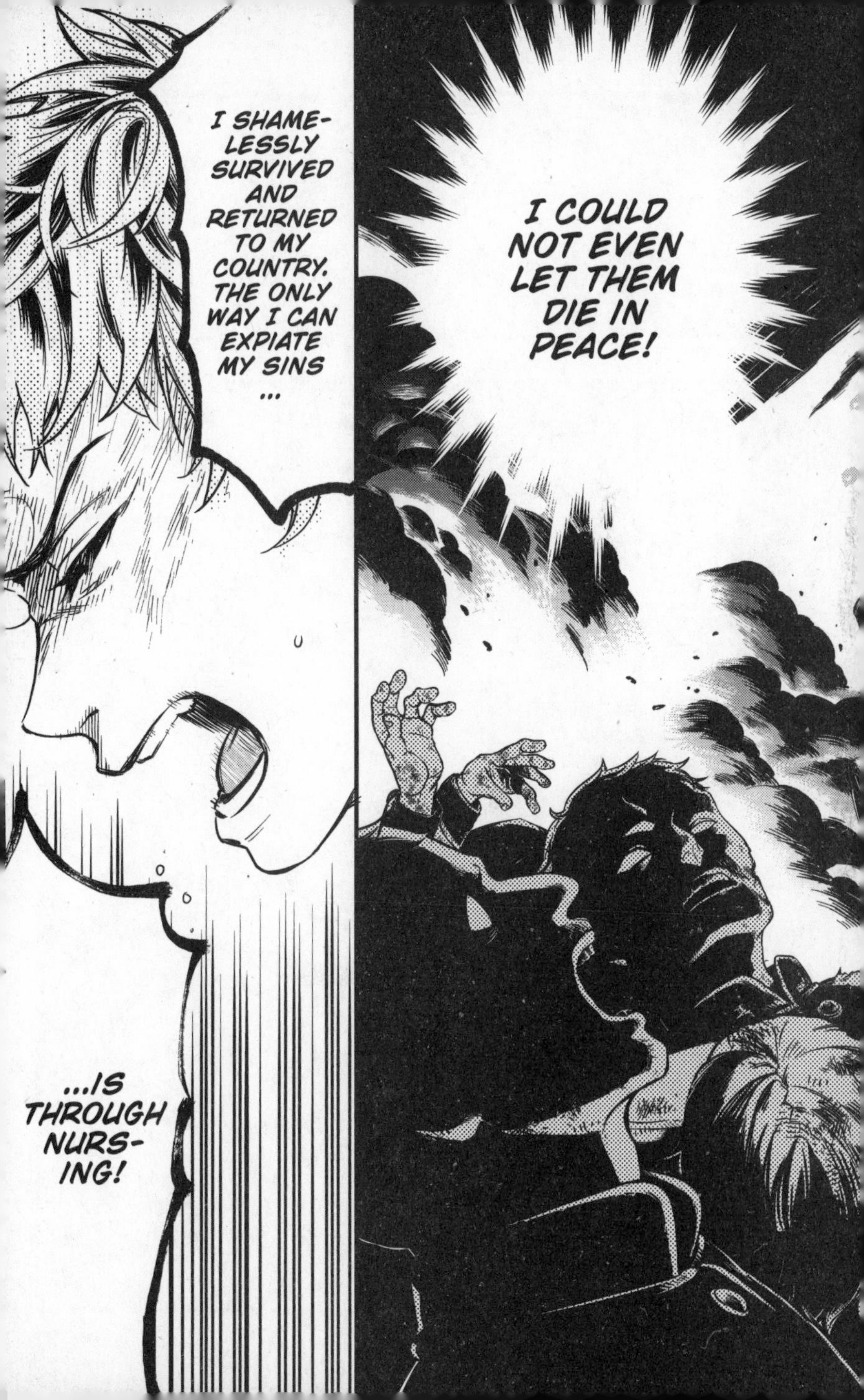
I COULD NOT EVEN LET THEM DIE IN PEACE!
I SHAME-LESSLY SURVIVED AND RETURNED TO MY COUNTRY. THE ONLY WAY I CAN EXPIATE MY SINS ...
...IS THROUGH NURS-ING!

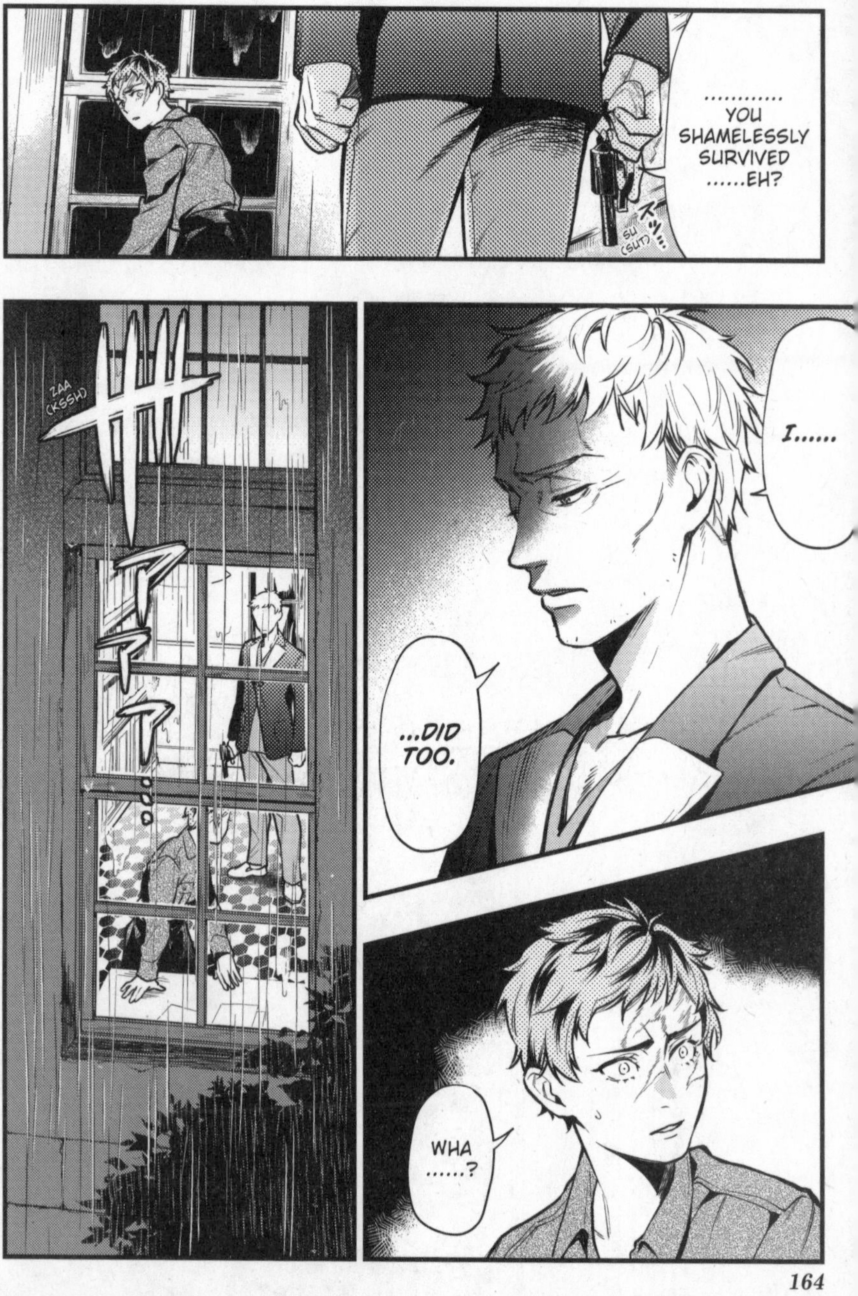
.... YOU SHAMELESSLY SURVIVED ......EH?
ズッ…
SU (SUT)
I......
...DID TOO.
WHA ......?
ZAA (KSSH)

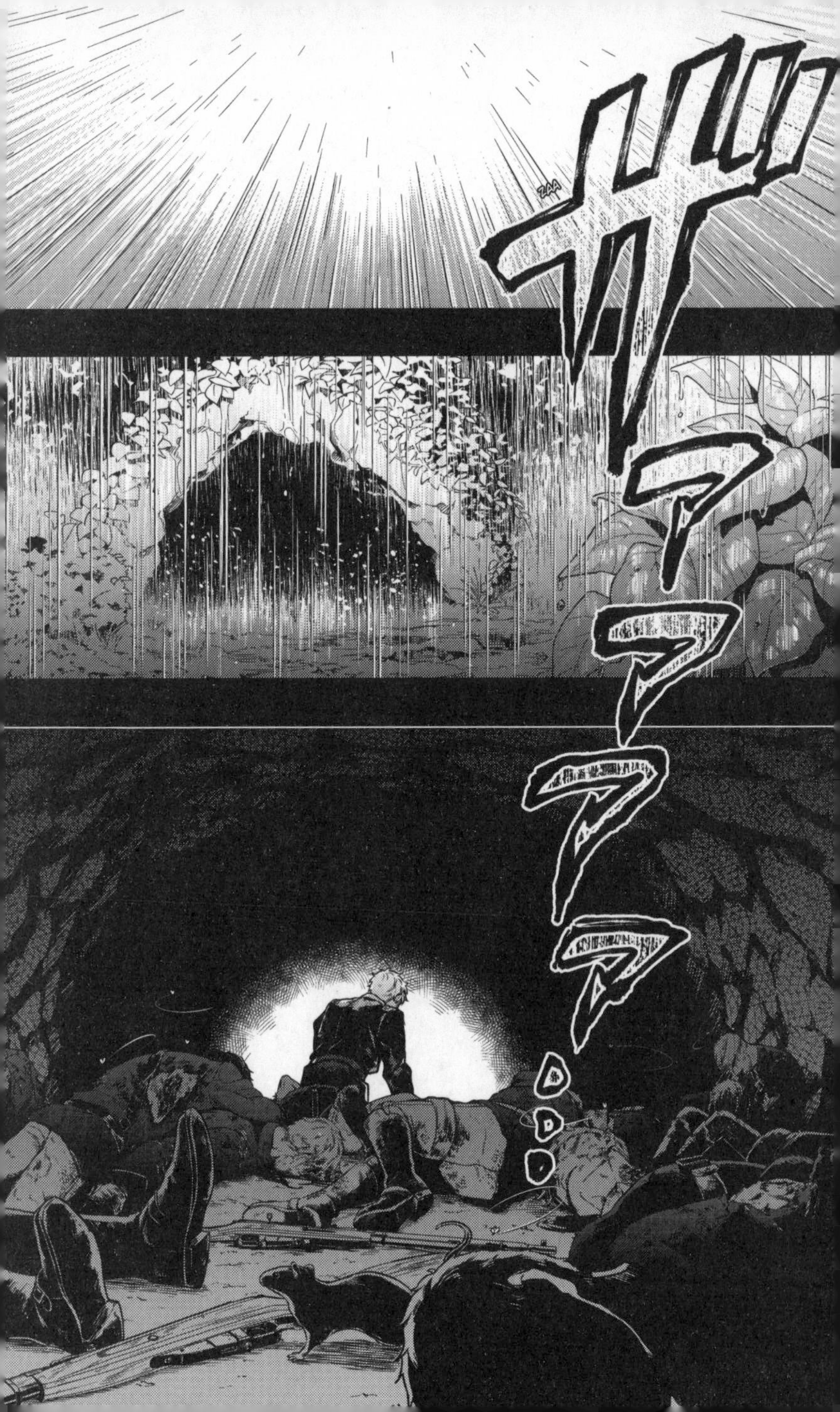
ザァァァァ
ZAA

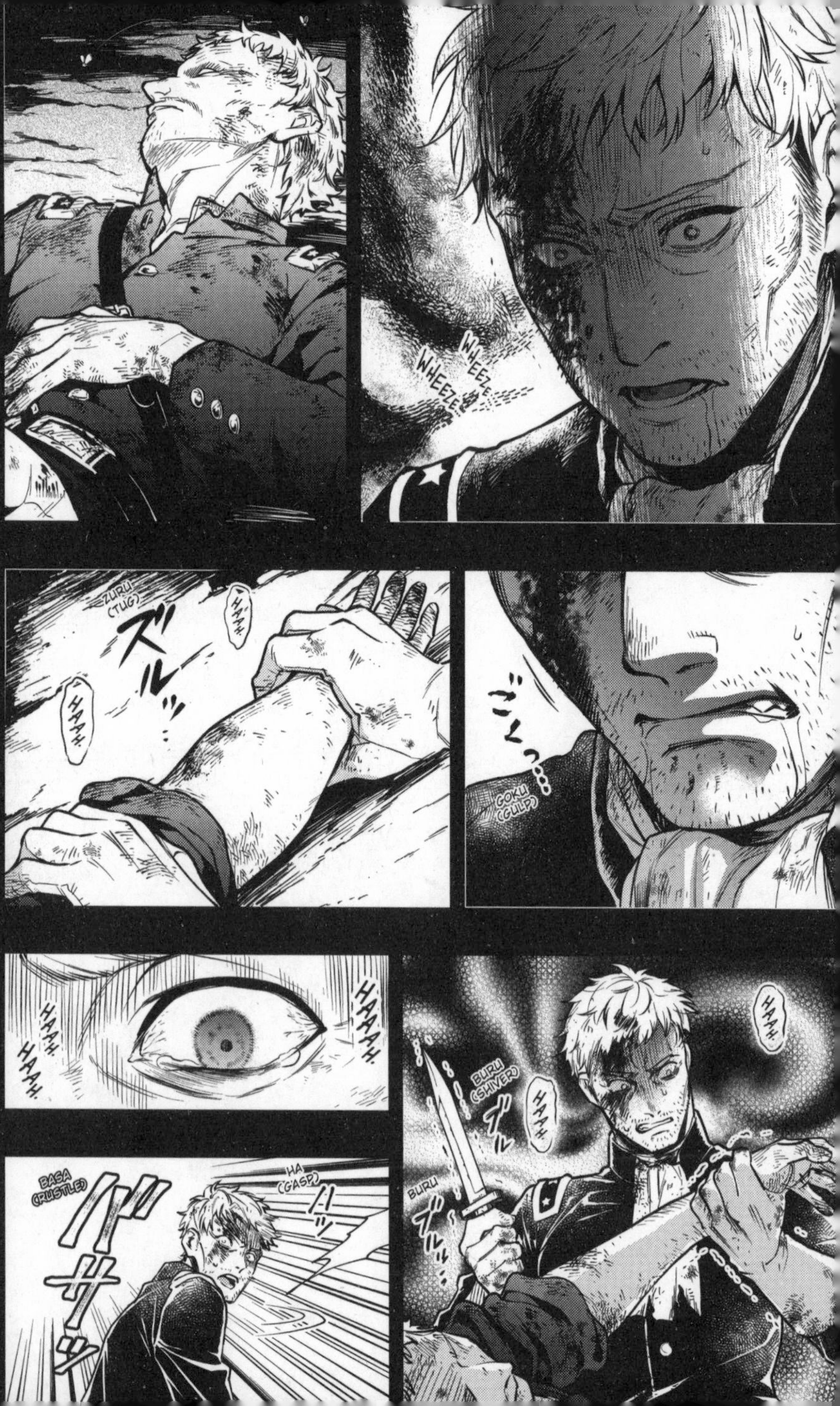
WHEEZE
WHEEZE
ごくっ
GOKU (GULP)
ZURU (TUG)
ズルッ
HAAAH
HAAAH
HAAAH
BURU (SHIVER)
ブル
HAAAH
BURU
ブルル
HAAAAH.
HAAAH.
HAAAH.
HA (GASP)
ハッ
BASA (RUSTLE)
バサッ

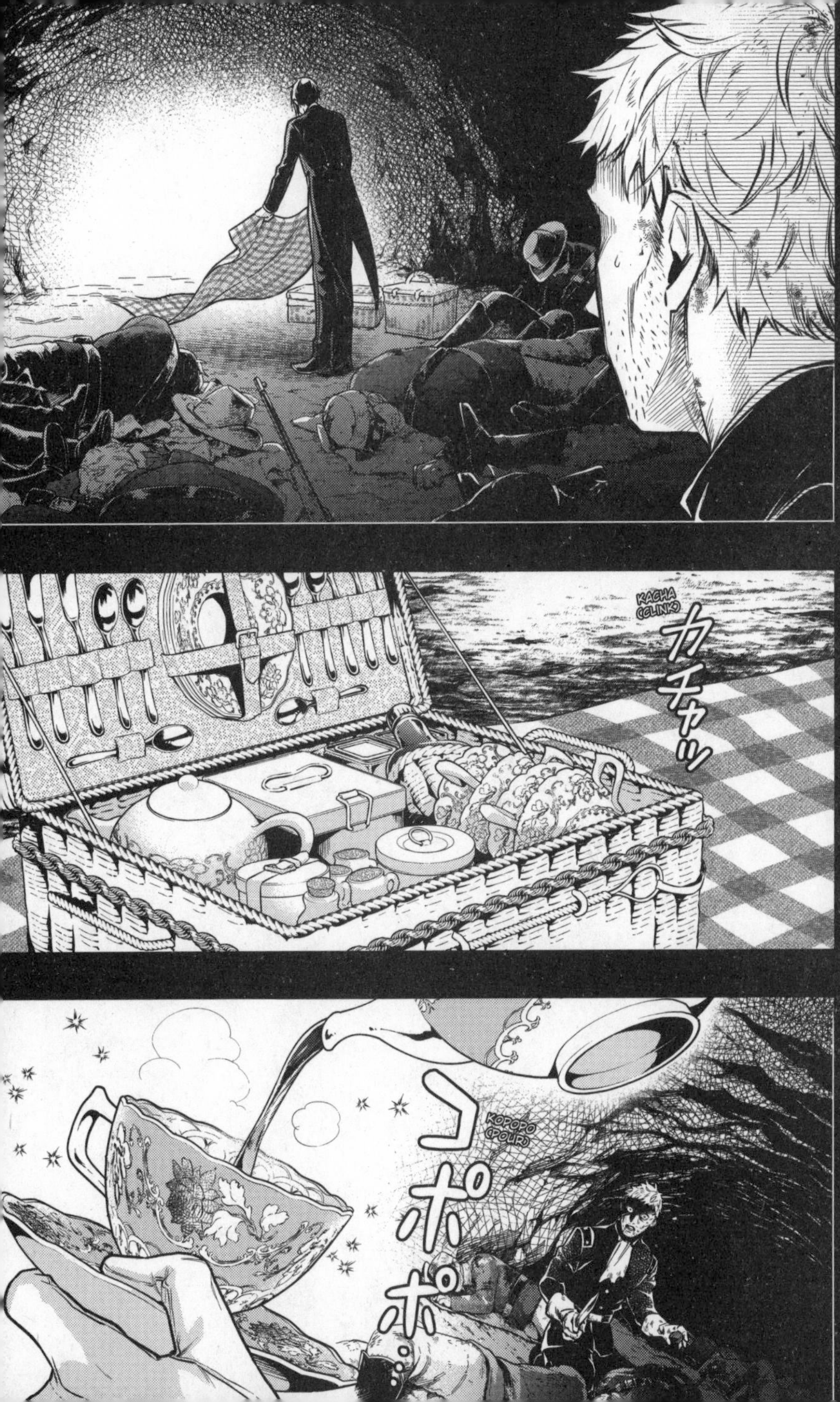
KACHA (CLINK)
カチャッ
KOPOPO (POUR)
コポポ…

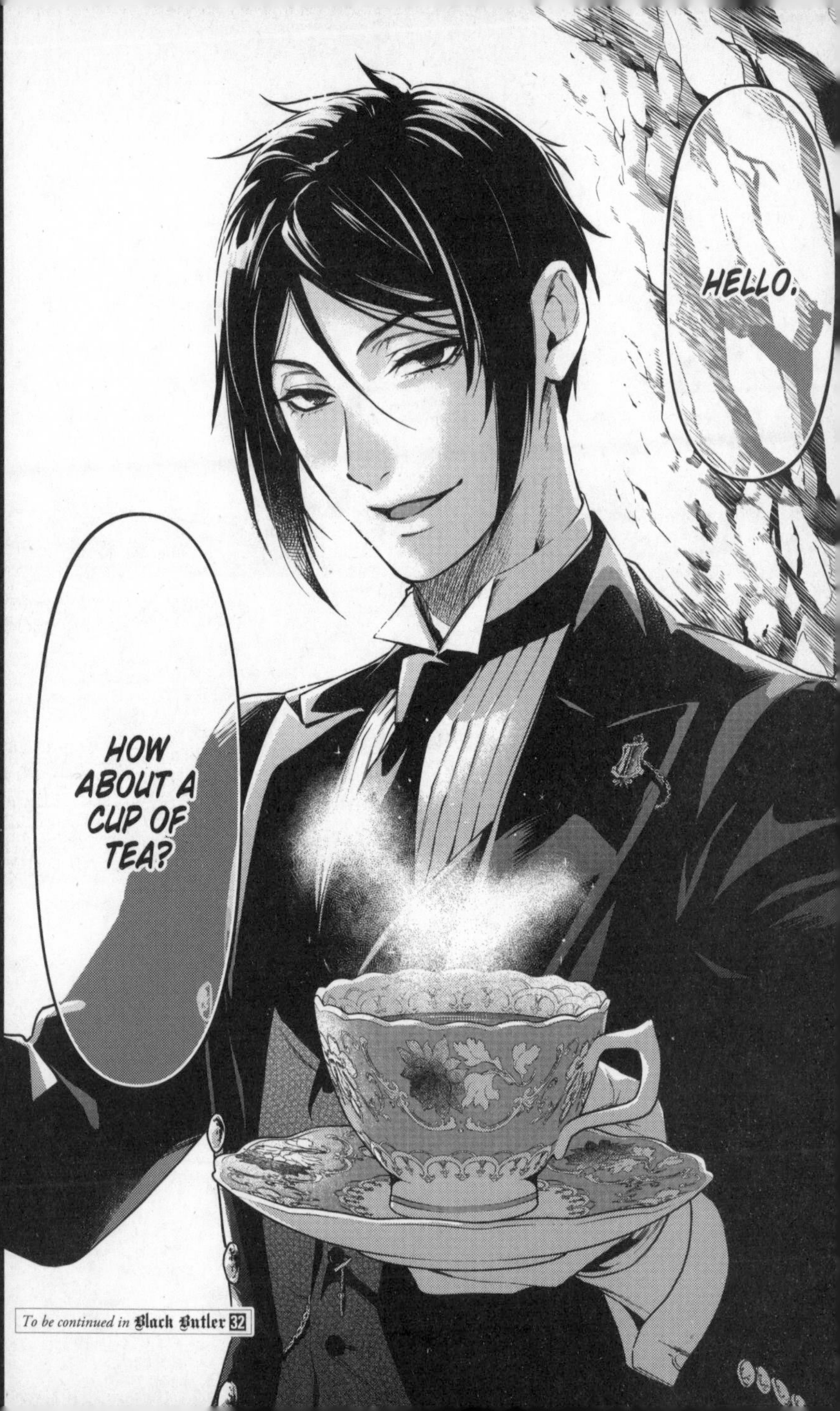
HELLO.
HOW ABOUT A CUP OF TEA?
To be continued in Black Butler 32

⇥ Black Butler ⇤

黒執事

❖

Downstairs

Wakana Haduki
7
Tsuki Sorano
Sumire Kowono
Jun Hioki
Mine
Sanihiko/KG/Tastu/Vas

*

Takeshi Kuma

*

Yana Toboso

❖

Adviser

Rico Murakami

Special thanks to You!

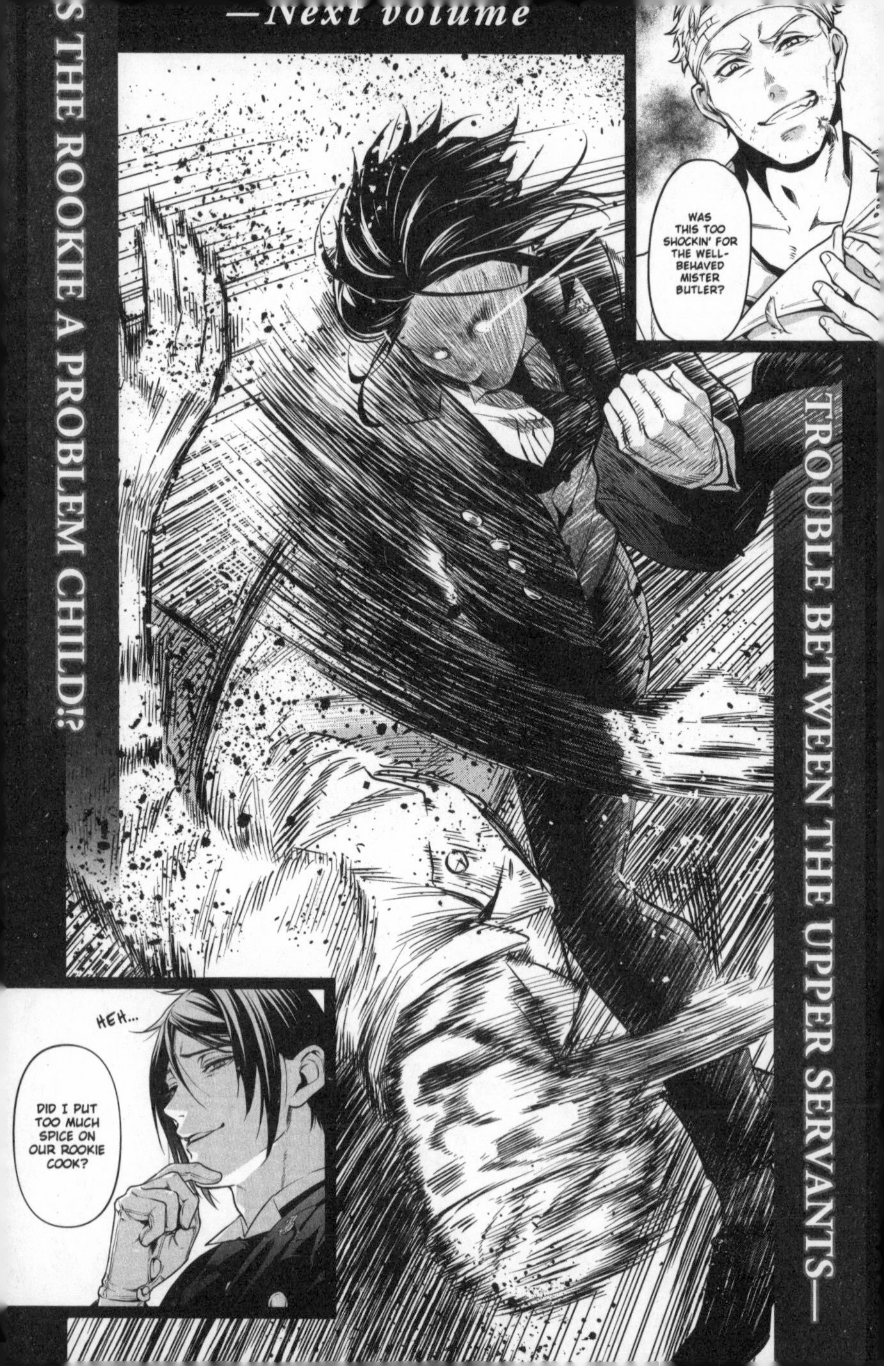
—Next volume
WAS THIS TOO SHOCKIN' FOR THE WELL-BEHAVED MISTER BUTLER?
TROUBLE BETWEEN THE UPPER SERVANTS—
S THE ROOKIE A PROBLEM CHILD!?
HEH...
DID I PUT TOO MUCH SPICE ON OUR ROOKIE COOK?

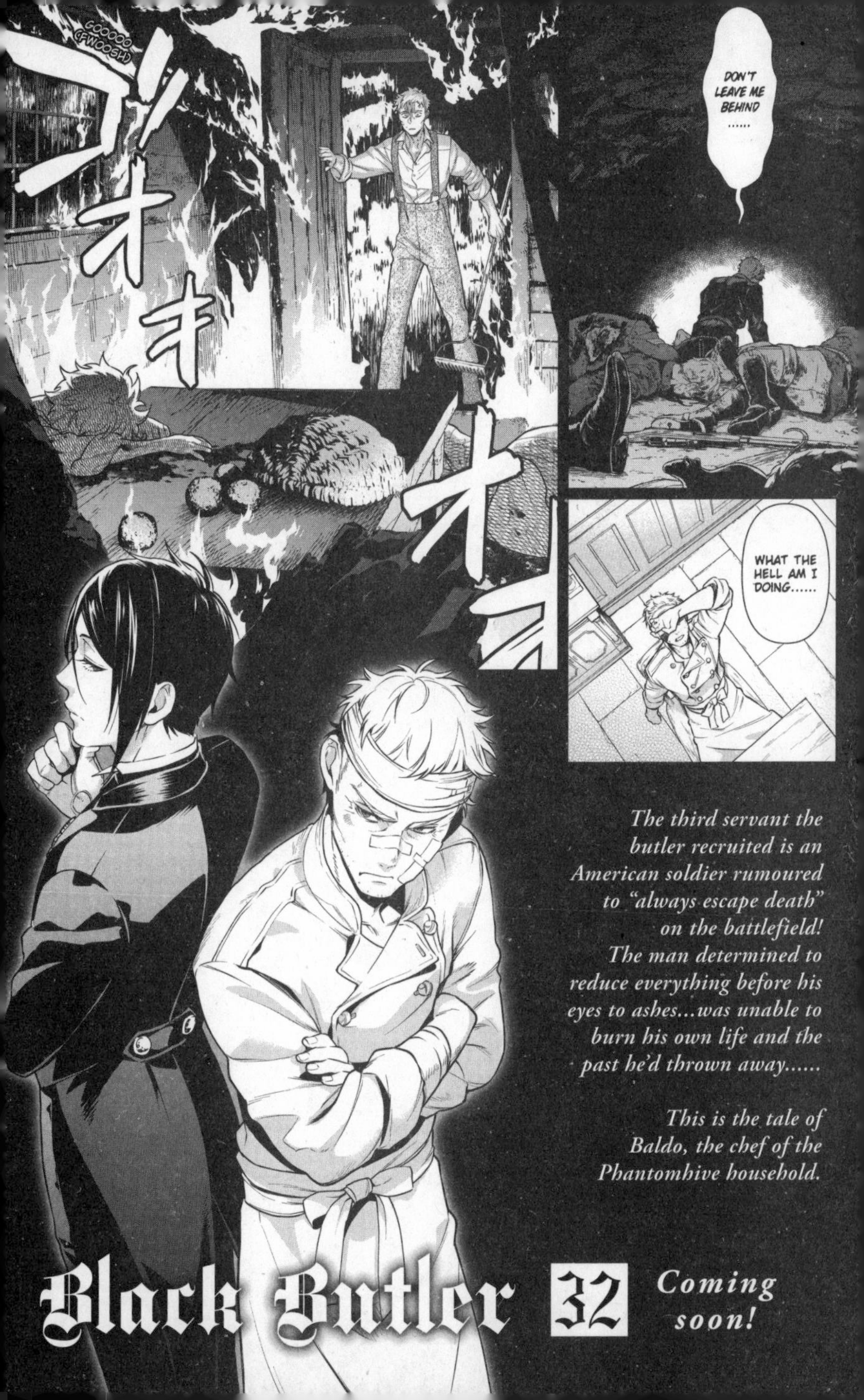
DON'T LEAVE ME BEHIND ......
WHAT THE HELL AM I DOING......
GOOOOO (FWOOSH)
The third servant the butler recruited is an American soldier rumoured to "always escape death" on the battlefield! The man determined to reduce everything before his eyes to ashes...was unable to burn his own life and the past he'd thrown away......
This is the tale of Baldo, the chef of the Phantomhive household.
Black Butler 32
Coming soon!

Translation Notes

Page 145
Bloodletting
Medical treatment where blood was
withdrawn from the body. It was frequently
used until the mid-nineteenth century.

Page 156
**"A single moment can be worth a
thousand gold pieces."**
A Chinese proverb that cautions against
wasting time, 一刻千金.

Page 161
The Sudan campaign
A colonial war in Sudan that began in 1881.
The city of Khartoum, where the British
army was stationed, fell in 1885.

Inside back cover
Rakutomi
A parody of the popular Japanese e-tailer
Rakuten.

Yana Toboso

AUTHOR'S NOTE

Black Butler is going to celebrate its fifteenth anniversary.

I do feel I've "drawn a lot of stuff," but I still can't believe it's been that long. I hope I can keep challenging myself to draw what I truly want to.

And so, this is Volume 31.

Black Butler

VOLUMES
1-14 **IN STORES
NOW!**

VOLUMES 1-16
AVAILABLE DIGITALLY!

Toilet-bound
Hanako-Kun

At Kamome Academy, rumors abound about the school's
Seven Mysteries, one of which is Hanako-san. Said to
occupy the third stall of the third floor girls' bathroom
in the old school building, Hanako-san grants any wish
when summoned. Nene Yashiro, an occult-loving high
school girl who dreams of romance, ventures into this
haunted bathroom...but the Hanako-san she meets
there is nothing like she imagined! Kamome Academy's
Hanako-san...is a boy!

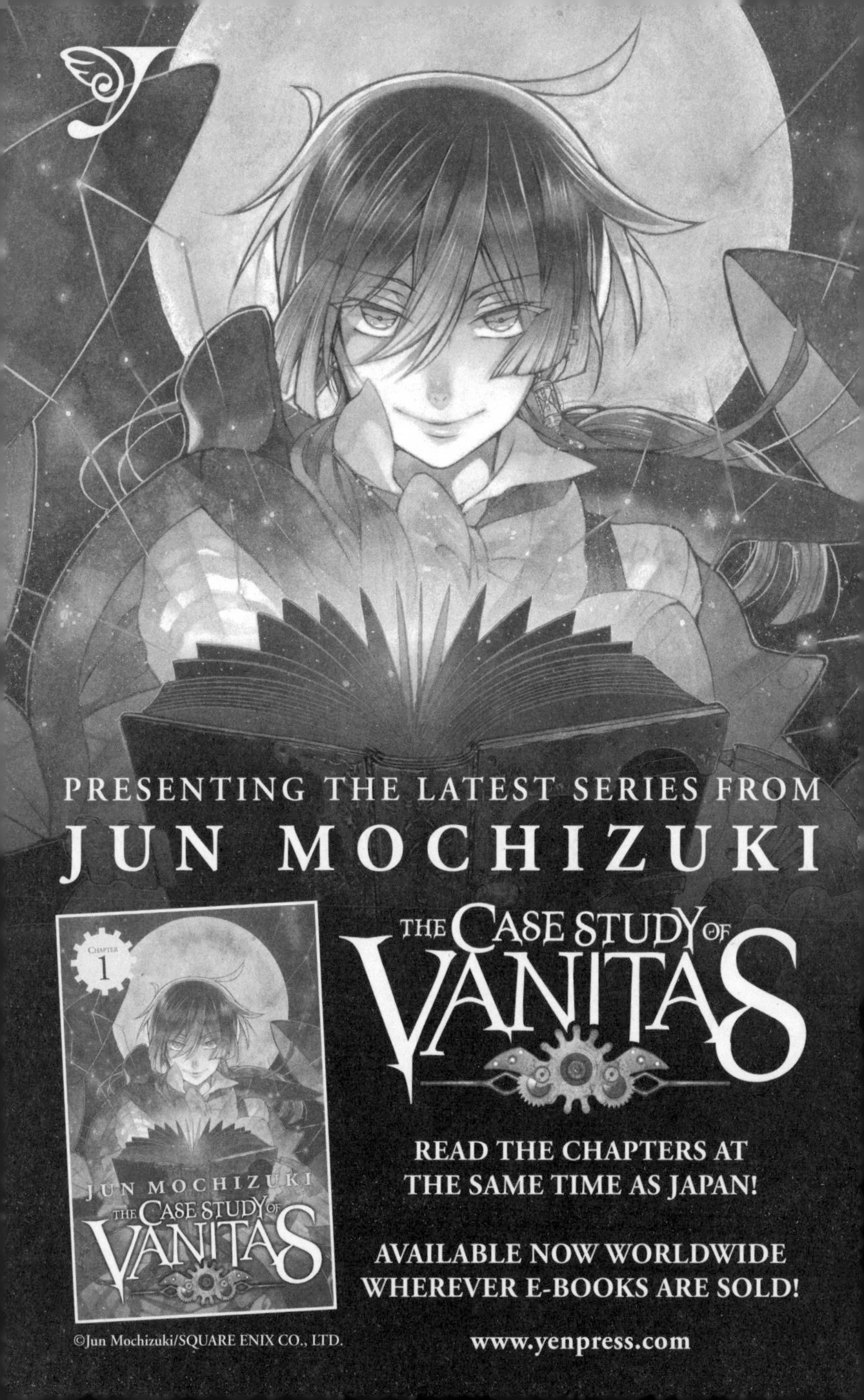
PRESENTING THE LATEST SERIES FROM
JUN MOCHIZUKI
CHAPTER 1
JUN MOCHIZUKI
THE CASE STUDY OF VANITAS
THE CASE STUDY OF VANITAS
READ THE CHAPTERS AT THE SAME TIME AS JAPAN!
AVAILABLE NOW WORLDWIDE WHEREVER E-BOOKS ARE SOLD!
©Jun Mochizuki/SQUARE ENIX CO., LTD.
www.yenpress.com

BLACK BUTLER ㉛

YANA TOBOSO

Translation: Tomo Kimura
Lettering: Bianca Pistillo, Alexis Eckerman

KUROSHITSUJI Vol. 31 © 2021 Yana Toboso / SQUARE ENIX CO., LTD. First published in Japan in 2021 by SQUARE ENIX CO., LTD. English translation rights arranged with SQUARE ENIX CO., LTD. and Yen Press, LLC through Tuttle-Mori Agency, Inc.

English translation © 2022 by SQUARE ENIX CO., LTD.

Yen Press
150 West 30th Street, 19th Floor
New York, NY 10001

Visit us!
† yenpress.com
† facebook.com/yenpress
† twitter.com/yenpress
† yenpress.tumblr.com
† instagram.com/yenpress

First Yen Press Edition: May 2022
The chapters in this volume were originally published as ebooks by Yen Press.

Yen Press is an imprint of Yen Press, LLC.
The Yen Press name and logo are trademarks of Yen Press, LLC.

The publisher is not responsible for websites (or their content) that are not owned by the publisher.

Library of Congress Control Number: 2010525567

ISBNs: 978-1-9753-4436-8 (paperback)
        978-1-9753-4437-5 (ebook)

10 9 8 7 6 5 4 3 2 1

WOR

Printed in the United States of America